Fun
Activities

Projects

BIG
BOOK
of Ideas

for Children's
Faith Formation

*Blessings!
Beth McNamara*

Edited by
Beth Branigan McNamara
with Gina Wright McKeever
and Sue Robinson

Crafts

Our Sunday Visitor Publishing Division
Our Sunday Visitor, Inc.
Huntington, Indiana 46750

Our Sunday Visitor Publishing Division
Our Sunday Visitor, Inc.
200 Noll Plaza
Huntington, IN 46750

ISBN: 0-87973-018-8
LCCCN: 00-130466

Cover and text design by Tyler Ottinger
Additional illustrations by Brenda Anderson, Peggy Gerardot and Tessie Bundick.

PRINTED IN THE UNITED STATES OF AMERICA

Introduction

What happens when three woman with fifty-plus years of experience with children between them, get together to share their love of children, their faith, and their ideas? The *Big Book of Ideas for Children's Faith Formation* happens!

Teaching children about Christian beliefs, attitudes, and values is an awe-inspiring task. We pray that the ideas in this book will spark your children's natural curiosity and creativity, helping them recognize God's presence in their daily lives. You and the children will enjoy oodles of easy activities and projects that are faith-centered, classroom-tested, and interactive. We trust that you will be energized, as we were, with these quick-to-prepare and fun-to-use activities.

ALL ☺
PRE 🧸
PRI ✋

The *Big Book* is arranged alphabetically in an A-to-Z format with a thematic index in the back. Each entry includes a symbol indicating the appropriate age level for the activity. The teddy bear "PRE" logo is for preschoolers. The hand "PRI" logo indicates activities for primary-grade children. The smiley face "ALL" logo means the activity can be used for preschool and primary-grade children.

You will find a variety of learning methods that nourish a child's belief in a captivating, loving God. Use a variety of ideas so the children will learn about Jesus in an imaginative and fun way, appropriate to their age and responsive to their level of understanding. Most importantly, each idea offers an encounter with faith that children can apply to their lives and won't forget.

May God bless you and inspire your important work with children.

Beth Branigan McNamara
Gina Wright McKeever
Sue Robinson

Beth Branigan McNamara has twenty-three years of experience in religious education. Presently she is a speaker, writer, and acquisitions editor for Our Sunday Visitor. She and her husband are volunteer faith-formation teachers, and reside in Minnesota with their two sons.

Gina Wright McKeever teaches fifth grade in Texas where she, her husband, and two daughters live. A past religious-education coordinator, Gina volunteers in the Early Childhood Faith Formation program and sacramental preparation programs in her parish.

Sue Robinson lives in Minnesota with her husband Paul and four children. She is a past religious-education coordinator, regular contributor to Christian Beginnings (published annually by Our Sunday Visitor), volunteer faith-formation teacher, and works with elementary special-education students.

Ability ☺ PRE

God gives every person many gifts that include his or her abilities. God gives us feet for jumping, eyes for looking, arms for stretching. The list of our abilities could go on and on.

❏ *You will need:*
Voices for singing
Bodies for moving

❏ *To do:*
Sing the following words to the tune of the *Farmer In The Dell*. Then have the children make up more verses.

Verse 1
I'm jumping up and down,
I'm jumping up and down,
Thank you, God, for feet that jump,
I'm jumping up and down.

Verse 2
I'm looking all around (2x)
Thank you, God, for eyes that look,
I'm looking all around.

Verse 3
I'm stretching to the sky (2x)
Thank you, God, for arms that stretch,
I'm stretching to the sky.

Absence ☺ ALL

When children are absent from the group let them know that they have been missed and you are looking forward to their return.

❏ *You will need:*
Paper circles
Ribbon
Markers
Stapler

❏ *To do:*
Cut out a circle and draw a happy face on one side and a sad face on the reverse. Staple a ribbon to the circle. Print "We really missed you" on the sad side and "We can't wait for you to come back" on the happy side. These thoughts may be hand-delivered or simply mailed in an envelope.

❏ *More to do:*
Keep a few postcards on hand and invite children who have free time to decorate them. Send the postcards to children who are absent or to let parents know just how wonderful their children are!

Acts of Kindness   ☺ ALL

Keep track of the kind acts that take place in your classroom every day by decorating a paper hand garland.

❏ *You will need:*
   String or ribbon
   Construction paper

❏ *To do:*
Cut a string or ribbon as long as you would like the garland to be and display at the child's level. Make hand cutouts to hang on the string as shown in the diagram. Each time a child does a kind act, invite her to decorate and display a hand for the garland. Before long you will probably notice a chain reaction of caring gestures happening everywhere you look

Advent Adventure   ☺ ALL

Take children on an Advent adventure. Discuss that during the Advent season we prepare for the birth of Jesus. Describe what an adventure the trip to Bethlehem must have been for Mary and Joseph. Include thoughts of anticipation and excitement. Using a suitcase will arouse excitement for this adventure.

❏ *You will need:*
   An old suitcase

❏ *To do:*
Choose four Advent themes that will symbolize the four weeks of Advent, for example, "Jesus is coming." Make a bumper sticker (see bumper sticker) to display the theme on the suitcase. Each class session use the suitcase to reveal a

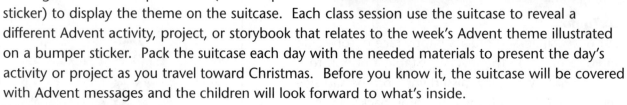

different Advent activity, project, or storybook that relates to the week's Advent theme illustrated on a bumper sticker. Pack the suitcase each day with the needed materials to present the day's activity or project as you travel toward Christmas. Before you know it, the suitcase will be covered with Advent messages and the children will look forward to what's inside.
Weekly theme suggestions:
Waiting for Jesus, Thinking of others, Sharing my gifts, A wonderful journey, The star that leads, Watching for Jesus
Ideas that come out of a suitcase:
Nativity story to read, angel to hide, Christmas ornament to make, Advent countdown project, blank cards to make Christmas greetings, parent gift materials, Advent chains or bracelets, skits or game ideas.

❏ *More to do:*
Keep the suitcase around the classroom even after the Advent season as a reminder that our journey with Christ does not end at Christmas.

Advent Calendar ☺ ALL

Take-home Advent calendars are a good way to help children prepare for the celebration of Jesus' birth.

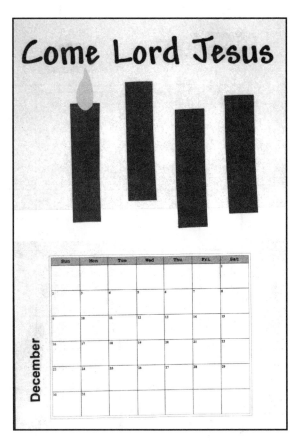

❑ *You will need:*

11" x 18" pieces of construction paper
Copy paper
Glue
Tree branches
Stickers

❑ *To do:*

Enlarge and duplicate the calendar provided on the next page. Fill in the dates of the month and a daily thought or activity such as the examples listed below. Duplicate for the children in your class. Mount the calendars on 11" x 18" construction paper or poster board. Place the calendar across the bottom of the paper. Using the pattern provided, cut out four candles and glue them across the top half of the paper. Staple or glue a pine branch (real or artificial) across the bottom of the candles. Print the words "Come Lord Jesus" across the top of the paper. Send home 25 stickers for the children to put on each day of December. Include four flames to add to the candles as each week passes.

❑ *Daily activities, thoughts and prayers:*

Be with us, dear Lord, as we prepare for the birth of Jesus. Give Mom or Dad a big hug today. Pick up your toys today. Draw a picture to send to a friend. Help make cookies or a special snack. Take a walk. As you say your prayers today, "God Bless" everyone in your family. Start making a paper chain of holiday colors to decorate the house. Call Grandpa or Grandma on the phone and tell them you love them. Read a Christmas story before bed. Do a puzzle and leave it out for everyone to see. Color a small paper plate to hang on your Christmas tree.

Collect some extra food from the cupboard to share with a food shelf, food pantry, or food kitchen. Hold hands when you say table grace today. Leave a love note under the pillow of someone in your family. Have a cup of hot cocoa together before bed.

Wear something red today. Draw a heart in the bottom of your shoe today to remind you that God loves you. Read the nativity story or a book about Jesus' birth. Look up Bethlehem on a map or globe. Talk about how you and Jesus were alike when you were babies. Look at one of your baby pictures. Watch a Christmas video or look at Christmas pictures together with your family. Bake cookies and share them with a neighbor. Before your celebrations today thank God for the special gift of Jesus. Merry Christmas!

A

Sun.	Mon	Tue	Wed	Thu	Fri	Sat

Advent Guessing Game ☺ ALL

Familiarize the children with some of the signs and symbols of Advent while having fun.
Tell the children that Advent symbols and signs tell us more about the season.

❑ **You will need:**

Enough note-size cards for the entire group with the
name or picture of an Advent symbol (such as a candle)
A large basket

❑ **To do:**

Invite a child to pick a card out of the basket. Invite the child to tell the other children something
about that symbol. This Advent symbol reminds us that Jesus brings light into our lives and helps
us find our way. Tell the other children to try and guess what the symbol is. Continue until all
the cards are gone. Symbols could include star, bell, Advent wreath, Christmas tree, candles,
wrapped package, nativity piece, straw, blue cloth, Christmas decorations, festive food items,
wrapping paper, felt heart, and pictures of people celebrating, etc.

Advent Magnets

Give the children visual knowledge of the nativity Scripture by putting together a refrigerator
manger scene.

❑ **You will need:**

Copies of the patterns on this page
Magnet strips
Markers or crayons and scissors

❑ **To do:**

Enlarge and copy the illustrations onto stiff paper or tag board and cut them out. Invite the
children to add color and to attach a small magnet piece to the back of each. A stable could be
drawn, cut out, and secured on the refrigerator with magnet pieces as well. During week one
send home Mary and the angel, telling the children about the angel's visit to Mary. For the weeks
of Advent that follow, continue telling the nativity story and adding the appropriate figures to the
refrigerator nativity.

Advent Prayer Cube   ☺ ALL

Introduce a new prayer each week during the four weeks of Advent with a prayer cube.
Make one for each child in your group to take home to enhance the season for their families.

❑ *You will need:*

Contact paper or Christmas wrapping paper
Square boxes (collect or purchase from a local paper or gift store)
Jingle bell
Copies of the weekly prayers

❑ *To do:*

Collect or purchase square boxes about the size that coffee
mugs come in. Put the jingle bell in the box. Cover the
boxes with Christmas wrap or contact paper. Glue the prayers
provided (one to each side) of the box. Cut out a picture
from a Christmas card or print the child's or family's name on
the blank side. During each new week of Advent turn the
cube to a new prayer.

❑ *Weekly Prayers:*

Wk 1 - Dear God,
We thank you for this special season of Advent. What a wonderful time of year
this is to grow closer to you and one another. Be with our family as we wait for
Jesus' birthday. Amen.

Wk 2 - Heavenly Father,
We thank you for our parents and the many ways they love and care for us each
day. Help us to always listen to our parents as Mary listened to the angel tell her
she was going to be Jesus' Mother. Amen.

Wk 3 - God Our Protector,
We thank you for always being with us and taking care of us just as a shepherd
cares for his sheep. Help us to always think of others first and care for them when
they need our help. Amen.

Wk 4 - Dear Lord,
For the sun, moon, stars, and all things bright and beautiful in our world we
thank you today. Just as the stars showed the shepherds and wise men to
Bethlehem may they always be a reminder to us of the great gift we have
received in Jesus. Amen.

❑ *More to do:*

Put everyday prayers or blessings on the sides of the cube. As the children line up
to go home or gather for circle time, toss the cube in the air and say the blessing
or prayer that lands up in your hand. Have the children take turns tossing too.

Air and God's Love ☺ ALL

God fills our lives with joy and happiness. Without God in our lives we become deflated. Here is a visual that carries the message.

❑ *You will need:*
   Unfilled balloon
   Ball point pen

❑ *To do:*

As you inflate a balloon, between each puff of air, discuss how God fills our lives with happiness. Gently tie a knot to keep air from escaping. Carefully draw a smiling face on the inflated balloon using a ballpoint pen. Toss the decorated balloon around the room for a few minutes. Retrieve the balloon from the children and untie the end to release the air. Watch what happens to the happy face when we let God leave our lives.

All Saints Super Cape ☺ ALL

On all Saints day we are all called to reflect on the special gifts we have received from God and how we share them with others. Ask the children to think about their gifts and how they can share them with others to be super saints.

❑ *You will need:*
   Large brown grocery bags
   Markers
   Scissors
   Yarn

❑ *To do:*

One brown grocery bag will make two capes. Cut out the two large panels of each bag. Round off the narrower top of each rectangle. Punch 2 holes on each of the rounded sides about 2" from the edge. Lace heavy yarn or ribbon through the 4 holes.

With marker print, "Super Saint (the name of child)" on the back of the cape. Let the children decorate the rest of the cape with markers. While all are wearing their capes, say a special prayer and ask for God's blessing on each child.

All Star Child of God   ☺ ALL

Highlight one child from your class each week. Put his or her picture and name on a large star in your classroom. As a class talk about what makes that person special and an All Star Child of God.

❑ *You will need:*
   Construction paper
   Glue
   Photo of each child
   Markers

❑ *To do:*
Cut out a large paper star for children when their turn comes. Glue a photo of the child in the center of the star. As you discuss that child's special qualities print them around the star. Display the star on a board labeled, "All Star Child of God."   Give each child a paper star or sticker to wear when he or she is the All Star.

Alleluia Banner   ☺ ALL

During Lent we stop singing Alleluia as a reminder of Jesus' sacrifice and the season. Make Alleluia banners with your children during Lent with the instruction that they go home and bury the Alleluia until Easter morning when we celebrate the Resurrection.

❑ *You will need:*
   Poster board
   Markers
   Glitter
   Stickers
   Beads
   Large garbage bags

❑ *To do:*
Duplicate and enlarge the Alleluia provided here. Mount it on a large construction paper or poster board. Have the children decorate the letters with marker, stickers, glitter, beads, etc. After the poster has dried, place each banner in a large plastic garbage bag and tape it shut. Send the banner home with the instruction that it be buried under a bed, the couch, deck, in the sandbox, etc. On Easter morning "dig up" the banner when looking for the Easter baskets and display in a prominent place in the house.

❑ *More to do:*
Alleluia Song (sung to the tune of "If You're Happy and You Know It")
Alleluia, Alleluia, clap your hands,
Alleluia, Alleluia, clap your hands,
Alleluia, Alleluia, Alleluia, Alleluia, Alleluia, Alleluia, clap your hands.
Add: stamp your feet, jump for joy, shout out loud, shake a hand.

Aloha = Love   ☺ ALL

Aloha means love. Use this Polynesian greeting with any lesson you may be doing on love. What a good boredom buster during the dark days of winter!

❑ *To do:*

Begin by telling the children that in Polynesian cultures the word "Aloha" is a greeting. When people meet on the street or welcome friends to their homes they say "Aloha" which means love. During circle time send an Aloha greeting around the circle. Have children give the greeting to the people on either side of them.

❑ *More to do:*

Write the word Aloha on blank postcards and have the children color on them.
Send them to special friends or shut-ins in your community.

Alphabet Creation Book   ☺ ALL

Celebrate the wonder of God's creation with a creation of the children's making.

❑ *You will need:*

Construction paper
Glue
Markers
Metal paper rings

❑ *To do:*

As a class list two or three things made by God for each letter of the alphabet. Include plants, animals, foods, families, etc. Print these on plain pieces of construction paper. Have the children draw the pictures that go with each item. Spread this project out over several days so that each child does pictures for several different letters. Laminate the finished pages and put together with metal book rings. Put the book in your reading or prayer corner for all to enjoy throughout the year.

America   ☺ ALL

How blessed we are to be born in the United States. While our country may not be perfect, we do enjoy many blessings and freedoms. Try patriotic banners in June and more in July or even in November for Thanksgiving.

❑ *You will need:*
    12" x 16" pieces of fabric
    1/4" dowels about 14" long
    Scraps of red, white, and blue fabric
    Glue
    Scissors
    Red or blue ribbon
    Markers

❑ *To do:*

Make patriotic banners. Give each child a white 12" x 16" piece of material. Print the words, "God Bless America" on each banner. Have the children decorate their banners with hearts and stars cut out of scraps of red, white, and blue fabric. Poke two equally spaced holes across the top of the banner. Guide a 1/4" dowel 14" long through the holes. Tie red or blue ribbon to the ends of the dowel for hanging the banner.

❑ *More to do:*

Make newspaper hats, decorate bikes, get out the rhythm band instruments and have a parade around the block. Enjoy blue punch, red Jell-O® and white frosted cookies for snack.

Angel in Me   ☺ ALL

Angels, God's special messengers, remind us of God's love and care for us.

❑ *You will need:*
    White or shiny gold paper
    Pencils
    Scissors
    Glue
    Construction paper
    Photos or self-portraits of the children

❑ *To do:*

To make these angels have the children trace both hands on white or shiny gold paper. Glue these with thumbs at the bottom to the back of a 4" paper triangle. At the top of the triangle glue a self-portrait or photo of the face of each individual child.

❑ *More to do:*

Include the angels with a special parent Christmas card or attach a string for hanging to make it a tree ornament. Make a bulletin board in your classroom of all of your angel children. Title the board, "God's Little Messengers," or "Angels From God."

Angel Hand Puppet ☺ ALL

Angels both heavenly and earthly fill our lives. Invite these angel hand puppets to fill the classroom.

❑ *You will need:*
   Face powder puffs
   Markers
   Star garland
   Yarn
   Yellow felt

❑ *To do:*
Draw a face on the soft side of the powder puff with the markers. Use glue to attach brightly colored yarn hair at the top of the face and a halo made from star garland. Cut out a large heart of felt to make wings. Glue the heart to the band across the back of the powder puff. Finish the angel by placing a garland halo on the top of its hair. Show the children how to slide their hand under the band to manipulate the puppet.

Animal Antics ☺ PRE

Celebrate God's animals with this fun game.

❑ *You will need:*
   Adhesive name tags
   Markers
   Pictures of familiar animals for younger children

❑ *To do:*
Print the name of a familiar animal on each name tag. For younger children use stickers of various animals. Place a tag on the back of each child. Invite the children to help one another decipher which animal is named on their back by giving clues and gestures. The game ends when all the children have identified their animal.

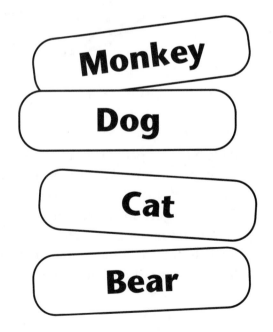

❑ *More to do:*
Invite children to move about the room like their favorite animal. Form a circle and call the animals each by name to enter into God's animal kingdom, the circle.

Animal Ark Game   🐻 PRE

Here is a circle game that provides an extension to the story of *Noah and the Ark*.

❑ *You will need*:

Brown paper bag cut into the shape of an *Ark* (see diagram)

❑ *To do*:

Place a brown paper bag, cut into an ark shape, in the middle of the floor. Invite the children to circle around the ark. Give each child an animal sticker to wear or hold. Select a person to be the leader, or "Noah." Noah moves around the outside of the circle and taps a child on the shoulder. That child gets up and calls out the name of the animal and runs around the circle, trying to get back to his or her place before Noah tags him. The other children with the same animal sticker move to the ark in the center. If Noah tags the child being chased, she joins the other animals in the ark. The last child to join the other ark animals becomes Noah next.

Animal Tube Puppets 🐻 PRE

Use an entire collection of these animal tubes for children to actively participate in telling stories about God's animals such as the *Good Shepherd*.

❏ *You will need:*
Magazines
Scissors
Stapler
Glue or clear contact paper
Empty tissue tubes

❏ *To do:*
Cut animal pictures from magazines. Staple, glue, or use contact paper to attach the picture to the outside of an empty tissue paper tube. Use markers or crayons to decorate the tube to look like the natural surroundings of the animal's habitat. Move the tubes around as the story is being told.

❏ *More to do:*
Invite the children to group the animals according to where they live, for example the jungle, farm, underwater, forest, zoo, etc. Remind the children wherever they look God has blessed our world with life.

Applause All Around 😊 ALL

Here are a few ways children can acknowledge a job well done by others in their community or to just give thanks and praise to God!

❏ *To do:*
Round of applause:
Clap hands together in a circular motion in front of your body at head and shoulder height.

Seal of approval:
With arms straight out, parallel to the floor, cross one arm over the other. Fold the arms back towards the chest and flap back of hands together making a clapping sound, just like a seal.

Silent applause:
Raise both hands in the air with elbows slightly bent, then shake hands loosely from side to side. Encourage children to pretend to cheer vocally but keep their voices silent.

Apples   ✋ PRI

What a wonderful gift from God! Apples are the fruit of the harvest that we enjoy all year long. Try these ideas in the fall or any time of year.

❑ *You will need:*

Large shiny apples
Short (6") white candles or votive candles
Raffia or ribbon
Small knife

❑ *To do:*

Make an apple candleholder for a parent or family gift. Make a hole in the top of the apple wide enough to push a candle in. A votive candle works too, just make the hole a bit wider. Tie a bow of raffia around the bottom of the candle or add a small pine branch. Include a copy of the Johnny Appleseed prayer.

Oh the Lord is good to me,
And so I thank the Lord.
For giving me the things I need,
The sun and the rain and the apple seed.   Amen.

❑ *More to do:*

Show the children the special surprise in the center of the apple: Cut the apple in half side-ways through the middle. Open it and there is a star for all to see. Use the half apple and tempera paint in a pie tin to print cards, wrapping paper, place mats or gift bags.

Arbor Day   ☺ ALL

In the spring many communities around the country celebrate the wonderful resource of trees. Attention is paid to the contributions of wood from making paper to building, just to name a few. Talk about how we use trees and how we can protect and nurture them for the generations to come. If possible plant a tree on your school grounds. Say a little prayer thanking God for the gift of trees and for the healthy growth of the new tree you planted. End with a puzzle tree project.

❑ *You will need:*

12" x 18" construction paper
Old puzzle pieces
Glue

❑ *To do:*

Cut out a tree trunk for each child in your group. Glue it to a large piece of construction paper. To make leaves for the tree have the children glue on a variety of old puzzle pieces. You could also use tissue or wall paper scraps. Title the picture "Thank you, God, for trees."

Arrival Message ☺ ALL

Meet each child personally at your classroom doorway with a welcoming action.

❑ *To do:*

A kind word, a welcoming gesture can make a huge difference in the experience a child has in your classroom. Take a few minutes to personally greet each child when they arrive.
You might say…
"Kevin, I'm so glad you're here today."
"It is so nice to start the day with a smile from you."
"Marisa, you look like you are ready for a great day."

❑ *More to do:*

If you can't be at the door to greet the children, leave a note or message in your place.
Leave a trail of stickers leading to a message on the board.
Leave a path of stones leading to an opening activity.

Ash Wednesday ☺ ALL

Ash Wednesday marks the beginning of Lent, a time we all strive to grow closer to God.

❑ *To do:*

Talk with the children about the season of Lent. Compare it to Advent when we get ready for Christmas. Remind the children that during Lent we prepare ourselves for Easter. Set some goals with the children—things they would like to do to grow closer to God. Come up with a service project and theme to explore throughout the Lenten season. (Many ideas for Lent will follow in this book.)

Set up a special prayer corner. Include a candle cross and anything else that would reflect your theme. Place a collection basket for the service project items you are looking for. Gather in your prayer space and pray together,

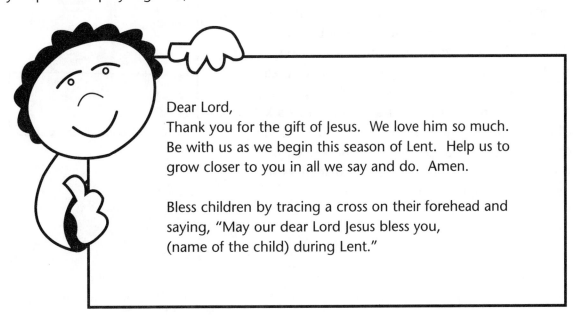

Dear Lord,
Thank you for the gift of Jesus. We love him so much.
Be with us as we begin this season of Lent. Help us to grow closer to you in all we say and do. Amen.

Bless children by tracing a cross on their forehead and saying, "May our dear Lord Jesus bless you, (name of the child) during Lent."

Attendance Sticks ☺ ALL

Children always love keeping track of their good attendance. Reward their efforts daily with the following ideas.

❑ **You will need:**
   Wooden paint sticks
   Photo of each child
   Glue
   Markers
   Stickers
   Soup can or basket

❑ **To do:**

Collect one paint stick per child from a paint or hardware store. Glue or tape a photo or name card of each child to the top of a stick. Each day the child comes to class, he or she puts a sticker on his or her stick. Place the sticks in a soup can or tall basket near the door of the classroom. Also keep the stickers nearby so that the children can be independent with this. Send the attendance sticks home at the end of the year as a reminder of their good work.

❑ **More to do:**

If you have themes that you develop throughout the year, change the types of stickers you use. Examples include, a flower, pumpkin, star, heart, or egg at the top of the stick with the photo or name in the middle. Have the children draw self-portraits for the top of the stick. Hang a clear shoe bag near the door to your classroom. Put each child's name on the front of one of the pockets. Place the attendance sticks in the appropriate child's pocket. When the children arrive, have them put their stickers on their sticks. To keep track of who is present, have the children then put their sticks in a can or basket. You will then know at a glance who is missing. Use the pockets of the shoe bag to put notes for home. At the end of the day have the children replace their sticks so they are ready for the next time.

Attitude of Gratitude   😊 ALL

Develop an "attitude of gratitude" with your children throughout the year. Focus on the daily blessings from God that we might take for granted. Talk to the children about the things in their lives for which they are thankful: loving parents, teachers, good food, clean water, warm homes, schools, just to name a few.

❑ *You will need:*
　Poster board
　Markers

❑ *To do:*
Write a thank you note to God from the whole class on poster board. Have an adult write while the children discuss the list. Sign the letter with the children writing or printing their own names. Have the children take turns drawing pictures that go with each item. Display the thank you note in a prominent place for all to see.

❑ *More to do:*
Reinforce an attitude of gratitude with this song.
Sing this song to the tune of "Are You Sleeping."
　　We are grateful,
　　We are grateful.
　　For our Moms
　　And our Dads,
　　So we sing God's praises,
　　So we sing God's praises,
　　Every day,
　　Every day.
　　(Add your own verses.)

Awards to Go   😊 ALL

Children love to be noticed for their accomplishments and the wonderful things they do. Notice every child in your group at least once a week using these great ideas.

❑ *You will need:*
　Pre-made awards (enlarge samples)
　Stickers
　Markers

❑ *To do:*
Keep pre-made forms on hand easy to access. Just add a name and reason and you are all set. Proclaim your praise on paper.

❑ *More to do:*
Try a seal of approval, round of applause or silent applause (see applause).

God gives us friends like ____

This person was a special friend when ____

Give a hand for ____
signed: ____
date: ____

The Sun Shines on...
this day because ____
Date: ____
Signed: ____

An Awesome God   ☺ ALL

"Our God Is An Awesome God," is the first line of a popular song. Celebrate the awesomeness of our God and try some of these fun ideas.

❑ *You will need:*
Neon-colored poster board
Markers

❑ *To do:*
Cut out, "Our God Is An Awesome God," in large balloon letters from neon-colored paper. Display them on a bulletin board or hallway wall. After discussing awesome with the children, print or draw the awesome works of God on the balloon letters. Invite parents and staff to do the same. From time to time share those writings with the children.

❑ *More to do:*
To continue the spirit of Awesome God, purchase neon shoelaces for each child. With permanent marker write Our God Is Awesome on each lace. Using the flower pattern provided and more neon colored paper or fun foam, make necklaces or shoe charms with the same message.

Our God Is An Awesome God

List Your Favorite Projects Here

_____

_____

_____

_____

_____

_____

_____

_____

_____

_____

_____

_____

_____

_____

_____

_____

_____

_____

_____

_____

Baby Jesus Sock Doll   😊 PRE

Remind the children that Jesus came into this world as a baby just like you and me with this easy-to-do sock project.

❑ *You will need:*
Small child or toddler size socks
1"-2" styrofoam balls
Fiberfill stuffing
Ribbon
Permanent markers
10" pieces of flannel

❑ *To do:*
Provide a sock and styrofoam ball for each child. Place the ball in the toe of the sock. Gather the sock under the ball and tie with white yarn. Next stuff the rest of the sock with fiber fill or clean white fabric scraps. Leave the bottom 2"-3" of the sock free of stuffing. Gather the bottom of the sock together and again tie off with yarn. Cut 10" triangles of light colored flannel to make the baby blanket.

Bag of Tricks   😊 ALL

Always have a bag of tricks ready for those times when you least expect the need for something extra. Sometimes when we least expect it, "the project that fizzles" or "the assistant that doesn't make it in to help" catches us off guard.

❑ *You will need:*
A sturdy bag to carry "tricks," such as a squish ball, favorite picture book, etc.
Materials for a simple craft
List of songs with words, and/or favorite hand puppet.

❑ *To do:*
Here are a few suggestions of what you can do with your bag of tricks. Keep in mind that you need to personalize the bag to fit your needs, personality, and interests.
A squishy ball to play a game of silent toss.
A favorite book to read aloud.
An ever-ready craft (see Friendship Pins).
A few favorite piggyback song ideas (see Songs).
A game idea (see Games).
A favorite hand puppet to see you through (see Hand Puppets).

Have a Ball ☺ ALL

Encourage spontaneous prayer or discussion with your children by tossing a large rubber ball back and forth during prayer time.

❑ *You will need:*
   Large rubber or soccer ball with each child's name printed on it with a permanent marker.

❑ *To do:*
The teacher begins the prayer, which might go like this. "Thank you, God, for the beautiful sunshine and the wonderful children in my class." The teacher then rolls or tosses the ball to a child in the circle. Upon catching the ball the child says his own prayer such as "Thank you, God, for my baby brother," and then passes the ball to another child and so it goes. After everyone has had a turn, the teacher closes the prayer and places the ball on the shelf in the prayer corner.

❑ *More to do:*
Use the ball to help the children focus on a topic or enter into discussion. Simply pose a question and roll or carefully toss the ball. The child who has the ball may answer or comment on the discussion.

Band-Aid Messages for Bruises ☺ ALL

Print short messages of faith on the bandages you pass out in class.

❑ *You will need:*
   Band-Aids
   Rubber stamps
   Small stickers
   Permanent markers

❑ *To do:*
As you take out bandages for the children, add a cheerful, short message such as "God heals," to the non-gauze, non-sticky sides of the bandage. Hold your hand gently over the injury and say a little blessing like, "God will help you heal," or "God, help (name) to feel better."

Baptism Water Blessing   ☺ ALL

Enhance your baptism lessons or observe the baptism of Jesus in January with the following ideas.

❑ *You will need:*
    Clear bowl
    Water
    Seashell
    Ribbon
    Permanent marker

❑ *To do:*

Plan a baptism party with cake and balloons for the children in your class. Sing "Happy Baptism Day" to the tune of "Happy Birthday." This could also be done in January around the time of the feast of the Baptism of the Lord. Use water to say a special blessing. Put a clear bowl of water in the center of the group. Pass the water around and one at a time have the children dip their fingers in the water and touch their foreheads saying, "God, bless my head," touch their lips saying, "God, bless my lips," and touch their heart saying, "God, bless my heart. Amen."

❑ *More to do:*

Collect a seashell for each child in your group. Tell the children that the seashell is often used as a symbol of the water used in baptism. Print each child's name on a shell as a reminder of his or her own baptism. If possible drill a hole in the shell and lace a ribbon through the hole for hanging. Add a small piece of paper with the blessing, "May God bless you and keep you always" or "You are God's child."

Baptism book   ☺ ALL

Children become familiar with many of the symbols of baptism through everyday living. Make baptism books to help them make important connections between their experience and a beginning understanding of these symbols of the sacrament.

❑ *You will need:*

Two sheets of construction paper per child
Pictures of children's baptism
Markers
Aluminum foil
Ribbon

❑ *To do:*

Use two sheets of construction paper folded together in half to create the following pages as you discuss baptism.

Cover – photo of child's baptism
Discuss why families decide to have their children baptized.

Page 1 – Have the children cut drops from aluminum foil. Encourage them to make a pattern as they paste them on the page.
Discuss all of the wonderful things water does for us such as cooling, cleaning, and refreshing, etc. Explain that God provides us all of that and even more.

Page 2 – Carefully light a candle away from the children. Allowing the children to watch, place a few drops of candle wax on the page. Remind them that lighting a candle must be done by an adult because the flame of a candle can burn you badly. Wait until the wax has completely dried and then let the children gently touch it.
Explain that parents and godparents are asked to hold a candle to remind them of the light God brings into our lives.

Page 3 – Have the children draw several smiling faces.
Tell the children that the community gathers together to pray for, support, and welcome the newest members.

Page 4 – Drawing of an open Bible or individual words cut from a newspaper.
Show the children a Bible. Tell them that we share God's Word when we celebrate Baptism.

Page 5 – A piece of white fabric.
A white garment is worn to remind us that we are God's Children.
When the books are complete invite the children to share what they have learned with their families.

Blanket Bounce ☺ PRE
Keep a blanket close by for quick community building fun.

❑ *You will need:*
Blanket
A small soft boat

❑ *To do:*
Invite the children to sit around the blanket and each take hold of an edge of the blanket so that they are able to manipulate the blanket together. The blanket can then be used in a number of ways. Here are a few ideas. Place the small boat in the center of the blanket and ask the children to make the boat move on the "Blanket Sea" at first very slowly telling them about Jesus calming the sea for the disciples. Make the sea stormy and when you say, "Jesus calmed the sea" have the children calm the blanket sea once again.

❑ *More to do:*
Tell a story that repeats a phrase to the children as they hold the blanket. When the phrase is said, the children will do that action with the blanket. For example, "The Shepherd looked HIGH (the blanket is lifted high and as the blanket balloons fly up the children look around) and the Shepherd looked LOW (the blanket is brought back down to the floor.)

Believer's Sign ☺ ALL

Explain to the children that a long time ago people who believed in Jesus began to use a drawing of a fish as a reminder of their relationship with God.

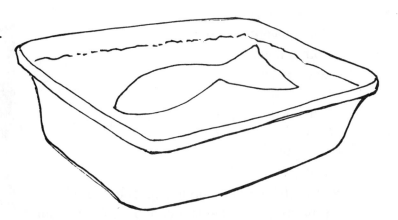

❑ *You will need:*
    Dirt or sand in a large plastic dishpan.

❑ *To do:*
Teach the children how to draw a fish pattern in the sand. Tell the children that when they see a drawing of a fish, it will remind them of Jesus.

❑ *More to do:*
    See Fish.

Believer's Song ☺ PRE

Teach this fun song about being a believer in God and the difference God makes in the children's lives. Add actions.

❑ *To do:*
    Sing the following words to the tune of "The Farmer in the Dell."

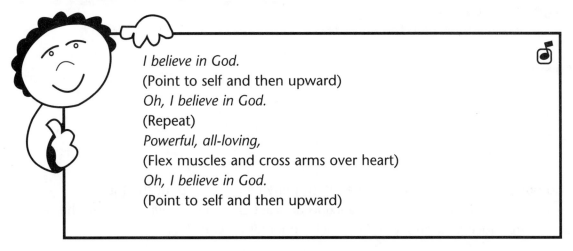

I believe in God.
(Point to self and then upward)
Oh, I believe in God.
(Repeat)
Powerful, all-loving,
(Flex muscles and cross arms over heart)
Oh, I believe in God.
(Point to self and then upward)

Add other verses such as: wonderful and giving, full of goodness, filled with love and kindness. Make up new actions with the children.

Belonging Tee Shirts ☺ ALL

On those important first days of school, children enjoy having something that reminds them of home and helps them to feel as though they belong.

❑ *You will need:*
 Child's favorite tee shirt
 Clothes hangers
 Paper plates
 Yarn
 Construction paper
 Tape

❑ *To do:*
Invite the children to bring in a favorite tee shirt. Hang the shirt from the hanger and display it around the room. As the days go by decorate a paper plate using yarn for the hair, construction paper and markers to create the face of the child. Attach the paper plate face to the hook of the hanger with the tee shirt. Display the finished product near the child's place or locker indicating where the child sits or hangs her belongings.

Belt Messages 😊 PRE

Enhance any lesson on any topic with this easy idea.

❑ *You will need:*
 Old belts
 Puffy paints
 Fabric paint

❑ *To do:*
Have each child bring in an old belt from home. With puffy fabric paint print the theme, message, or symbols from the lesson you are working on the belt. To tie in with the belt theme you could add, "Surrounded by God's love," or "Held together by God."

Bethlehem Bread ☺ ALL

The town of Bethlehem is the place of Jesus' birth. The word itself means, "house of bread." How ironic that we remember the sacrifice of Jesus with bread when we receive communion.

❑ *You will need:*
 Frozen bread dough
 Aluminum foil

❑ *To do:*

Bake bread together with your class. Use frozen bread dough, thaw according to directions and have the children make their own shapes. Place each shape on an aluminum foil sheet with the child's name written on it with permanent marker. Place the foil sheets on cookie sheets to bake. Enjoy for snack.

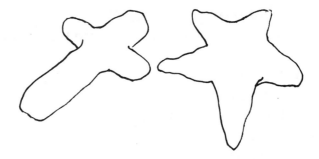

Bible Song ✋ PRI

Introduce the Bible as a very special and important book. Help the children learn the importance of God's Word.

❑ *You will need:*
  Bible
  Bible storybooks

❑ *To do:*

Make a special place for the Bible in your prayer corner. As often as possible refer to and read stories from children's Bible.

❑ *More to do:*

Sing to the tune of "Ten Little Indians."

  Hear God's Word and listen carefully,
  Telling us to love one another,
  Pass the news to all the others,
  The Bible is Good News.

Biggest Me Ever ✋ PRI

Teach children that each one of them is very special by making these fun paper dolls.

❑ *You will need:*
  Roll of newsprint, cut into 4' lengths,
  Crayons
  Scissors
  Tape or stapler
  Old newspapers

❑ *To do:*

Trace the bodies of each child on a piece of newsprint. Invite the children to draw clothes on their body tracings and to add facial features similar to their own. Lay each child's tracing on a second sheet of paper that is the same size. Staple the sheets together in several places inside the line of the body tracing to hold the sheets together. Cut out each tracing, cutting through both papers. Tape or staple the sheets together along the edge, leaving a large opening. Wad up newspaper and stuff into the body shape and tape the torso shut.

Bike Blessing   ☺ ALL

Remind the children that God is with them always with this bike blessing.

❏ *You will need:*
  Index cards
  Dark permanent marker
  Stickers
  Spring clothespins

❏ *To do:*
Using the marker print the message "God is with me!" on
the index card. Decorate the card with markers and stickers.
Clip the card to the spokes of a child's bike and encourage
them to do the same at home. Tell the children that each
time the child hears the clapping sound, he or she will be
reminded God is near. If some of the children do not have
bikes, the blessing card is easily attached to a backpack or curtain.

❏ *More to do:*
Personalize the bike card with a photograph of the child.

Billfold Carries God's Love   ☺ ALL

A billfold is a place to keep very important things. Make these little billfolds to hold a cross,
prayer card, and other reminders of God's love.

❏ *You will need:*
  Legal-size envelopes
  Laminating machine or clear contact paper
  Prayer cards
  Photos
  Paper crosses

❏ *To do:*
Have the children color and decorate the front
and back of a legal-size envelope. Laminate the
front and back of it. Carefully slice open the
envelope opening with a razor blade or scissors.
Have the children cut out little paper crosses to
put in the wallet. Also include a little prayer
card that says God is always near. If possible
add a photo of the child and his or her family.

Bird Peanut Butter Cup ☺ ALL

Remembering our feathered friends in the winter when food is scarce is another way to share our blessings.

❑ *You will need:*
Peanut butter
Birdseed
Nylon net
String

❑ *To do:*
Mix a cup of peanut butter and a cup or more of birdseed together. The mixture should be very thick and as dry as possible without being crumbly. Divide the mixture into fourths and roll into balls. Place each ball in an 8″ circle of nylon net. Gather the net at the top and tie with a string.

Bird Feeder Perch ☺ ALL

Caring for God's creatures also shows respect to all living things. This bird feeder is a simple project any child of any age can do as a sign of respecting life.

❑ *You will need:*
Clear vinyl plastic plant liners
Twigs (or drinking straws)
Hole puncher

❑ *To do:*
Punch holes around the edge of the plant liner tray. Slide the twigs or drinking straws through the holes forming perches for the birds to stand on as they eat. Hang the feeder by tying three strings to three different holes. Bring the three strings together and secure them together in a knot. Hang from a tree branch and fill with birdseed.

❑ *More to do:*
Decorate the plastic dish with permanent markers.

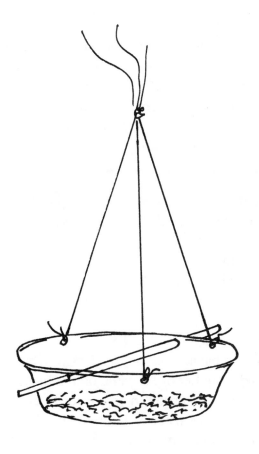

Birthday Vest ☺ ALL

Birthdays are so fun for young children. Make a birthday vest or tee shirt for the children in your class to wear on her or his special day.

❑ **You will need:**
Birthday fabric
Vest pattern
Volunteer who sews
White tee shirt, one size fits all
Fabric paints

❑ **To do:**
Purchase a vest pattern and a birthday party fabric or plain fabric that could be painted with fabric paint. Recruit a parent who sews to make a one-size-fits-all vest for the birthday girl or boy to wear on their special day. If plain fabric is used, have the vest sewn first and then decorate it. With fabric paints decorate a white tee shirt for your class birthday shirt. Print the words "Happy Birthday to you," on the front of the shirt and "God bless you on your birthday" on the back. Decorate with balloons, hearts, and stars.

❑ **More to do:**
Include a birthday blessing sung to the tune of "Happy Birthday."

> *May the Good Lord bless you,*
> *May the Good Lord bless you,*
> *May the Good Lord bless (child's name),*
> *Happy Birthday to you!*

Blanket Gathering ☺ ALL

Make a class blanket to use for prayer or gather time, inside or out.

❑ **You will need:**
A plain, light-colored blanket
Permanent markers

❑ **To do:**
Lay the blanket out on the floor or table. Spread newspaper underneath the blanket. Have each child write her or his name on the blanket with permanent marker. If you have a small group you may want to assign them a place to print their names around the edge of the blanket. This could then be their place to sit on the blanket when you are using it. If time and space allow have the children decorate the blanket with their artwork.

Blessings on the Go   ☺ ALL

Always bless your children as you send them off each day.
An extra hug, a little squeeze will help them on their way.

❏ *To do:*

Try these little blessings with your children as they come and go. Sprinkle a bit of glitter on their heads or in their shoe. Tie a brightly colored ribbon to their belt or around their wrist. Stamp a heart print on the top of their hand or the bottom of their shoe. Give them a little spritz of water as you say, "God bless you and keep you."

Boat in a Bottle   ☺ ALL

The children will enjoy using bottles to tell the story of Jesus calming the sea.

❏ *You will need:*

    16-ounce clear plastic bottles
    Blue food coloring
    Cutout boat and fish shapes from plastic ice cream tub lids
    (colored with permanent markers) or use heat laminated fish and boat stickers
    2-3 brightly colored pony beads
    Cooking oil
    Vinyl caulk

❏ *To do:*

Fill a 16-ounce clear plastic bottle halfway with water. Tint water with blue food coloring to look like the sea. Top the tinted water off with a small amount of cooking oil. Drop the "boats" and "fish" and beads into the bottle. Secure bottle cap with a small amount of clear vinyl caulk on the inside of the cap. Twist the cap tightly in place without allowing the water to contact the caulk. Allow plenty of time for the cap to dry in place before moving or shaking the bottle.

Bobbers Keep Us Afloat ☺ ALL

Make a fishing bobber necklace to add some fun to your summer lessons or Vacation Church School curriculum.

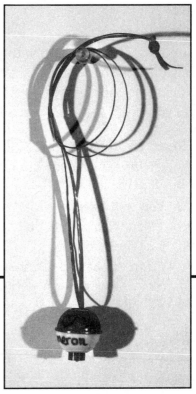

❑ *You will need:*
    Fishing bobbers
    Fine-lined permanent markers
    Twine or plastic lace

❑ *To do:*

Collect or purchase a fishing bobber for each child in your group. With a fine-lined permanent marker write, "God's Love Keeps Us Afloat," and the child's name. Push on the peg at the top of the bobber. A small metal eyehook will come out of the bottom. Slip the twine or plastic lace through the hook and let go of the peg to secure it in place. Tie the two ends together to make the necklace.

❑ *More to do:*

Bobber song
To the tune of, "I'm A Little Teapot."
    I'm a little bobber short and round,
        (Cup hands together to show short and round.)
    Floating in the water is where I can be found.
        (Move hands with fingers together to show floating.)
    When a fishy comes and happens to bite,
    I'm down in the water out of sight.
        (Clap and squat down on the floor as the last two lines are sung.)

Box of Bible Fun ☺ ALL

Call this the Box of Bible Fun or Box of Family Faith and encourage your families to check it out to use at home. The contents will depend on what is available to you and what you wish to accomplish. Here's just one idea for this take-home.

❑ *You will need:*
    A sturdy cardboard box
    A Bible story such as Noah's Ark and the animals
    Contact paper with brightly colored animals
    Flavored gelatin mix
    Animal molds

❑ *To do:*

Cover the box with the animal decorated contact paper. Rewrite these simple directions on the inside of the box.

❑ **_Directions for the box:_**

As a family read the story about Noah's Ark and the animals. Read the story aloud and make the gelatin following the package directions. Pour the gelatin into the molds and chill. When the gelatin is ready to eat, enjoy the cold treat as a family and talk about the faith Noah had in God and the promise we are reminded of when we see a rainbow. Please return the box, book, and mold when finished. If possible include a new box of gelatin mix, making it ready for the next family.

Box of Spring ☺ ALL

Invite the children to collect from outside or bring from home symbols / signs of spring or new life during the Easter Season.

❑ **_You will need:_**

Empty shoe boxes
Opportunities to collect signs of spring
Brightly colored wrapping paper or fabric or stickers
Magazine pictures of favorite things

❑ **_To do:_**

Simply decorate the shoebox. Discuss a variety of signs/reminders of spring and new life that the children can see and give them the opportunity to collect some of these treasures. Ideas include: dried flowers, seeds kept between two circles of clear contact paper, bird feathers, cross made from sticks, a favorite rock, spring confetti, a plastic egg, an Easter picture. The possibilities are endless. Label the box with a gift tag that reads: "Box of spring" or "Gifts from God." "Collected by (child's name)."

Bread in a Bag ☺ ALL

Children will begin to learn the importance of shared bread in our Christian communities.

❑ **_You will need:_**

Bisquick mix
Milk
Small Ziplock Baggies
¼ cup measuring cups
Tablespoons
Flour

❑ **_To do:_**

Have each child measure a 1/4 cup of Bisquick to put in his/her baggy. Then add a tablespoon of milk. Tell the children to close the bags securely and mix by manipulating the baggy with hands until soft dough forms. Place a small amount of flour on a table and allow the children to shape their dough. Place on an ungreased cookie sheet and bake at 450 degrees until golden brown. Enjoy!

Bread Song 🐻 PRE

Sing to the tune of "The Farmer in the Dell."

> *We are making bread, oh we are making bread*
> *Oh come and lend a helping hand, oh we are making bread.*
> *Mix the milk and flour; mix the milk and flour.*
> *Push and pull and push and pull and knead the bread.*
> *I can hardly wait; I can hardly wait,*
> *I can hardly wait to taste the good bread that we baked.*
> *Sharing the tasty bread, sharing the tasty bread,*
> *A sign of God's great love for us, the gift of bread!*

❏ *More to do:*

Encourage the children to help you make up actions to compliment the song.

Bubble Echo 🐻 PRE

Share this bubble echo with your little ones as they play with bubbles.

❏ *You will need:*

Bubbles, bubbles, and more bubbles
Lots of energy!

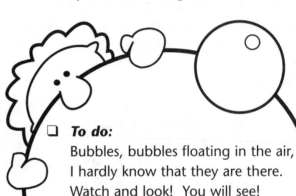

❏ *To do:*

Bubbles, bubbles floating in the air,
I hardly know that they are there.
Watch and look! You will see!
Bubbles floating down on me.
In the air God's love is found,
Just look and see it's all around.

Bumble Bee 🐻 PRE

Remind the children to be thankful for all of God's incredible gifts of creation with this fun action rhyme and bumblebee.

❏ *You will need:*

Construction paper
Markers or crayons
Snap clothespins
Glue

❏ *To do:*

God made the birds to sing from the trees,
God made the trees to blow in the breeze,
God made the bees that provide honey for me,
And God made me to be thankful for all of these!

Duplicate and enlarge the bumblebee pattern provided.
Have the children color and cut out two bees. Glue these to the flat sides
of a clothespin. Attach to a copy of the above poem.

Bumper Sticker 😊 ALL

Spread the good news of God's love for us making bumper stickers.

❑ *You will need:*
   White contact paper
   Permanent markers

❑ *To do:*
Cut 4" x 18" strips of white contact paper. With permanent marker write your God message. Ideas would be, "Rolling Along With God" or "God Zone." Make the message fit any of the themes you might be working on. After printing the words have the children color the rest of the bumper sticker.

Button Covers 😊 ALL

Make felt button covers to reinforce the theme of your lesson.

❑ *You will need:*
   Felt scraps
   Scissors

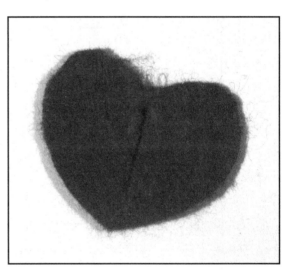

❑ *To do:*
Cut little shapes of felt to coordinate with the theme you are working on. Hearts for Valentines Day, pumpkins for the harvest, stars for Christmas, flowers for spring. The shapes should be 2" or 3" wide so that they fit comfortably over shirt buttons. Cut a small slit in the center of the cutout and push the button through it.

❑ *More to do:*
Add glitter paint or small beads to make the button covers more interesting.

B

List Your Favorite Projects Here

Candle Warms Hearts   PRI

This candle gift idea is a perfect one for children to make for parents or for staff to make for volunteers.

❏ *You will need:*

4" or 5" flowerpot saucers
Votive candles
Potpourri
Raffia or ribbon

❏ *To do:*

Place the candle in the center of the saucer. Put potpourri around the bottom of the candle. Tie a bow of ribbon or raffia around the candle. Attach a greeting, prayer or thank you card to the candle.

Candy Cane   ALL

There is a legend that long ago a candy maker wanted to honor the birth of Jesus in a special way. He decided to make a candy in the colors red and white. White for the goodness of Jesus and red for the sacrifice he made for us. The candy maker also decided to make the candy in the shape of a "J" for Jesus. Hence we have the candy cane.

❏ *You will need:*

Red poster board
Heart pattern
Clear drying glue
Hole punch
Ribbon
Candy canes

❏ *To do:*

Have the children trace and cut out red hearts from poster board that are about 5" across and 6" long. With clear drying glue, glue a candy cane to each side of the heart. Punch a hole at the top of the heart and string a ribbon through it for hanging. To the center of the heart glue a picture from an old Christmas card, print the words, "Jesus is Love," or have the children print their names.

C

Christmas Bake-Off ☺ ALL

How many more days until Christmas? Have fun with a cookie sheet countdown.

❑ *You will need:*
Aluminum foil
Tag board
Markers
Cookie cutters
Scissors
Pencil
Glitter
Markers
Construction paper
Tape

❑ *To do:*

Use aluminum foil to cover a piece of tag board to look like a cookie sheet. Use a permanent marker to print the numbers 1-25 in descending order. Hang the cookie sheet in a place the children can see and reach. Provide a basket of Christmas cookie cutters. Have the children create paper cookie cutters that will be used to tape over the number of days left until Christmas. Each day during the month of December tape a cookie cutter over the number of days. Be sure to take some time to discuss the cookie cutters and their symbolism each day.

Christmas Bells ✋ PRI

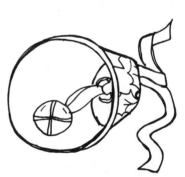

❑ *You will need:*
Paper cups
Bright Christmas ribbon
Small Christmas tree balls or jingle bells
Glue
Scissors
Christmas stickers

❑ *To do:*

Decorate the cups with stickers and pieces of ribbon and glitter. Punch a hole in the bottom of each cup and thread a ribbon through. Fasten a Christmas ball to the ribbon on the inside of the cup. Tie a knot in the ribbon about three inches up from the ball to keep it from slipping up through the cup. Tie the ribbons from the top of the cups together. Add a bit of holly and ring in the holidays!

❑ *More to do:*

Cover the cup with aluminum foil and bunch up a small amount of aluminum foil to make a clapper.

42

Christmas Card Holder ☺ ALL

After the children make this delightful holder for their families' Christmas cards, send home a note encouraging the families to keep the holder on or near their dinner table. Each night choose a card to read as a family and share the meaning and illustration on the card. Then pray for the people or person who sent them the card.

❑ *You will need:*
  Shoe box
  Contact paper or construction paper
  Glue
  Christmas tinsel or ribbon
  Christmas stickers

❑ *To do:*
Cover the box with contact paper or construction paper. Print "God bless our friends and family" or "We are thankful for friends and family." Decorate the box with tinsel or ribbon and stickers.

Christmas Countdown to Bethlehem ☺ ALL

Help the children prepare daily for the coming of Jesus by creating the nativity.

❑ *You will need:*
  Blue construction paper
  Stable outline on brown paper
  Paper crèche figures
  (See patterns of Joseph, Mary, and Shepherd with sheep, Wisemen and Jesus in manger.)
  Glue
  Foil star stickers

❑ *To do:*
Help the children glue their stable outlines onto the blue construction paper backgrounds. Each week provide the families with a new paper figure for the crèche and a week's supply of foil star stickers. Ask the children to say a prayer for someone each day and add a star to the sky. Shortly before Christmas send home a special star to place over the stable and the baby Jesus to be placed underneath.

Christmas Journey 😀 PRE

Bring the Christmas story to life by taking the children on a Christmas journey with this delightful finger play.

❑ **To do:**

Five happy shepherds watching their sheep - (*Hold up five fingers*)

One saw an angel and jumped to his feet. - (*Hold up one finger*)

Four barn animals sound asleep - (*Hold up four fingers*)

One saw an angel and didn't make a peep. - (*Hold up one finger*)

Three Wise Kings watching the sky - (*Hold up three fingers*)

One saw an angel and began to wonder why. - (*Hold up one finger*)

Two loving parents full of love - (*Hold up two fingers*)

They both saw the angel, and were filled with joy.

One little baby asleep in the hay - (*Cradle arms to create baby Jesus*)

God's gift to us on Christmas day.

❑ **More to do:**

Change various headpieces to create the characters.
Paper crown – Kings
Dish clothes and rope – Shepherds, Mary, Joseph
Holiday garland halo - Angel

Christmas Nativity Ornament 😀 ALL

Send home this sparkling reminder of the gift of Jesus.

❑ **You will need:**
Margarine lids
Star pattern
Clear glitter
Glue
Sticker of small picture (prayer card) of the nativity
Hole punch

❑ **To do:**

Ahead of time, use the star pattern to cut out stars from the margarine lids and punch holes in the top of each. Have the children put the nativity sticker or glue the nativity picture on to the plastic star. Then place small amounts of glue all around the star and sprinkle clear glitter over the entire star.

C

Christmas Sky ☺ ALL

Decorating the Christmas sky in your classroom will make the world and your classroom a better place.

❑ *You will need:*
Fish net
Construction paper
Star pattern
Pencil
Scissors
Child-safe crèche figurines
Clothespins

❑ *To do:*

Hang a loosely woven fish net low enough for the children to reach yet high enough under which a crèche may be displayed. Trace and cut out many bright yellow stars. Discuss how kind acts brighten the world for others and us. Remind the children that Jesus came to teach us how to make the world a brighter place filled with God's love. Invite the children to share acts of kindness they have done for others and as they do attach one paper star per act with a clothespin. As the stars are added watch the sky and your classroom brighten.

Christmas Star Game 🐻 PRE

Use this fun game to remind the children of the star that led shepherds and kings to the baby Jesus.

❑ *You will need:*
A star cut from poster board and covered with shiny gift-wrap.

❑ *To do:*

Hide the star somewhere in the room while the children cover their eyes. Then say to the children, "Shepherds, shepherds, where's the star? You need it to find your way, afar." Then allow the children to look for the star, giving them clues such as "close" or "far," "hot" or "cold." When a child finds the star, give that child an opportunity to hide the star while the other children cover their eyes. Begin, "Wisemen, wisemen, where's the star? You need it to find your way, afar."

Celebration Tree   😊 ALL

Make a celebration tree for your classroom that can be used all year long to observe the seasons and holidays of our faith.

❏ **You will need:**
    Tree branch
    An ice cream bucket or coffee can
    Plaster of Paris
    Fabric

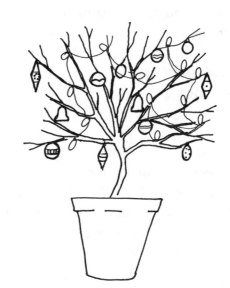

❏ **To do:**
Find a large bare tree limb with lots of branches. Saw the bottom off straight. Sink the branch in an ice-cream bucket or 3-pound coffee can with plaster of paris. (Plaster of paris can be purchased in a hobby or craft store.) Mix the plaster according to directions. Let it harden overnight. Cover the bucket or can with fabric or place it in a larger flowerpot.

As the seasons come and go make and hang different items on your tree. At the beginning of the year hang photos of the children, fall leaves, apples, or pumpkins. At Christmas time string colored lights on the tree and add ornaments. Gather gifts or collection items under the tree. Make snowflakes and hearts for the New Year and flowers and eggs for spring and Easter.

Chair Prayer   😊 ALL

Add a little interest to your community prayer by changing the environment now and then. How about reminding children that we need to take time with God by putting a chair in the area you gather for prayer.

❏ **You will need:**
    Old wooden straight back chair
    Cloth
    Bible
    Candle
    Cross

❏ **To do:**
Round up a wooden straight back chair from the attic, a volunteer, or parent. Place it in a corner of your classroom where there is room for the children to gather. Place a cloth on the seat of the chair with a Bible, candle, cross, etc. Hang a small wreath or pot of flowers from the back of the chair and there you have a neat new prayer place!

Church = People   ☺ ALL

When discussing the topic of the Church with children, the most important message for them to receive is that Church is people, a community of people who gather to give thanks and praise to God and to care for one another. The church is people!

❑ *You will need:*
Poster board
Markers or crayons

❑ *To do:*
Draw a large picture of a church on poster board. Print the name of your church across the top of the paper. Have the children print their names and draw a picture of themselves in the church. Hang this picture in a prominent place in your classroom as a reminder of church and community.

Circle of Kindness   ☻ PRE

Explain the importance of being kind to one another. Our belief in God and the care that we show for one another connects us to one another. Help children visualize this message.

❑ *You will need:*
Red handkerchief or red fabric scrap for each child
Basket

❑ *To do:*
Ask the children to share how we can show others we care for them. Each time a child offers an idea that conveys care for others invite them to take a piece of fabric from the basket. Once everyone has a fabric piece invite the group of children to stand and hold on to another child's fabric. Discuss how just as the fabric connects us to one another so do our kind actions.

Clay for Creating   ☺ ALL

Use this simple recipe to cook up some creativity in your classroom, one of the many gifts with which God blesses us.

❑ *You will need:*
Salt
Flour
Cream of Tartar
Food coloring
Cooking oil
Zip-lock baggies

❑ *To do:*
Mix 1 1/2 cups salt with 3 cups flour in a large mixing bowl. Add 6 teaspoons cream of tartar. Stir in 3 cups boiling water. If a tinted clay is desired tint boiling water with food coloring before adding to dry ingredients. Mix in 3 tablespoons of cooking oil. Knead onto a floured counter top until soft and pliable. This clay lasts longer if refrigerated and kept sealed in airtight zip lock bags.

Cloud Gazing   ☺ ALL

After what may seem like an endless number of cloudy days, take the children outside for some cloud gazing. Try to find different shapes. Take turns describing a shape in the sky and invite others to find the shape before it changes. Remind them that God gives us both these beautiful clouds and our imaginations.

❑ *You will need:*
Construction paper
Fiberfill batting
Glue

❑ *To do:*
Recreate the cloud shapes on construction paper using fiberfill and glue.

Color, God's Design   ☺ ALL

Send this fun color palette home as a reminder to families to look for God in all places.

❑ *You will need:*
Paper plate or tag board
Paintbrush
Small tissue paper squares in a variety of colors.

❑ *To do:*
Cut a paper plate or tag board to look like the palette of a painter. Place a square of tissue paper on the palette. Using the brush paint water over the small square to make the color run on to the palette. Continue adding more color to the palette in the same manner. After the watermarks are dry use a marker to print the message "The world is God's design."

Cookie Creations   🐯 PRE

When planning a class party it is always fun to have the children decorate their own cookies for the celebration.

❑ *You will need:*
Sugar cookies, wafer cookies, or graham crackers
Clean craft sticks
Frosting
Cookie sprinkles

❑ *To do:*
Give each child a paper plate, clean craft stick, a couple of cookies, and a couple of tablespoons of frosting. Have them spread their own frosting and then sprinkle the top with cookie sugars or small candies.

Corn Cob Kernels   ☺ ALL

Children are reminded to give thanks as they make corncobs to decorate the room.

❑ ***You will need:***
Tag board
Dried field corn with husks
  or colored popcorn
Glue

❑ ***To do:***
Cut a cob shape for each child out of tag board. In the middle of the cob write, "Thank you, God, for all good things." Remove the corn kernels from the cob as well as the husks. Have the children glue the kernels of the field corn to the paper cob. Staple or tape a few dried husks to the top of the corn.

Corner Stone Prayer Card   ✋ PRI

Reinforce and strengthen family prayer time with this corner stone prayer card.

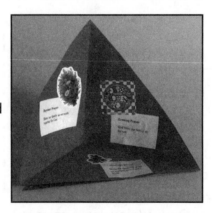

❑ ***You will need:***
8 1/2" squares of construction
  paper (one per child)
Copies of the three prayers
  provided or have them copied
  directly onto the paper
Stickers
Markers or rubber-stamps

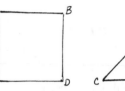

❑ ***To do:***
Fold the square into a triangle by bringing two opposite corners (A/D) together and crease the fold. Open to the square. Fold into another triangle using the opposite corners (B/C) and crease. Open to the square. Make a straight cut on the fold from the corner (D) to the center where the two folds intersect (E). Overlap cut corner (D2) to meet corner C, while corner B meets cut corner (D1). Staple or tape the overlapping side in place. Have the children use markers, rubber stamps, or stickers to decorate their corner stones.

Mealtime Prayer
Bless the food that gives us strength to do God's work.

Daytime Prayer
Bless our family as we work together for God.

Evening Prayer
God bless our family as we rest.

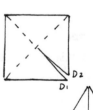
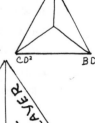

Cornucopia ☺ ALL

Use the cornucopia or "Horn of Plenty" to celebrate the harvest and Thanksgiving.
Cornucopia bulletin board.

❏ *You will need:*
   Large sheet of brown or gold paper
   Magazines
   Glue
   Scissors
   The letters, "Our Cornucopia of Blessings"

❏ *To do:*
Make a large cornucopia basket out of the
brown paper. Try a two dimensional basket by
scrunching the paper up and stapling it in place.
Have the children go through the magazines
and cut out pictures of things that they are
thankful for. Share these pictures during gather time and then staple them around the opening of
the cornucopia basket on the wall. Add the letter cutouts, "Our Cornucopia of Blessings."

Bugle Snack Cornucopia ✋ PRI

Mini-cornucopias made with Bugle corn snacks make wonderful place cards and table decorations.

❏ *You will need:*
   Bugle® corn snacks
   Colored popcorn
   Birdseed or dried beans
   Clear drying glue

❏ *To do:*
To make a folded place card, cut
the paper into 3" x 6" rectangles
and fold in half. With the fold at
the top, have the children write
their names on top left of the card.
Next have them glue the Bugle to
the lower right of the card. Glue
the seeds to the opening and area
around the opening of the Bugle. Be generous with the glue, as it will dry clear.
If possible dry over night.

C

Corny Thanksgiving Ideas ☺ ALL
Use these ideas as you plan your harvest and Thanksgiving lessons.

Corny Bird Feeder
Help care for God's creation by feeding the birds.

❑ *You will need:*
Dried field corn
Twine or string

❑ *To do:*
To make a bird or squirrel feeder, tie a string around the top of an ear of corn and hang in a tree.

Blessing corn
Native Americans tied corn up to dry to represent the blessings from Mother Earth and Father Sky.

❑ *You will need:*
Ear of dried field corn with husks per child (these could be donated by a local grower or
    purchased from a garden or grocery store)
Raffia
Thanksgiving blessing

❑ *To do:*
Tie a raffia bow around the center of the ear of corn. Attach a card with a Thanksgiving blessing
such as, "Thank you, God, for our harvest blessings." Hang the corn from the raffia on the wall or
use it as a table decoration.

Cotton Ball Toss ☺ ALL
Cotton ball toss is a fun and easy party game that can be adapted to any holiday and can be
played inside or out.

❑ *You will need:*
Cotton balls
Chalk and chalkboard
Water

❑ *To do:*
Draw shapes with chalk that coincide with the holiday you are celebrating: Pumpkins for
Thanksgiving, hearts for Valentines Day, etc. The children stand 3' to 6' back from the board
depending on their age and toss wet cotton balls at the symbols on the board. The cotton balls
should not be soaked, just wet enough to stick to the board for a few seconds.   To play outside
toss the cotton balls at the side of the building or on the sidewalk.

Cranberry Harvest Wreath 🖐 PRI

Cranberries are usually abundant in the fall of the year. Try making these little wreaths to celebrate the harvest with your children.

❑ **You will need:**
Fresh cranberries
12" lengths of heavy florist wire
Raffia

❑ **To do:**
Bend one end of each piece of wire so that the berries will not slide off as the children are stringing them. Show the children how to string the berries end to end. Leave about 2" of wire open at each end. Secure the berries by twisting the ends of the wire together and folding it over to one side. Tie a raffia bow over the folded wire to finish it off.

Creation Chant 🐨 PRE

Give God thanks for the beauty of creation with this fun chant.

❑ **To do:**
Red, yellow, green and blue,
These are colors, it is true.
Flowers, birds, trees and sky,
God loves us. That is why!

Creation Color Palette 🐨 PRE

Give thanks to God for all of creation with this Creation Color Palette.

❑ **You will need:**
Poster board
Brads
Scissors
Markers or paint

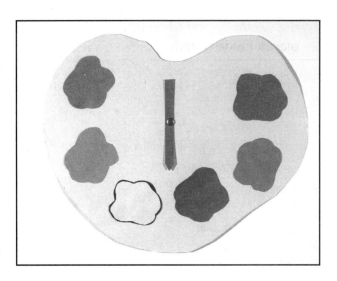

❑ **To do:**
Ahead of time make a painter's palette from tag board as shown in the diagram. Cut a paintbrush shape from tag board and attach to the painter's palette as shown using a brad fastener. Invite the children to take turns spinning the paintbrush and identifying something that God has provided for us that matches the color the brush indicates.

Crèche Take-Along ☺ ALL

These take-along nativity scenes are just the best. Children and their parents love the fact that they can play with the figures and carry them wherever they go.

❑ *You will need:*
  Plastic milk jugs
  Toilet tissue rolls
  Left over scraps of material
    (nylon netting works well, too)
  Glue
  Scissors
  Markers
  Raffia or ribbon

❑ *To do:*

To make the stable have an adult cut out the middle area of the milk jugs opposite the handle. Leave about 2" to 3" along the bottom, top, and sides of the milk jug. Place a few pieces of raffia or straw in the bottom of the stable and tie a bow on the handle. Use the tissue rolls to make Mary Joseph and Jesus. Tie and glue fabric scraps to the tissue rolls to make their clothes. Leave space near the top to draw their faces right on the cardboard. Cut the tissue rolls in half to make Baby Jesus. Also, cut a triangle blanket to wrap him in.

Crepe Paper Ball Filled With Surprises   PRI

Crepe paper surprise balls are fun for children to receive as a gift and just as much fun for children to make to give away.

Small gifts are rolled up into a ball. As the children unroll their balls, they receive little surprises along the way. Use this idea to make gifts for your little ones or have them help you make them to give away to those in need. This might be a great project for the older children in your community to make for the younger children.

❑ *You will need:*
  Rolls of crepe paper in a variety of colors
  Small toys, Stickers
  Candies, Balloons
  Coins, Erasers
  Tape, Ribbon

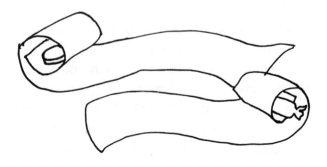

❑ *To do:*

Adjust the lengths of crepe paper to the number of items to be rolled up in each ball. There should be about 8"-10" between items. Start with one toy or coin and place it at the end of the crepe paper. Gently wrap the paper around it and then roll it several times before adding the next gift item. Turn and wrap the paper so that it makes the shape of a ball. When finished tape the end of the ball and tie a ribbon around it.

Crosses   ☺ ALL

Fast Food Tray Cross

Make sturdy three-dimensional crosses out of fast food trays during Lent or at any other time of the year.

❑ *You will need:*

    Fast food tray for each child
    Tissue paper
    Glitter
    Stickers
    Ribbon
    Glue
    Paper punch
    Scissors

❑ *To do:*

Cut the corners (the cup holders) out of each tray. Punch a hole at the top and lace a ribbon through it for hanging. Decorate the crosses with whatever is handy, glitter, beads, stickers, small silk flowers etc.

Collage Cross   ✋ PRI

Send home the message that Jesus lived, died, and rose for everyone with this cross of many faces.

❑ *You will need:*

    Cross pattern
    Tag board or poster board
    Magazine pictures of people
    Glue

❑ *To do:*

On poster board or heavy paper, draw and cut out a cross shape. Have the children search magazines for a variety of pictures of people to cut out and glue on the cross.

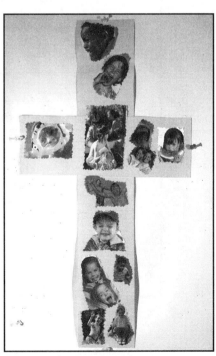

C

List Your Favorite Projects Here

_____

_____

_____

_____

_____

_____

_____

_____

_____

_____

_____

_____

_____

_____

_____

_____

_____

_____

_____

_____

_____

_____

Daffodil Celebration PRE

Make a spring daffodil to celebrate the season.

❑ *You will need:*
   Styrofoam egg cartons
   Construction paper
   Scissors
   Glue

❑ *To do:*

Cut out the egg cups from the egg cartons. Snip the sides of the cup from top to bottom to make the petals of the flower. Glue this to the flower pattern provided and glue to the paper. Add a stem and leaves.

Daily Blessings ALL

Remind the children to give thanks to God for all of their daily blessings with this easy-to-make-blessing reminder.

❑ *You will need:*
   Index cards
   Ribbon
   Markers
   Pictures cut from magazines
      of daily blessings such as food.

❑ *To do:*

Give each child several cards. Ask them to think about all of the things that God blesses them with every day. Brainstorm with them: family, friends, food, clothing, homes, etc. Then tell them to draw or paste pictures of these things/people, one per card. Staple a loop into one end of the ribbon to serve as a hanger. Then staple the index cards down the ribbon. Encourage the children to hang their blessings in a place where they will see them and remember to thank God for them every day.

Daisy Designs   ☺ ALL

Use up your wallpaper and wrapping paper scraps to make this cute designer daisy for spring.

❑ *You will need:*
   Brightly colored scraps of wallpaper and wrapping paper
   Buttons
   Glue
   Scissors
   Construction paper

❑ *To do:*
Using the pattern provided, have younger children cut out the flower and glue it to the paper. Add a stem and leaves. Glue buttons to the center of the daisy. Older children could cut out individual petals for the daisy, using a variety of patterns of paper and glue them into place.

Darkness and Light   ✋ PRI

God brings light to darkness. Bringing God into our homes makes them a brighter place to live.

❑ *You will need:*
   Empty milk carton
   Scissors
   Construction paper
   Markers

❑ *To do:*
Help children to make houses using empty milk cartons with the bottom cut away. Cut windows and doorways in the milk cartons. Decorate the outside by covering the carton with construction paper. Add details with the markers. When finished shine a flashlight from the bottom of the house to light up the inside.

Dateline Highlights   ☺ ALL

Keep track of the highlights of your year by making a number line dateline around the walls of your classroom.

❑ *You will need:*
   Number line
   A variety of pictures or symbols of the holidays and holy days
   Clear contact paper or lamination machine
   Tape

❑ *To do:*

Make a number line of the number of days between the beginning and end of the time you are together. These can be purchased or made. To make a number line cut a 6" width of rolled paper long enough to accommodate the number of days of your session. Tape the number line along the top of your classroom wall. With pictures, words, and symbols mark the highlights of the year above and below the number line. Include Thanksgiving, Advent, Christmas, New Years, Epiphany, Valentine's, Lent, Easter, children's birthdays, and any other special days you'd like to remember. If possible cover the pictures and symbols with clear contact paper or have them laminated so that they keep their color. Refer to the number line throughout the year as a teaching tool.

Day and Night   ☺ ALL

Remind the children that we can thank God with prayer each day for the blessings of our days and nights. This prayer reminder may be sent home with a short morning and evening prayer tucked inside each side.

❑ *You will need:*
  Two paper plates
  Markers
  Stapler
  Prayers
  Yarn
  Hole punch

❑ *To do:*

Decorate the top half of the whole plate with a bright shining sun. Turn the plate over and decorate the backside top half with a sleepy moon. Cut the undecorated plate in half. Staple the half plates to the decorated whole plate forming a pocket on each side so the moon and sun remain exposed.

Dear God Letter   ☺ ALL

Make poster-size letters to God that the children color themselves.

❑ *You will need:*
   12" by 18" construction paper or poster board
   Markers

❑ *To do:*

Print "Dear God" at the top of the poster board. Have the children color in the spaces of the prayer petitions.

Deck the Halls   ☺ ALL

Try making hand garland to border your bulletin board, bookshelves, doorways etc. for any holiday of the year.

❑ *You will need:*
   Construction paper
   Scissors
   Glue

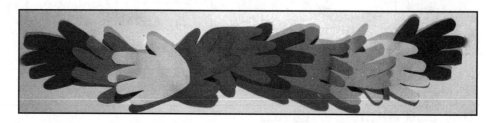

❑ *To do:*

Have the children trace and cut out two or three sets of their handprints. (Have staff cut out duplicate sets of hands depending on how much you have to make.) Glue or staple these together in a line to make a garland. At Christmas or in the spring make green handprints. In the fall, use orange, gold, and brown colors.

Delicious Doggie Delight   ☺ ALL

A sweet treat that older children can help make. What makes it fun to eat is that it looks like doggie chow.

❑ *You will need:*
   Stick margarine
   2 cups chocolate chips
   1 cup peanut butter
   8 cups rice/corn cereal
   2 1/2 cups powdered sugar (save for end)

❑ *To do:*

Melt margarine, chocolate chips, and peanut butter in double boiler or microwave. Pour melted ingredients over cereal in large bowl. When cereal is covered with chocolate mixture add powdered sugar and stir until covered. Refrigerate a couple of hours before eating. Serve in a new, clean dog dish for lots of giggles.

Departure Song 😺 PRE

At the end of every class make sure the children remember that God cares for each one of them.

❏ **To do:** 🎵

Sing to the tune of "If You're Happy and You Know It."

Be safe and happy as you go (Stomp with feet twice)
Be safe and happy as you go (Stomp with feet twice)
Keep Jesus in your heart
From you he'll never part.
Be safe and happy till we meet again. (Stomp with feet twice)

Describe It ☺ ALL

Here is a game that can be used at any time to recognize the beauty in the world God has given us.

❏ **To play:**

Select a person to be the "describer." His or her task is to look around and find an object to describe for the others in the group. The rest of the children try to guess what the item is. When it is guessed correctly, take time to recognize the item as a gift from God.

Desert Salt Painting ✋ PRI

Before special moments in his life, Jesus often went off by himself to pray. He prayed in the temple, hills, and even the desert. Remind the children to follow his example with desert salt painting.

❏ **You will need:**

Styrofoam meat trays
Salt
Powdered tempera paint
Pattern of Jesus
Glue

❏ **To do:**

Combine a few tablespoons of powdered tempera paint with about four cups of salt. Add paint until you have the color you wish. To create a desert scene, use blue, yellow, orange, brown, and red. Spread glue thinly over the meat tray. Have the children sprinkle desired colors over the meat tray. Shake off excess sand back into the pie tin. As the pictures are drying have the children add color to the Jesus pattern and cut it out. When the pictures are completely dry, add Jesus with glue and print, "Every day Jesus prayed."

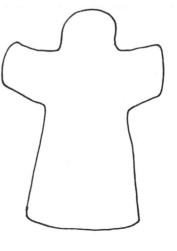

Dew Drop Picture ☺ ALL

Take an early morning walk in the wet grass and return to the classroom to make dewdrop pictures to hang in your classroom.

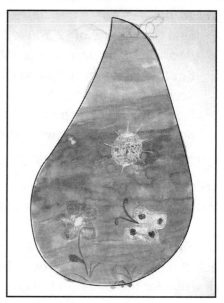

❑ **You will need:**

Large white construction paper
Crayons
Blue watercolor paint and brushes
Fishing line
Several dewdrop patterns

❑ **To do:**

Trace, and cut out the dewdrop. Using crayons have the children draw a spring or outdoor picture on the paper cutout. After coloring use blue watercolors and paint over the whole dewdrop. The paint will not stay on the crayon. Dry over night. Punch a hole in the top of the dewdrop and string a piece of fishing line through it for hanging.

Ding Dong Christmas Poem ☻ PRE

Delight little ones with this fun Christmas tale.
Copy and send home on an Advent card for families.

❑ **To do:**

Ding dong,
It won't be long,
Before the baby Jesus comes.
Make haste and ready the manger bed,
A warm, soft place to lay His head.
Ding dong,
It won't be long,
Till Christmas bells will ring.

Dinosaur Bone Soup ☺ ALL

This is an activity to build community during a few days of a cold spell. Children are more likely to eat a nutritious dish they prepare rather than one an adult suggests they eat.

❑ **You will need:**

Vegetables contributed by the children
Electric crock-pot or slow cooker
Browned soup bones
Canned tomato juice
Seasonings

❑ *To do:*

Early in the week ask children to bring their favorite vegetable to class for a pot of soup. The children should help clean and cut their selection for the soup. The day before you wish to eat the soup, place the children's ingredients into an electric crock-pot along with some partially browned soup bones, canned tomato juice, and desired seasonings. Cover and cook over night. The children are sure to feel a sense of pride and community as they fill their tummies with warmth and nutrition.

Calling the soup bones dinosaur bones just makes it a little more interesting.

Directory of Families ☺ ALL

Make and distribute family directories as a way to build community.

❑ *You will need:*

Copy paper
Copy machine
Staples
Pictures of their families drawn by children.

To do:

Before beginning this project get written permission to have each child's address, phone number, immediate family member's names and ages in the directory. Depending on the number of children in your program or class, plan to have one or two families on each page. Type out the following information about each family: Names of parents, names and ages of children, address, and phone number. Below this information add the family picture drawn by each child. Be sure that each child autographs his or her work. Make enough copies for each family, staple together, and distribute.

Dirty Worm Snack   😊 ALL

A fun treat to eat when working on a spring or creation unit.

❑ *You will need:*
  Instant chocolate pudding
  Crushed chocolate cookies or graham crackers
  Candy worms

❑ *To do:*

Mix up the pudding as directed and pour into small paper cups, about 3/4 full. Sprinkle crushed cookies over the top and add a worm. Beware! Lots of giggles will follow.

Disciples Are We   😊 ALL

Explain that the disciples were friends of Jesus who tried to live their lives as Jesus did. They spread God's word and love to others. Remind them that they are friends of Jesus as well with this fun song.

❑ *To sing:*
  To the tune of "BINGO."
  I am a friend to God's own son and Jesus is his name.
  J-E-S-U-S, J-E-S-U-S, J-E-S-U-S and Jesus is his name.
  He helps and leads me every day and Jesus is his name.
  J-E-S-U-S, J-E-S-U-S, J-E-S-U-S and Jesus is his name.
  I follow his example, being kind, strong and good.
  J-E-S-U-S, J-E-S-U-S, J-E-S-U-S and Jesus is his name.

Discovery Dig   PRE

Introduce new symbols each season with this activity.

❑ *You will need:*
  Zip-lock freezer bag
  Uncooked rice
  Small plastic toys such as Easter-eggs
  Bunnies
  Chicks
  Butterflies
  Caterpillars
  Grass
  (Any of these symbols could be cut out of construction paper.)

❑ *To do:*

Fill the freezer bag 3/4 full with the uncooked rice and a symbol of the season. Encourage the children to carefully dig for their treasure. Encourage the children to describe what they discover and what it tells about the season or about God.

Dominos Game 😊 ALL

Make up a dominos game for the children to use as they work in your classroom.

❑ *You will need:*
Tag board
Variety of religious or holiday stickers
or paper cutouts (80 total of 20 different designs.)
Clear contact paper or laminating machine

❑ *To do:*
Cut the paper into 40 3" x 7" pieces. Place one sticker or cutout to each end of the paper cards.
Have the stickers or cutouts facing the ends. Mix up the stickers and cut outs and be sure to have
about 4 of each in your cards. To play the game the children match up the ends of the cards on
the floor and come up with quite a creation!

Donations in Decorated Places 😊 ALL

Throughout the year we are always collecting items to share with those less fortunate. Decorate
boxes, grocery bags, use baskets or even clean garbage bins to collect food, personal hygiene
items, mittens, socks, baby clothes, etc.

❑ *You will need:*
Cardboard boxes
Wrapping paper
Ribbon
Pictures drawn or colored by the children

❑ *To do:*
Wrap plain cardboard boxes in wrapping paper to collect heavier items such as food, or hygiene
items. Collect mittens, hats, and socks in garbage cans. Tie ribbons on the handles and tape
pictures drawn by the children to the front of them. Collect baby clothes in large baskets lined
with receiving blankets or at Christmas time use a life-size manger or cradle.

Doorknob Welcome 😊 ALL

Spread the peace of Jesus to others with this doorknob decoration.

❑ *You will need:*
Tag board
Markers
Jingle bells
Ribbon

❑ *To do:*
Cut the paper into 4" x 12" pieces. Two inches from the top of the paper
trace and cut out a 2" circle. On the paper print one of the following sayings,

D

"Peace to all that enter," "Peace be to you," or "Peace of Jesus to you." Have the children color around the words. Punch holes along the bottom of the paper and hang jingle bells from them.

Doormat Designs ☺ ALL
Welcome in the season with doormats made from a carpet samples.

❏ *You will need:*
Carpet squares
Acrylic paints
Sponges cut out into seasonal shapes
Stencils
Paintbrushes

❏ *To do:*
Using the paints and brushes print a seasonal message. Decorate with stencil designs and/or sponge designs. Encourage the children to be creative with their designs.

❏ *More to do:*
Decorate a new doormat for the start of each season – Lent, Easter, Advent, and Christmas.

Double Decker Sandwich ☺ ALL
Make a double-decker sandwich to reinforce mealtime prayer at home.

❏ *You will need:*
White card-stock paper
Markers
Hole puncher
Paper fasteners
Copies of meal prayer

❏ *To do:*
Enlarge, copy, and cut out the patterns provided here for the sandwich. Have the children color each part of the sandwich. Place a copy of the meal prayer in the middle. Punch a hole in each and put together with a paper fastener.

Double Dice Petitions ☺ ALL

Play the dice game and each time someone gets doubles they add a line to a spontaneous prayer or thanksgiving or petitions.

❑ *You will need:*
Pair of dice
Pie tin

❑ *To do:*
Have the children sit in a circle. One at a time the children shake the dice in the pie tin. If they do not get a pair they pass the pie tin and dice to the next person and they shake the dice. If someone gets doubles they stop and add a petition to a prayer. Chose a prayer topic such as thanksgiving or families or friends. Before passing the pie plate, begin the prayer, "Dear God, we are so grateful for our families." Again, have the children add a petition to the prayer when they get doubles.

Dove Centerpiece ✋ PRI

As Jesus was baptized by John in the river, "the heaven was opened to Jesus, and he saw the Spirit of God coming down like a dove and lighting upon him." (Cf. Matthew 3:16) Introduce your children to the symbol of the dove by making this centerpiece.

❑ *You will need:*
1/2 of a Styrofoam ball
Jar lid
Glue
Styrofoam packing worms
Pipe cleaners
Yellow construction paper
White construction paper

❑ *To do:*
Glue the flat side of the half Styrofoam ball inside the jar lid. Stick one packing worm on the end of a pipe cleaner and poke the other end into the Styrofoam ball. Use the wing pattern to cut wings and a tail feather from white paper and the beak pattern to cut a beak from yellow paper. Glue the wings to the center of the packing peanut and the beak to the front as shown. Encourage the children to add as many doves as they would like to their centerpieces.

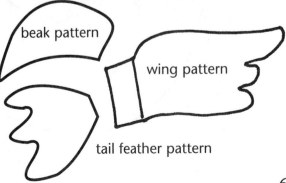

beak pattern

wing pattern

tail feather pattern

Dove Mobile 🖐 PRI

God sent Noah the dove with a twig in its mouth as a reminder to keep the faith, "Dry land is just ahead." God sends us daily reminders that sometimes go unnoticed. Take time to notice and record the signs to keep the faith with this dove mobile.

❑ *You will need:*
  Twine
  Green construction paper
  White tag board
  Marker
  Hole punch
  Scissors

❑ *To do:*

Cut out a dove using the pattern. Attach a 12" to 15" piece of twine to the mouth of the dove. Discuss some ways we are reminded that God is always with us. For example when a rainbow comes out after a rain. Encourage the children to notice these signs throughout the day. At the end of the day talk over some signs they noticed. Provide each child with a piece of green construction paper to cut a small leaf. Attach the leaves to the twine. Continue in the weeks that follow to add leaves when a sign is noticed. To make a hanger open a paper clip and pull it through the hole at the base of the dove's neck.

Dragonfly ☺ ALL

❏ *You will need:*
Standard clothespins
  (type without the spring)
Markers
Bright pipe cleaners
Tissue paper

❏ *To do:*
Wrap a pipe cleaner around the top of the
clothespin to form the head and antennae.
Use a marker to make a face on the flat side
of the round top as shown. Cut wings from the tissue paper and pull through the slip as shown.

Dreamcatcher ☺ ALL

A Native American ritual that will capture the spirit of the year. The tradition holds that if a dream catcher is placed above a child's bed, any bad dreams will be kept away and the good dreams will stay within. Use the symbol to remind children that God helps us keep the good and push out anything bad.

❏ *You will need:*
Plastic butter tub lids
Yarn
Stickers
Beads plastic straws
Scissors
Hole punch

❏ *To do:*
Cut away the center to the plastic lid leaving
at least a half-inch rim. Use the hole punch
to make holes all the way around the rim as
shown. Make a web by threading yarn in and
out of the holes in no particular order.
Decorate the web with beads and stickers.
At the end of the year gather up any leftover
craft materials for this project. For younger
children pipe cleaners may be used to easily
attach beads. Make simple plastic beads by
cutting the straws in 1/2" to 1" sections.

D

Dribble, Drip, Drizzle   ☺ ALL

Build a class prayer table. Collect a few building materials such as bricks and boards from members of your community. As few as two bricks and one board are needed.

❑ *You will need:*
Building bricks
Boards
Latex paints
Paint brushes
Drop cloth or newspapers
(Don't forget towels, soap, and water for clean up.)

❑ *To do:*
Place the building materials on the drop cloth. Give each child a paintbrush and some paint inviting the children to dribble, drip and drizzle the paint over the building materials. When the paint has dried work together to set up the prayer table in a special place. These building materials make it easy to take the table down and redesign anywhere anytime.

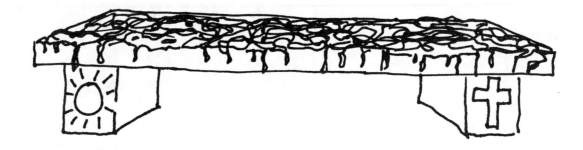

Duck, Duck, Swan Game   ☻ PRE

This game is perfect to teach children that often we follow the actions of others.

❑ *To play:*
The children stand in a line in an area that allows plenty of room to move around. The leader shows an action for the children to follow like rubbing his or her tummy while saying, "Duck." The next child does the same action and says, "Duck." The third child says, "Swan" while introducing a new action. The play continues in this manner until all the children have had a chance to be the "Swan" or as time allows. After playing this game discuss how our kind words and actions can be followed by others to make this an even better world to live in.

Earth Care Cards   ☺ ALL

God has surrounded us with living beauty in nature. As adults it is our job to teach young children to respect and care for the earth and its resources. Have the children help create a set of earth prayer cards. This is an activity that may begin with Earth Day in April and continue throughout the year.

❑ *You will need:*

3" x 5" index cards
Magazines full of nature pictures
Scissors
Glue

❑ *To do:*

Invite the children to search for magazine pictures of things in nature they are thankful for. Glue the pictures to the index cards. Distribute the cards at a prayer time and ask the children to share what is pictured on their card while saying a prayer of thanks to God.

Leave the cards in an area where the children can always be reminded of the wonderful gift of life that God has surrounded us with. Use the cards to lead discussions of how we can care for the earth. Recycling, reducing, reusing!

Earth Day Promise Tree Mural   ☺ ALL

Celebrate creation and the many gifts of God with this spring Earth Day mural.

❑ *You will need:*

Large bulletin board or wall space
Brown paper
Green construction paper
Scissors
Markers

❑ *To do:*

Make a large tree with branches in the center of the bulletin board. Title the bulletin board, "Our Earth Day Promise Tree." Use the patterns provided and have the children trace and cut out a variety of leaves. With adult help have the children write down ways that they will help take care of the earth. Examples would be not littering, picking up trash, planting new flowers and trees, etc. Staple the leaves to the tree.

Our Earth Day Promise Tree

Easter Basket ☺ ALL

A tisket, a tasket, you will certainly need an Easter basket.

❑ *You will need:*
   Plastic produce pint containers
   Ribbon
   Easter grass
   Pipe cleaner
   Glue

❑ *To do:*
Weave the ribbon in and out of each row on the sides and bottom. Use glue to secure the ends of the ribbons. Add a pipe-cleaner handle. Put a little Easter grass in the bottom. All that's left is to fill the basket.

Easter Bell ☺ ALL

Ring in the Good News of Jesus' Resurrection with flower pot bells.

❑ *You will need:*
   3" clay flower pots
   Paints
   Stickers
   Twine
   1/2" bead or jingle bell
   Ribbon

❑ *To do:*
Have the children decorate the outside of the flower pot with paints or stickers. Allow to dry. To make the hanger cut the twine in 24" lengths. Pull the twine through the bead and fold in half so that the bead is at the folded end of twine. Make a double knot 3" above the bead and pull the ends of the twine through the bottom of the bell making sure the knot is secure and does not go through the hole. Make a new double knot on the top of the bell; again making sure the knot holds the twine in place. To make a loop for hanging tie a knot at the end of the twine. For decoration tie a bow of ribbon above the knot at the top of the pot.

Easter Bunny 🙂 ALL

The familiar Easter symbol represents the new life of spring.

❑ *You will need:*

Easter grass
1/4 sheets of green construction paper
11" x 1" strips of white paper
Three 5" x 1" strips of white paper
Cotton balls
Glue
Stapler
Tape

❑ *To do:*

Secure the two strips of white paper into individual loops. Staple the small loop (head) to the larger loop (body). Staple a small loop to each side the head to make ears. Glue a cotton ball on the body in place for a tail. Secure the base of the body onto the green paper with a piece of tape. Add Easter grass around the base of the body to hide the tape.

Easter Butterfly 🙂 ALL

Celebrate the new life of spring with this butterfly mobile.

❑ *You will need:*

Tag board
Markers
Paper punch
Ribbon
Jingle bells

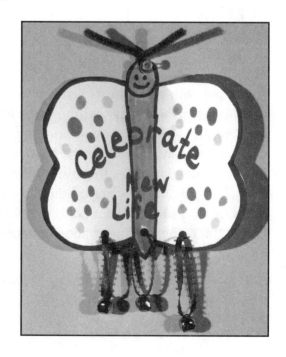

❑ *To do:*

Using the pattern provided cut out one butterfly per child in your group. Attach pipe cleaners to the head of the butterfly for antenna and have the children color the rest of it with markers. With adult help write the words, "Celebrate New Life" on the butterfly. Punch three holes along the bottom of the butterfly. Hang the bells with ribbon from the holes. Punch a hole at the top of each wing and lace ribbon through them for hanging.

Easter Egg Surprise ☺ ALL

Try this fun, simple Easter egg gift for you to make for the children or for the children to make for others.

❑ *You will need:*
   Plastic Easter eggs
   Candy to fill each egg
   8" circles of brightly colored nylon net
   Ribbon

❑ *To do:*
Fill the plastic eggs with candy and cover with the nylon net. Gather the excess netting at the top of the egg and tie with a ribbon. Add a second piece of ribbon for hanging the egg. Attach a little prayer card with a greeting such as, "Easter blessings to you."

Easter Lily ☺ ALL

The white Easter lily fills the church on Easter morning as a sign that Christ has risen. Here is an idea that uses hands to create this Easter flower symbol.

❑ *You will need:*
   White construction paper
   Tape
   Green pipe cleaner
   Brown pipe cleaner
   Pencil
   Paper cup or pastel colored sheet of paper

❑ *To do:*
Use the pencil to trace the child's hand onto the white construction paper. Cut out the hand shape and roll the pinky so it meets the thumb. Secure in place with a piece of tape. Through the bottom opening (where the wrist would be) slide a green pipe cleaner to form the stem of the flower. Hook the top of the green pipe cleaner to make the stamen of the flower. The finished flower may be placed in a vase (paper cup) or glued to a pastel colored sheet of paper with the message "Christ is risen."

E

Easter Song   😊 ALL
Sing to the tune of "BINGO."

❏ **To Sing** 🎵

Jesus rose on Easter day and that makes us so happy.
H-A-P-P-Y, H-A-P-P-Y, H-A-P-P-Y and that makes us so happy.
Jesus brings new life to us and that makes us so happy.
H-A-P-P-Y, H-A-P-P-Y, H-A-P-P-Y and that makes us so happy.
Jesus is with us today and that makes us so happy.
H-A-P-P-Y, H-A-P-P-Y, H-A-P-P-Y and that makes us so happy.
Encourage the children to make up new verses for this joy-filled tuned.

Echo Rhymes   😊 ALL
This is a fun way to teach a poem, story or rhyme to little ones.

❏ **To do:**

The leader says one line and the children repeat or "echo" it back. Try this creation echo.
In the beginning (echo)
There was God. (echo)
Making light, making dark. (echo)
Dotting sky with stars. (echo)
Parting sea from land. (echo)
Making plants and animals. (echo)
Sending fish to swim at sea. (echo)
Thennnn God, (echo)
Made you and me. (echo)
And God said, (echo)
This is greaaaat," (echo)
For I love you!" (echo)
Create your own echo using any story or poem and keeping the repeated phrases short.

Edible Insects   😊 ALL
Provide the materials and let the children explore the wonder of God's bugs by creating their own kind of edible insect. As the children are designing these treats they can learn some insect vocabulary.

❏ **You will need:**

Jellied orange slices, Jumbo gum drops
Strings of licorice, Mini pretzels

❏ **To do:**

Use the jellied candies as the "body." Use a knife to make slits in the jellied candies. This will make a place to slide in pretzel "wings."
The licorice may be cut into short pieces for "legs" and "antennae."

Egg Carton Treasure Box   ☺ ALL

Make little treasure boxes for the children to use to collect the wonders of creation or special little trinkets they gather along the way.

❑ *You will need:*
Egg cartons
Spray paint
Stickers
Glitter
Glue

❑ *To do:*
With spray paint, paint the outside, top, and bottom of the egg cartons. Allow to dry overnight. Have the children decorate the outside of their carton with glitter and stickers. Be sure they add their name to the top, too.

Egg Pocket   ✋ PRI

Peek into an egg with an Easter symbol inside.

❑ *You will need:*
Construction paper
Easter grass
Easter stencils for tracing
Scissors
Pencil
Glue

❑ *To do:*
Fold a sheet of construction paper in half. Cut out a large egg shape. On one of the egg shapes, cut an opening on the center as shown. Put glue around the outer edge of one of the eggs and glue the two eggs together. Stuff the opening of the egg pocket with grass. Have the children select an Easter symbol to trace and cut out of construction paper. Decorate with markers and place the symbol inside the grass-lined opening. Print the Easter message, "Alleluia!" on the egg.

Elephant Ears   ☻ PRE

You don't have to have elephant ears to hear God's word.
Explore the many ways God speaks to us in the world around us.
Make elephant ears to wear while saying the elephant poem.

❑ *You will need:*
Gray construction paper
Stapler
2" strips of paper long enough to fit around childrens' heads

❏ *To do:*

Enlarge and copy the elephant ears provided. Trace them and cut out of gray construction paper.
Staple the ears to 2" wide strips of paper sized to fit around the children's head.

You don't have to have elephant ears to hear God's word.
You can hear it each day in the song of a bird.
God speaks to us in so many different ways,
In the rain and the sunshine of our days.
Through the mountains and the seas,
And the rivers and the trees.
We hear God's voice,
Each and every day.
We know our God is always near,
We don't need elephant ears to hear.

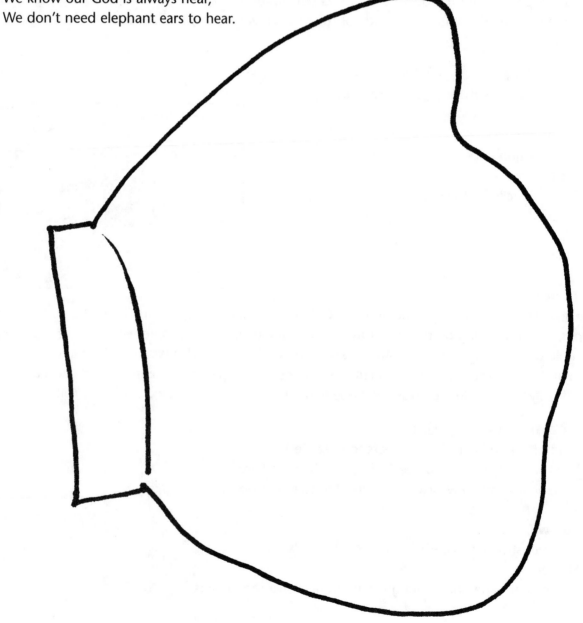

78

Embroidery Hoop Tambourine   ☺ ALL
Jump, jingle, and jive and celebrate the wonder of God with this neat tambourine.

❑ *You will need:*
   4" to 6" wooden embroidery hoops
   (These may be purchased inexpensively
      in twos at craft and fabric stores.)
   Ribbon
   Jingle bells

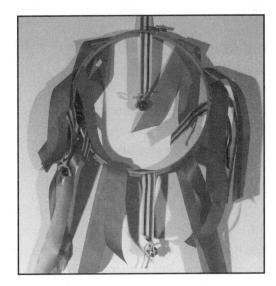

❑ *To do:*
Tie a variety of colors and lengths of ribbon to the
hoop. Also tie on 3 jingle bells. Use these fun
tambourines with your rhythm band instruments or
for a parade around the block

Emotion Circles   ☺ ALL
God gave us so many emotions to show what we are feeling in our hearts. This activity will help
children express their emotions in a creative manner.

❑ *You will need:*
   Large sheet of paper for each child
   Crayons or markers
   Circles in various sizes to use for tracing.

❑ *To do:*
Before distributing any materials discuss emotions you have observed children expressing. Talk
about a variety of emotions and various situations without identifying any specific children or
situations. Talk about how emotions show what our hearts are feeling. Provide each child with a
sheet of paper, markers, and circles. Ask the children to think of a time when they felt "love."
Encourage them to trace or draw a circle the size "love" is to them using the color they think
represents the feeling of "love." Use the same process to express other emotions such as sad,
lonely, happy, embarrassed, wonder, anger, etc.

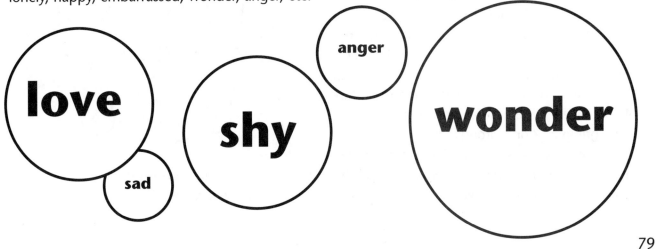

Empty Tomb ☺ ALL

Begin to teach young children about the Resurrection with an empty tomb made of papier-mâché.

❑ **You will need:**
Large bowl
Aluminum foil
1" to 2" strips of newspaper
To 1 cup of water add enough
   flour to make paste or papier-mâché

❑ **To do:**
Cover the bowl with aluminum foil. Coat the foil covering with three layers of newspaper strips that have been dipped in the paste mixture. When the papier-mâché has dried remove the bowl. Use a scissors to make a door in the papier-mâché' frame. Use gray and brown paints to resemble the look of stone. Place a small stone in front of the door during Lent and rolled away from the door during the Easter season.

End of the Year Autograph Pots ✋ PRI

A real flowerpot with everyone's name written on it is a wonderful keepsake of the year together.

❑ **You will need:**
4" clay flower pot
Fine point permanent markers
Pebbles
Potting soil
Bedding plants such as marigolds,
   petunias, or impatiens

❑ **To do:**
Have the children write their own names on the bottom of the pot. In groups of 2 or 3 have the children write their own names on each other's pot. (Every child writes his or her name on every pot.) It works best to have the children sit at a table and pass the pots down the line for each to sign. Adult guidance is needed to keep the children from getting mixed up and off task. If you have a large group you may have to do the signing in 2 or 3 sittings. Plant each pot after everyone has signed it. Put a few pebbles in the bottom of each pot for drainage. Fill the pot about half full with potting soil. Add the plant and fill in with more dirt around the edges. Water and enjoy!

Envelope Gift Bag  PRI

A great project that will be enjoyed by young and old alike. Make these little gift bags to give to the children or for the children to make to give to others.

❑ *You will need:*
A variety of greeting card envelopes
Ribbon
Rubber-stamps
Markers
Decorative-edged scissors

❑ *To do:*
This project can be a bit tricky so be sure you have a little extra help on hand. To make the bags, first seal the envelope. Next cut off the top 1/2 to 1/3 of the envelope. Make a 1" fold on each of the 3 folded sides of the envelope. Open the envelope and fold to the inside of the original envelope folds. Re-crease the side folds to the center to make a bag. Tape the corner flaps (that are made when the sides and bottom are folded in) to the bottom of the bag. Punch holes in the topsides of the bag and tie a ribbon through them to make a hand holder. Decorate with rubber stamps and stickers. Hint: adjust the width of the first folds around the envelope depending on the size of the envelope.

❑ *More to do:*
Make extra gift bags to fill with goodies for shut-ins or your neighborhood food pantry.

Envelope Puppet ALL

This simple and creative puppet idea will make any story you have to tell more fun and interesting.

❑ *You will need:*
Legal or standard size envelopes
Stickers
Markers
Scissors

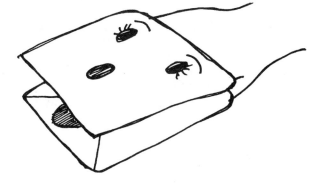

❑ *To do:*
Fold the envelope in half the short way and then unfold it. Carefully cut the fold along the solid or address side of the envelope. Wet and seal the other side of the envelope as you normally would and fold it back in half again. To make the puppet talk place the thumb in the bottom opening and the next two fingers in the top. Have the children add facial features as well as ears, hair etc.

81

E

Epiphany Board Game　　 PRI

Set this large game board up in the classroom to help children
learn about the journey of the kings or wise men: Gaspar, Melchior, and Balthasar.

❏ **You will need:**
28 sheets of paper
Masking tape
Marker for each child
(See game pieces.)
Dice

❏ **Game preparation:**
Print these messages on the sheets as indicated.

Sheet 1-2　　blank

Sheet 3　　　You see the star in the east. Move ahead 1 space.

Sheets 4-6　　blank

Sheet 7　　　Cloudy sky. Move back 2 spaces.

Sheets 8-13　　blank

Sheet 14　　You listen when Herod asks about the newborn King. Move back 1.

Sheets 15-16　blank

Sheet 17　　You see the star just ahead. Move ahead 3 spaces.

Sheets 18-19　blank

Sheet 20　　You are excited to find the baby with Mary. STOP here to present
　　　　　　the gifts to baby Jesus. (Decorate this sheet with a large, bright, yellow star)

Sheet 21-23　blank

Sheet 24　　You are told in a dream not to return to Herod. Move ahead 2 spaces.

Sheet 25-27　blank

Sheet 28　　King's home! (Decorate with 3 crowns)

❏ **To do:**

Tape the sheets in order 1-28 on the floor. The game is played by rolling the dice and moving the
number of places the dice shows. Follow the directions on the game board. Every player must
stop at the star (sheet 20). Play until all the kings have reached their home.

Epiphany Cake and Celebration   ☺ ALL

Celebrate Epiphany or the journey of the three kings with a class party. The wise men followed the bright guiding star to Bethlehem where Jesus lay in the stable. The Kings brought gifts of gold, frankincense, and myrrh for the newborn King. Epiphany means appearance. Today in many countries, this is the holiday in which children receive their gifts, rather than at Christmas. Eat a cake for your special kings' party, but be prepared for a hidden surprise inside. Tradition says that whoever finds the candy coin or prize in their cake is king for the day.

❑ *You will need:*
> Cupcakes or single layer cake
> Candy coins or other surprise to hide in the cake
> Prizes for the children who find the coins
> Extra frosting

❑ *To do:*
Cut the cake in serving size pieces. In one or two pieces of cake hide a candy coin. We have found it works best to go in through the bottom of the cake. Use extra frosting to doctor up the cake if necessary. The children will have fun finding the coins and enjoying their cake! Play a little trick on the children and add a coin in each child's cake so that they can all be king for a day.

Epiphany Crowns   ☺ ALL

Remember the special visitors baby Jesus had by making everyone king for a day.

❑ *You will need:*
> Construction paper
> Markers
> Sequins
> Glitter
> Glue
> Scissors
> Stapler
> Tinsel holiday tree garland

❑ *To do:*
Enlarge and trace the crown pattern provided. Fit each crown to the children's heads before decorating and joining ends together. Staple a string of holiday garland to the lower edge of the crowns. Have the children decorate the rest of their crowns with sequins, glitter, beads, and markers. After the decorations have dried, staple the ends of the crowns together.

Evening Prayer Card   ✋ PRI

Help children make this three-sided prayer card as a reminder to say an evening prayer. The prayer could be to ask for help to be more like Jesus in their hearts, words, and actions.

❑ *You will need:*

  4 1/2" x 5 1/2" sheet of stiff paper such as cardstock
  Tape
  Newspapers
  Scissors
  Heart stickers
  Marker

❑ *To do:*

Fold the sheet into thirds lengthwise and crease.
Open the folded paper and decorate the three sections as follows:

Print, "Jesus, help me to be more like you in my"

    (place the heart sticker – symbol for heart).

Print, "Jesus help me to be more like you in my"

    (glue some cutout words from the newspaper – symbol for words).

Print, "Jesus help me to be more like you in my"

    (make hand shapes with a marker – symbol for actions).

Tape the 4 1/2" ends together forming a triangle as shown. Before sending this home with the children demonstrate how it is used. Each evening roll the card over from side to side asking to grow more like Jesus in heart, words, and actions.

Evergreen Mobile   ☺ ALL

Hang ornaments and a Christmas prayer from an evergreen branch.

❑ *You will need:*

  Fresh or artificial evergreen branch about 12" long and thick enough to hold about five ornaments.
  Ribbon
  Ornaments such as jingle bells or glitter painted pinecones
  Small candy canes
  Paper stars, etc.
  Fishing line or string
  Ribbon
  Copies of the Christmas blessing below

❑ *To do:*

Provide a fresh or artificial branch for each child. Tie a ribbon to the ends of the branch for hanging. Use fishing line or string to hang the ornaments from the branches.

"May the blessings and joy of this Christmas season be with you throughout the year."

Exercise ☺ ALL

Exercise is a way to keep our bodies fit for God's work but it can also be a celebration of our creation! Here is a creative movement activity that will exercise the body as the mind imagines.

❑ *To do:*

Walk the children through this activity telling a story similar to this.

Stretch tall, reach up high (higher and higher) and pretend to receive a huge "gift" box from God. Bending at the knees pretend to bring the gift down to the floor. Let go of the gift and, because the gift was so big, shake out your hands.

❑ *Work-out*

Bending at the knee, lift the gift from the floor. Show how excited you are to receive this great gift from God by hopping around the room while shaking the imaginary gift from side to side over your head. Set the box down and take a rest. Show how strong you are by lifting the gift up and down off the floor several times. Bend down low and stretch up high as you lift the imaginary box. Place the gift back on the floor. Bend at the waist, place your fingers under the gift and pretend to swing the gift from side to side. Set the box back down.

❑ *Cool-down*

Pretend to open the gift box and look inside to find that it is YOU inside the box. Curl up tightly into a ball on the floor and pretend to roll out of the box. Then stretch out lying down on the floor. Curl up tight again and then stretch further out. Curl up very tight once more. Stretch all the way out on your back and relax. As you relax on your back, take deep breaths and think of what a wonderful gift our bodies are and how we can keep them fit for God.

As the children are relaxing talk about ways we can keep our bodies fit with proper rest, nutrition, and exercise.

Exercise Equipment for Good News ☺ ALL

Faith is very similar to the muscles in our bodies. It must be used and worked to be strong and healthy. Make a gym bag to fill up with exercise equipment for God to help build strong faith and healthy kids.

❑ *You will need:*
 Large grocery bag
 Stapler
 Markers
 Stickers

❑ *To do:*
Cut 1/2 of the bag off the top. Cut 2" by 12" strips off the cut-off part of the bag. Staple these strips, one to each side of the bag for handles. With adult help have the children write, "My exercise bag for God."

❑ *More to do:*
Fill the bag with a child's Bible story or small prayer book. Make a small cross by tying two sticks together with raffia or string. Trace the child's hand on a piece of toweling or terry cloth and write the words, "Working out for God." On a plastic water bottle write the words, "Refreshed and reborn in Jesus." Add an item from nature such as a seashell or flower as a reminder of the wonder of creation. Check out a surplus or discount store for sweatbands for the head and wrists.

Exploring God's World with Binoculars 🦁 PRE

Make a pair of cool binoculars to check out the detail and beauty of God's creation.

❑ *You will need:*
 Toilet tissue tubes
 16" lengths of string
 Stickers
 Stapler
 Paper punch

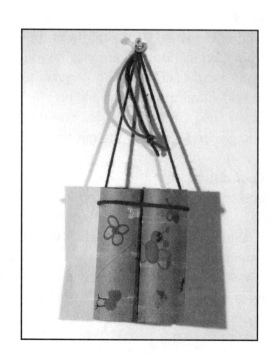

❑ *To do:*
Staple two toilet tissue tubes together. Punch a hole 1" from the end on the outside of each roll. Lace one end of string through each hole and tie. Decorate with stickers.

Eyes Have It   ☺ ALL

In God's eyes we are all equal. Together, as a group, make a mural of eyes.

❑ *You will need:*

Markers

Roll or large sheets of paper

❑ *To do:*

Help the children draw their pair of eyes on the paper at their approximate height. Provide colorful markers for each child to personalize their own pair of eyes. Hang the mural low enough for the children to admire it at their level. Across the top print "In God's eyes we are all equal."

E

Eyes of Love ☺ ALL

To love others is to look for the best qualities in them. If we look at others only noticing their faults we can overlook the good qualities.

❑ **You will need:**
Tag Board
Scissors
Glitter
Sequins
Glue

❑ **More to do:**
Pass the pair of heart-shaped glasses to a child and ask him or her to complete the phrase, "When I look with eyes of love, I see." Continue to pass the glasses and invite the children to complete the phrase until everyone has had the opportunity. Have each child make a pair of glasses and decorate his/her own glasses.

❑ **To do:**
Make a pair of heart-shaped eyeglasses from tag board and decorate them. Holding the glasses in your hand share a time when you were having a bad day and only remember the negative happenings. Here's an example: I woke up late one morning and felt kind of crabby. My baby sister bugged me. The dog wouldn't leave me alone. My mom wanted me to eat breakfast but I didn't feel like it. Then I found these cool glasses and when I put them on, I noticed how funny my baby sister is. It felt good to see how excited my dog was that I was around to play with him. Wow, my mom made a delicious breakfast for me. What a great start to my day.

Tell the children that we can show others how to look through "new eyes" – "eyes of love" – by our example and actions.

Faith and Feathers ☺ ALL
Faith is believing even when we cannot see. Try this delightful activity to give children a beginning understanding.

❑ *You will need:*
Feathers

❑ *To do:*
Give each child a feather. Tell the children to throw the feathers up into the air. Watch the feathers come down. Ask the children what controls the way the feathers fall. When they answer air, ask if they can see the air. Explain that God is like the air in that we cannot see God's presence but we know God is there.

Fall Bulbs ☺ ALL
In the fall think ahead to spring by planting bulbs that will bloom in the spring.

❑ *You will need:*
Bulbs such as tulips, daffodils, crocus
Bone meal

❑ *To do:*
Plant the bulbs. If you do not have a garden area, a great place to plant the bulbs is in the grass near an entrance. Usually the bulbs will grow and bloom before the grass will need to be cut. Once the flowers are done blooming, just cut the grass as usual. Watch and see; the flowers may come up the next year. Seeing new life in the form of flowers is a great treat for the whole community.

Fall Forest Right in Your Room ☺ ALL
Create a "forest" to enhance your prayer area.

❑ *You will need:*
Large cardboard boxes
Brown paper bags
Glue
Markers

F

❑ *To do:*

Pile two or three large cardboard boxes on top of one another. Secure them with packing tape. Draw a very simple outline of a tree, as shown. Take the children for a walk giving each one of them a paper bag. Have the children collect leaves of various kinds, colors, and sizes. Point out textures, colors, sights, and sounds of the season. Back in the classroom, discuss all the things you experienced on your walk together. As you tape each leaf on the "tree," thank God for one of the textures, sights, colors, or sounds you experienced on your walk.

Fall Lessons of Faith ☺ ALL

Fall is the time of year when you only need to look around outside and you will see God is providing. Here is an idea that will help carry a fall message of faith to the homes of the children: "Faith is knowing the animals will be warm and fed this winter."

❑ *You will need:*

Brown paper lunch bag
Dark marker
Scissors

❑ *To do:*

As fall approaches take the children outside to look for signs of animals preparing for the cold. Watch as the squirrels collect acorns and other nibbles of food to store. Look for hiding places animals might tuck in to escape the winter winds. Sprinkle seeds for animals to find and store. Make a pretend tree using a brown paper lunch bag for the families to fill with signs in nature that the animals will be protected from the winter cold.

Draw the outline of a tree trunk on the bag. Cut out a hole where the found items may be placed. Send the bag home with the children. Invite families to store nuts, seeds, and soft pieces of cloth, string, straw, and whatever else they might collect in the bag until the end of autumn. On a cold day encourage the families to set the items out for an animal to use.

Family Prayer Journal   ☺ ALL

Begin a family prayer journal to go back and forth from the homes of children to church as a way to reinforce and encourage prayer as well as community.

❑ *You will need:*
    Notebook with or without lines
    Contact paper
    Permanent marker
    Copies of various prayers for mealtime, bedtime, etc.

❑ *To do:*
Cover the notebook with colorful contact paper. On the cover print, "Family Prayer Journal." On the inside page attach the following instructions for using this book.   This journal is to go from home to home as a way for families to share their prayer ideas with one another. Invite families to write their favorite prayers or prayer ideas in the book. Names are not necessary, just the ideas. Invite the children to draw pictures in the journal, too. Also invite people to share any special prayers they might have for the healing of a sick relative, etc. On the instruction sheet invite families to try out the prayer ideas included to get started. Only provide a few so that people do not get overwhelmed. Depending on the meeting days of your program send the journal home with a different family each week.

Family Tree and Beyond   ☺ ALL

Each of us belongs to a family unit consisting of people who love us very much. Some families are made up of a mother, father, and a child. Some families are made with a parent and three children. Children are born into families and others are adopted. Extended family members play an important role in many children's lives. When charting family members, always be sensitive to the variety of family units. Below is a family project for creating the family's tree.

❑ *You will need:*
    Brown paint
    Green paint
    Pie tin
    Paint brush
    Large sheets of paper

❑ *To do:*

Using brown paint, paint the outline of a tree trunk on the sheet of paper. Let the trunk dry. Invite each family member to add a leaf to the tree by dipping one of his or her hands into the green paint and onto the tree trunk. After the paints have dried label the names and birth dates of each of the family members next to their leaf. Hang for all to see and celebrate the family.

❑ *More to do:*

Go beyond the traditional "family tree" model so as not to exclude anyone. Invite children and their families to use their creativity for showing their family. One possible model might be a pond filled with water life or a school of fish continuing to grow. The possibilities are endless, so go beyond!

Father's Day Gift – Soap on a Rope ☺ ALL

❑ *You will need:*

See recipe for Lenten soap balls
34" of cotton rope.

❑ *To do:*

Tie the two ends of the rope together. Using hands shape soap dough around the knot of the rope. Let dry completely before wrapping this gift.

Father's Day Medallion ☺ ALL

The fathers will love to be presented with these Father's Day Medallions.

❑ *You will need:*

Scissors
Red cardstock paper
White construction paper
Markers
Glue
Yarn

❑ *To do:*

Cut a 4" circle from the red cardstock paper and a 3 3/4" heart from the white construction paper. Invite the children to print, "#1 Dad" or a similar sentiment on the white heart. Then glue the heart to the circle and print their names on the back. Punch a hole at the top of the medallion and string a yarn through it. Present these to the Fathers as they arrive to collect the children or wrap them for the children to give on Father's day.

Father's Day Tool Can ☺ ALL

A natural looking tool can to hold Dad's necessities at home or work.

❑ *You will need:*

A variety of sticks about 6" long and 1/4" to 1/2" thick.
An empty, washed out soup can
Glue
Rubber bands
Raffia

❑ *To do:*

Go on a nature hunt with the children and have them collect a variety of sticks. With adult help break the sticks down into lengths that will fit around the soup can. Use clear drying glue to glue the sticks to the can. Put rubber bands around the sticks to hold them in place. Dry over night. Remove the rubber bands and tie a raffia bow around the center of the can. Attach this little poem.

Thank you God for my Dad,
He is the best I've ever had.
We love to tease and play and run
It seems we are never short of fun.
God bless my Dad!

Feathered Friends Bookmark ☺ ALL

Make a cute birdie bookmark with feathers included.

❑ **You will need:**
Card stock paper
Brightly colored feathers
Glue

❑ **To do:**
Enlarge and copy this bookmark pattern on card stock. Color the birds with marker and glue on the feathers.

File Folder Advent Activity ☺ ALL

Make a stand-up nativity scene using a file folder and character cutouts.

❑ **You will need:**
White paper
Blue file folders
Glue
Markers
Scissors

❑ **To do:**
Enlarge and copy the stable and nativity characters provided here. Have the children color the pictures and cut them out. Glue the stable to the center of the open file folder. Put the remaining figures in an envelope to go home. During each week in Advent have the children glue a different cutout to the nativity scene. By the time Christmas comes, all of the characters will be in place.

Make a stand-up nativity scene using a file folder and character cutouts.

Finger Paint Recipes   😊 PRE

Finger painting is a tactile delight especially for younger children. Exploring the feel of paint between the fingers is very fun and can be a bit messy.

With pudding
❑ *You will need:*

   Vanilla instant pudding mix
   Milk
   Mixing bowl
   Hand mixer
   Food coloring
   Bowls

❑ *To do:*

Mix up the box of instant pudding with milk according to package directions. Pour into individual bowls. Tint the pudding to the desired color using drops of food coloring.

With corn syrup
❑ *You will need:*

   Corn syrup
   Food coloring
   Wax paper

❑ *To do:*

Tint corn syrup with food coloring. Pour a small amount of the mixture onto the waxed paper and let the creating begin. After the children have created a picture give the artwork plenty of time to dry away from ants and humidity. The paint will have a very high gloss shine when dried.

With liquid dish soap
❑ *You will need:*

   Powdered tempera paint
   Liquid dish soap
   Hand mixer
   Mixing bowl

❑ *To do:*

Use the hand mixer on low speed to blend small amounts of powdered tempera paint into liquid dish soap. Use small amounts of this finger paint on heavy absorbent paper.

Fingerprint Fun ☺ ALL

Our fingerprints identify who we are and are as unique as each one of us. God made us different in our appearances, experiences, and thoughts. Here is a unique way to see our differences.

❏ *You will need:*
   Fine tip markers
   Paper
   Washable ink pad

❏ *To do:*
Demonstrate how the children should roll their fingertip on the inkpad and then roll the fingerprint on the paper. Then encourage them to use the markers to decorate the fingerprints creating a picture. To help get some children started you may need to give them a few ideas. An example would be, by adding yellow stripes and wings you can change a fingerprint into a bee. Display the finished pictures on a bulletin board titled, "God made us as unique as our fingerprints."

Finger Puppet ☺ ALL

Make simple finger puppets to share faith stories with the children.

❏ *You will need:*
   Felt scraps
   Sequins
   Beads
   Tacky (fabric glue)

❏ *To do:*
Check your parent list and recruit someone who could sew up a variety of finger puppets. Cut 2 matching felt pieces for each puppet. Top stitch the felt pieces together leaving the bottom open. Glue on facial features, hair, etc. with fabric glue and tell your story.

Fish, a Christian Sign ☺ALL

Early Christians who were in fear of openly expressing their faith used the fish as a secret sign to let others know who they were. People would draw a fish on their doorpost or trace it in the dirt when talking to someone. Try these fun fish craft ideas.

❑ *You will need:*
Fish crackers
Construction paper
Glue

❑ *To do:*
Draw the shape of a fish or the letters of the children's name with glue and add the fish crackers.

❑ *More to do:*
Twist pipe cleaners into the shape of a fish. Slip it on a ribbon to make a necklace.

Fish Caught in the Net ☺ALL

A game of tag brings home the message.

❑ *To play:*
Four children form the "net" by holding hands. The rest of the children are the "fish in the sea." The "net" children try to tag the "fish" children. When a child is tagged he/she joins hands with "net." The game ends when all the children are tagged and attached to the "net."

Fishermen and Jesus ☺ALL

Jesus realized how much work he had to do. He wanted some friends who would help him. Use this action story in class to tell the children what he did...

One day Jesus was walking	Walk in place.
by the Sea of Galilee.	Make waves with your arms.
He looked out over the water	Hand shading eyes.
and saw two boats there.	Look out, hold up two fingers.
Peter and Andrew were	Hold fishing reel.
fishing from one boat.	Pretend to fish.
In the other boat, James and	Sew and tie knots.
John were mending a net.	
Jesus called to them,	Cup hands around mouth.
"Come and Follow me."	Motion with arm to come.
The men looked at each other	Look at others.
Yes, each of them nodded.	Nod.
They rowed their boats ashore	Row a boat.
to tell of God's love with Jesus.	Hug yourself.
Today we follow Jesus	Walk in place.
by sharing our love with others.	Shake each other's hands.
We celebrate God's love for us	Join hands and
as we join hands and greet	wave to one another.
the New Year!	

❑ *More to do:*
Trace one foot of each child. Print, "I can follow Jesus by (child tells you what to print or draws a picture)."

Fishing Net 😊 ALL

This crepe paper fishing net has many uses. You will find it helpful in making bulletin boards or decorating for parties and special events. See Luke 5 for inspiration.

❏ *You will need:*
    Packaged crepe paper
      that is folded in sheets
    Scissors

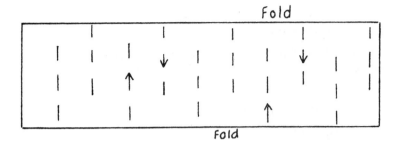

❏ *To do:*
Make cuts in the crepe paper 2" wide from one folded side to within 1" of the other folded side. After cutting one side in one direction, turn the paper and cut in between the first cuts, but going the other direction. After all the cuts are made gently shake out the crepe paper and stretch it to make a fishing net or spider web. Add construction paper fish and share the story of Jesus and the fishermen (see Mark 1:16-20).

Flannel board 😊 ALL

Make this flannel board to use as a tool to tell stories.

❏ *You will need:*
    Cardboard
    Flannel fabric
    Wide masking tape
    Pictures to tell story
    Clear contact paper
    Double stick tape or coarse sandpaper or Velcro

❏ *To do:*
Cover a front side of a piece of cardboard with flannel fabric. This does not need to be store bought; you may want to reuse an old flannel shirt or a baby blanket. Secure the edge of the flannel to the back of the cardboard using wide masking tape. Make any pictures flannel-board ready by clear contacting or heat laminating them. Then using double-stick tape secure the small piece of Velcro, sandpaper, or flannel to the back of each laminated picture.

Flat Bread ☺ ALL

Use this wonderful recipe to make flat bread for a special celebration or when you are learning about the Eucharist.

❏ **You will need:**
6 tbsp margarine
1 tsp. salt
3 cups flour
3/4 cup warm water
Frying pan
Mixing bowl
Spoon
Spatulas
Cooling rack
Rolling pin

❏ **To do:**
Put an adult in charge of the frying pan. Melt 6 tbsp. margarine in the pan. Pour melted margarine into the mixing bowl. Add water, salt, and 2-1/2 cups flour. Mix. Add 1/2 cup flour so that mixture is not too sticky. Have the children form balls, then flatten them with your hand or a rolling pin into about 8" circles. Preheat the frying pan, Fry each circle about 3-4 minutes, turning once. Cool on racks. Serve while warm.

Floral Wreath ☺ ALL

Use grocery bags to make neat flower wreaths for spring.

❏ **You will need:**
Grocery bag
Pipe cleaners
Silk flowers
Ribbon
Scissors
Glue

❏ **To do:**
Cut the bottom of the grocery bag off without cutting the sides.
Beginning at one end, gently fold down the sides of the bag toward the outside. Continue rolling until the bag is all rolled up into a ring. Twist 4 to 6 pipe cleaners around the ring to hold it in place. Add ribbons and silk flowers to decorate.

Flowers 🙂 ALL

Fancy, fun tissue-paper flowers.
Use these cute flowers to decorate the grocery bag wreath from above or to fill May baskets.

❑ *You will need:*

Tissue paper in a variety of colors
Pipe cleaners

❑ *To do:*

Enlarge and duplicate the patterns provided.
Trace and cut out 3 different size flowers from the
tissue paper. Next, make a 1/2" bend at the end
of a pipe cleaner. Beginning with the smallest
flower poke it through the straight end of the
pipe cleaner and pull it to the top of the pipe
cleaner to the bent end. Add the next 2 tissue
flower pieces. Gently twist the tissue paper
around the top of the pipe cleaner.

F

Foil Star Gift   ☺ ALL

Use these foil stars to decorate a variety of things to use as teacher or parent gifts.

❑ *You will need:*
   Foil stars
   Candle or bar of soap

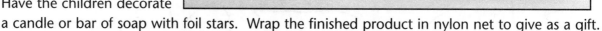

❑ *To do:*

Have the children decorate a candle or bar of soap with foil stars. Wrap the finished product in nylon net to give as a gift.

Follow This Way   ☺ ALL

Lead children to a special destination with a path of paper plates to mark the way. The message may be a blessing or clues as to what is planned for the class session.

❑ *You will need:*
   Paper plates
   Masking tape
   Markers

❑ *To do:*

Print one word of the message on each plate. Tape the plates in order leading a path to where you would like the children to go. This is an exciting way to invite children into the classroom especially at the start of the year.

Following Jesus With Both Feet ☺ ALL

A reminder that no matter where we go Jesus is always with us.

❏ *You will need:*
   Sandpaper sheets
   Markers

❏ *To do:*
With marker trace the feet of each child on one sheet of sandpaper. With help of an adult print the words, "Jesus is always with me."

❏ *More to do:*
Put a sticker in the bottom of the child's shoe as a reminder of God's presence.

Fork Painting ☺ ALL

Use a fork instead of a paintbrush to make all kinds of neat pictures and designs.

❏ *You will need:*
   Plastic forks
   Tempera paint
   Construction paper

❏ *To do:*
Put the paint in a pie tin. Dip the fork in the paint and go to town. To make a Christmas tree drag the fork the long way across the bottom of the paper. Decrease the length of the lines all the way up the paper to make a tree. To make a cross drag the fork once down the middle of the paper and then once across.

Frame It Up   ☺ ALL

Give children an important reminder of God's presence to put on their walls.

❑ *You will need:*
Margarine containers
Yarn
Glue
Large stickers of "Jesus and the children."
Stick-on picture hanger

❑ *To do:*
Glue the yarn around the inside bottom of the margarine tub. Place a large sticker in the center of the tub. Fasten a picture hanger to the back of the tube for hanging on the wall.

Friends in a Circle   ☺ ALL

Here's a great way to remind the children to pray for one another throughout the week.

❑ *You will need:*
Construction paper hearts
Large construction paper circle
Markers
Scissors
Glue

❑ *To do:*
In the middle of the circle print, "God Bless."
Glue the hearts around the edge of the circle.
Print the names of friends on each of the hearts.

Friendship Blessing   ☺ ALL

Try this friendship blessing when you are playing outside.

❑ *To do:*
To the tune of "London Bridge" sing this song.
Use the same bridge with your arms and have the
child receiving the blessing stand between the two children.

God is with you day and night, day and night, day and night.
God is with you day and night, God bless (child's name).

Friendship Bracelet ☺ ALL

Remind the children of the special gift of friendship with a friendship bracelet.

❏ *You will need:*
  8" piece of leather (boot lace)
  Red, blue, green and yellow beads

❏ *To do:*
Have the children lace the beads on the leather one at a time. As they lace the beads give them a brief explanation of the symbolism of each bead. The red bead reminds us of the heart and the love we have for our friends. The blue bead reminds us to be faithful and true. The light of Jesus our best friend is seen in the yellow bead. The green bead reminds us of the precious gift of life which we have received. Tie a knot at the end of the bracelet so that it fits securely.

Friendship Window ☻ PRE

At the start of the year some children are hesitant to even enter the building. Help identify your classroom by painting the children's handprints in a window that can be seen when they arrive.

❏ *You will need:*
  Tempera paint
  Pie tin
  Soap
  Water
  Toweling

❏ *To do:*
Pour tempera paint in a pie tin. Invite children to dip one hand in the paint and place their handprint on the window glass. Wash excess paint off hands with soap and water. Now each time the children arrive they will see their hand print in the window along with those of their friends who are waiting to play.

Frogs   ☺ ALL

Make a funny paper plate frog to go with the frog poem below.

❑ *You will need:*
    Small paper plate
    Construction paper
    Glue
    Markers
    Small plastic bugs

❑ *To do:*
Fold the paper plate in half and crease it. Paste on 2 pre-cut eyes to the top of the folded plate. Tape a red paper tongue to the inside crease of the plate. Glue a small plastic bug to the end of the tongue. Tape or glue paper legs to the bottom of the folded plate. Color the rest of the plate green.

❑ *More to do:*
Frogs Poetry

    God talks to everyone,
    God even talks to frogs.
    They listen from their lily pads,
    And from their swamps and bogs.
    God talks to everyone,
    God even talks to frogs.
    There's not a place God can't be found.
    The voice of God is all around.
    Ribbit, ribbit, croak, croak!

Frosted Christmas Tree Snack   ☺ ALL

A finger-licking good, do-it-yourself snack guaranteed to be enjoyed by all.

❑ *You will need:*
    Sugar ice-cream cones
    Canned frosting
    Green food coloring
    Cookie sugars and small candies
    Paper plates
    Disposable knives or craft sticks

❑ *To do:*
Mix a few drops of food coloring in the can of frosting. Turn the cones upside down on a paper plate. Have the children frost the cone and then add candy ornaments. Eat these for a holiday party or send them home to be shared with mom and dad.

Gabriel Had Surprising News   PRI

Tell the children that it was the angel Gabriel who told Mary that she was going to have a baby. He also told her that her baby would be a great King and that the baby's father was God. Gabriel said, "Nothing is impossible with God." See Luke 1: 29-38. Remind the children that nothing is impossible with God. Teach them this short mantra. Encourage them to begin their day with it.

❑ *To do:*

Simply say,
God is with me.
God loves me.
God will help me.

❑ *More to do:*

Give the children prayer cards as a reminder to pray this mantra. On cardstock weight paper about 2 1/2" x 4", print the mantra. On the back of each card place a heart sticker or another symbol of God's love for us. Cover each card with clear contact paper.

Game Ideas That Require No Materials   ALL

Games are a great way to build community among a group of children. Here are a few game ideas that can be played at a moment's notice without any extra preparation.

Shoe commotion

❑ *To do:*

Standing in a circle the children take off one shoe and place it in the middle of the circle. Instruct the children to each take a shoe from the center that is not their own. Holding hands and the shoe the children must try to return the shoes to the proper owner without breaking the circle. The commotion begins when the circle is moving in every direction. Keep encouraging the group to work together helping each other to get their shoe back.

Reverse hide and seek

❑ *To do:*

One child hides and the other children in the group must try to find the hiding child. Without saying anything the "seeker" joins the "hider" as soon as the hiding place is revealed. The play continues until all the "seekers" are hiding with the "hider."

Quiet game

❏ *To do:*

Invite the children to work together to keep quiet for a predetermined time limit such as 1 to 2 minutes. If a child speaks during the time limit he must stand until someone else speaks out. The previous speaker then returns to the play. At the end of the time limit share what everyone was thinking about in the quiet.

Who is the leader?

❏ *To do:*

All but one child sit in a circle. The one child turns his or her back to the group. While the child is not looking the teacher points to a child to be the leader. The excluded child turns around and watches as the circle of children follow whatever actions the leader is doing. Actions might include flapping your arms, rolling your head, clapping, clicking your tongue, twisting body with hands on hips, etc. By the actions of the group the excluded child must try to determine who is leading the group.

Game Pieces ☺ ALL

Here is a simple idea for making board game pieces

❏ *You will need:*

    Bulldog binder clips
    Laminated picture

❏ *To do:*

Slide a picture between the clips so the piece stands on the black base as shown in the diagram.

Garden Poem ☺ PRE

The perfect companion for any planting or growing lesson.

❏ *To do:*

Invite the children to repeat the following after you and add actions.

    Children, children how does your garden grow?
    Tell me, tell me. I want to know.
    First add the dirt, then add the water and a bit of sun,
    Now watch very closely we're in for some fun.
    Within a few days the tiny seeds will begin to grow,
    And a new life before us will start to show.
    Thank you, God, for the dirt and the sun and the rain,
    For the blessing of new life we praise God's name.
    Amen! Amen! Amen!

Garland   ☺ ALL

A garland of candy, noodles, cereals, pretzels, and noodles of fun.
Make a fun, holiday garland for the Christmas or Easter tree with leftover snacks and candy.

❑ **You will need:**
    Large sewing needles
    Heavy thread or light-weight yarn
    Licorice cut into 1" sections
    Life savers
    Pretzels
    Gumdrops
    Cheerios, Fruitloops etc.

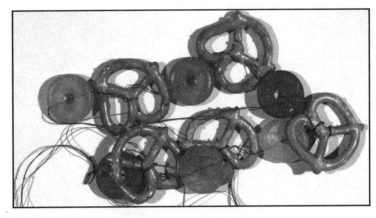

❑ **To do:**
Sort out the items to string into separate bowls. With adult help thread the needles and make knots in the end of the string. Leave about 6" at both ends of each string so that they can be tied together to make one long garland. Let the children make their own patterns. Because these treats will probably be favorites to eat allow for the snacking of broken pieces or give each child a few items to eat before beginning. When each child has completed her/his string, tie the sections together and hang on the tree.

Gethsemane   ✋ PRI

The garden where Jesus knelt and prayed reminds of us the importance of prayer in our lives.
Help the children remember to follow Jesus' example of prayer.

❑ **You will need:**
    Construction paper
    Praying Jesus pattern
    Pencils
    Scissors
    Glue
    Popsicle sticks
    1/2 of a Styrofoam ball

❑ **To do:**
Copy twice the pattern of Jesus praying for each child. Then ask the children to color and cut it out. Glue one copy of Jesus praying to one side of the Popsicle stick and the other copy to the other side. Place the bottom of the Popsicle stick into the Styrofoam ball so that the picture of Jesus praying is upright. Around the bottom encourage the children to print the first few words of prayers that they like to say.

Getting to Know You Chain ✋ PRI

An old idea with a new twist. With adult help, help the children write things about themselves on the links of a paper chain.

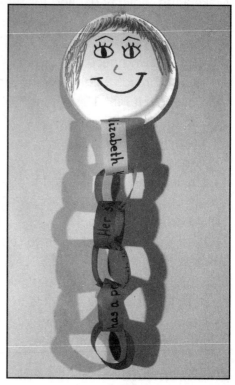

❑ *You will need:*
Construction paper strips
8" paper plate
Hole punchers (if possible use the shaped punchers)
Markers
Glue or stapler

❑ *To do:*
Have the children draw a picture of themselves on the paper plates. While the children are working on this take them aside one at a time to write some things about themselves on the paper strips for the chain. On the first link print the child's name. Then add things like, Jake likes pizza, he likes to play soccer, etc. After writing on 6-8 paper strips, have the children glue or staple them together to make a chain. Staple the chain to the bottom edge of the plate. Hang the plates for all to see.

Gift ideas (see Index for Individual gifts)

Gift Box, Not So Empty ✋ PRI

Gift giving is very fun to do but we can't purchase gifts for everyone. Lead children to more non-material gift ideas, gifts from the heart instead of always those that require money. God's greatest gift was Jesus. Jesus who continues to give to us with lessons he taught. Set this activity up during Advent as a reminder that there are gifts that do not require any money.

❑ *You will need:*
An empty wrapped gift box in which the lid can be removed.

❑ *To do:*
Lead the children in a discussion of possible gift ideas for their friends and classmates.
Talk about God's many gifts to us, especially Jesus. Then sitting together as a group, invite the children to take turns holding the empty gift box while sharing what they would put inside the box and whom they would like to give it to. When possible encourage non-material items. After all those wishing to share have had a chance, place the gift box where children can draw pictures of gift ideas for others. Encourage them to write the name of the person the gift is for on the picture. As time passes and the box begins to fill, take pictures from the box and share the names of whom they are for.

Gifts of God ☺ ALL

Wrap up a box and use it to illustrate the many gifts of God.

❑ *You will need:*

Paper box
Light-colored wrapping paper
Ribbon
Magazine pictures
Markers

❑ *To do:*

Wrap up each box and tie with a bow. Glue magazine pictures or draw pictures of the gifts of God to the package. Add a gift tag that says, "The Gifts of God."

Give a Hand Card ✋ PRI

Children may need to work in pairs to "give each other a hand" tracing each other's hands for these cards.

❑ *You will need:*

Half a sheet of cardstock paper (8 1/2" x 5 1/2")
Markers
Scissors
Pencil

❑ *To do:*

Fold the sheet in half to make the card. Turn the card so the fold is on the left side. With the help of another child, trace the other's hand on her or his card front with wrist resting on the fold. Cut away paper from the hand as the picture shows. Under the hand on the inside of the card print the message "God's love reaches out to you." Use markers to add color and pictures.

God's love reaches out to you!

Glad Tambourines ✋ PRI

Make gleeful taps on these tart tin tambourines.

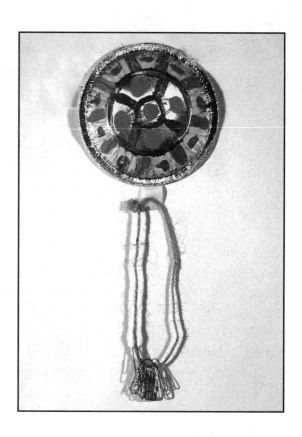

❑ *You will need:*

Aluminum tart tin
    (found in the baking aisle of the grocery store)
Acrylic paints in variety of colors
Masking tape
Paintbrush
Twine
20 or more paper clips

❑ *To do:*

Decorate the outside of the tart tin using the acrylic paints. Let dry completely. Then clip the paper clips to the twine and wrap the clipped twine around the rim of the tart tin. Glue masking tape to secure the twine in 3-4 places. And let the joyful sounds begin!

Glitter Pine Cones ☺ ALL

Collect pine cones on a nature walk to make a simple Christmas ornament.

❑ *You will need:*

Pine cones of any size
Glue
Glitter
Ribbon

❑ *To do:*

Tie a ribbon for hanging on the wide end of the pine cone. With a paintbrush have the children put glue on the edges of the pine. Over a pie tin have the children sprinkle glitter on the pine cone. Gently shake off the excess glitter and allow to dry.

❑ *More to do:*

Have each child decorate a variety of pine cones and tie them together in a bunch to make a door hanging. At Easter time paint the pine cones pastel colors for the egg tree or basket.

Glove Wind Sock ☺ ALL

Use canvas work gloves to make a fun garden wind sock.

❑ *You will need:*

One canvas garden glove per child

Twine

Ribbon

Small felt cutout

Sequins

Buttons

Tacky fabric glue

❑ *To do:*

Before turning the project over to the children, tie a 18" piece of twine to the cuff of the glove. It works well to thread the twine in a needle to sew and knot it to the cuff. With adult help have the children print, "Blowing in the wind with God." Decorate the gloves by gluing buttons and sequins to them. Cut a variety of lengths of ribbon to glue to the fingertips of the glove.

God 😊 PRE

Who is God? We can tell a lot about God from Jesus' actions. John 3:16 tells us that "God is a God of love." Remind the children of the love God has for each one of us with this easy-to-sing song.

❑ *To sing:* 🎵

To tune of "The Farmer in the Dell."

Oh God loves me!

Oh God loves me!

I will clap my hands for

God loves me!

Sing several times, each with a new action.

God Bless You! ☺ ALL

Remind children of the importance of praying for those they love.

❑ *You will need:*

3" x 18" ribbon or fabric strips

Construction paper

Fabric glue

Stapler

❑ *To do:*

To make a bow fold an 18" piece of ribbon together overlapping the ends by 1"-2". Staple the middle of the bow to hold in place. Cover the staples by folding a 6" piece of ribbon over the staples and tape the back in place. Also tape the second piece of ribbon to the back of the center of the bow with the right side facing out. Glue or staple a scalloped edged card that says, "God Bless," to the top of the ribbon below the bow. Below this sign add smaller ones that have the names of family members and friends that the child would like to bless each day.

God Hunt   🐻 PRE

Make a back pack and go on a God hunt looking for signs of God in the world around you.

❑ *You will need:*
    Grocery bags
    Staplers
    Markers

❑ *To do:*
From the top of a mid-sized grocery sack cut two strips each approximately 1 1/2"wide. These strips will be straps. After the children have decorated their bags, staple the straps in place as shown. Take your God hunt inside or out. Collect flowers, rocks, feathers, seashells, photographs of friends, wrapped food, etc. As you walk, talk about the wonders of God. Share your finds with one another during circle time.

"God" Times Roll   ✋ PRI

Recognizing God's presence in the classroom and recording these times can be an ongoing activity. Use this as a yearlong journal of the "God" moments you share in class. Invite the children to record these special times as they happen. Leave this displayed in a permanent area that is always accessible to the children. Keeping it in the children's view will serve as a reminder to be on the lookout for events, actions, and experiences that reflect God's presence in our lives.

❑ *You will need:*
    String
    Wooden dowel
    Calculator printing tape
    Empty paper towel tube
    Markers

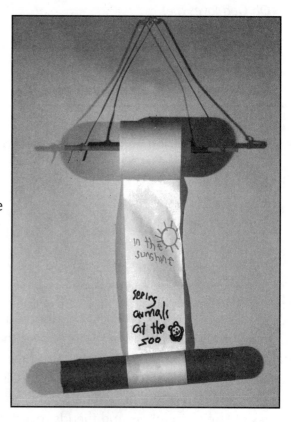

❑ *To do:*
Place a wide roll of calculator printing tape through a wooden dowel. Attach a string to both ends of the dowel so the roll easily hangs from a hook. Attach the free end of the paper roll to an empty paper towel tube.

Golden Rule Bulletin Board Lesson 😊 ALL

As a class make this bulletin board to help children learn the two part golden rule Jesus taught us, "Love God above all else" and "Love your neighbor as yourself."

❑ *You will need:*

A cloth tape measure
A red paper heart
Two white paper circles for each child
Markers
Tape

❑ *To do:*

Introduce the first part of the rule by distributing one white circle to each child and asking that they use the markers to make a picture on the circle of something they love very much. As the children are making their pictures, share and print on the heart the first piece of the rule, "Love God above all else." Adhere it to the top of the tape measure. Display this heart and tape measure to a bulletin board where the children can see it. As the children finish their circles ask them to bring the finished pictures to you so they may be attached to the tape measure below the heart. Remind children that this is the first part of the golden rule, to love God above all else. Later introduce the second part of the rule, to love one another. Ask the children to print their names on the other white circles. Tape these together in a chain so that the names read across. Add this to the bulletin board placing it perpendicular to the tape measure. As you display the name chain, tell the children that Jesus also taught us to love one another as ourselves.

Good News Mega Phone 😊 ALL

Make a Good News Mega Phone to share the, "Good News of God."

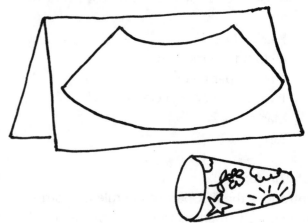

❏ **You will need:**
  12" x 18" sheets of construction paper
  Markers
  Scissors

❏ **To do:**
To make a pattern, fold the paper into a 12" x 9" rectangle. Use the 9" side to mark off a small semicircle. Draw around the pattern. Cut on the lines and decorate with markers. Roll the paper overlapping the sides. Tape or glue in place and announce the, "Good News of God."

Gorp 😊 ALL

The best snack ever!
Use up your leftovers and make a fun delicious snack.

❏ **You will need:**
  Leftover snack items, such as pretzels, cereals, crackers, candy, raisins, peanuts, and marshmallows.
  Large mixing bowl
  Paper cups

❏ **To do:**
In a large mixing bowl combine any leftover snack items. Mix with a large spoon and serve in a paper cup.

Got God? 😊 ALL

Spark some interest and get people thinking with this fun saying on a chain.

❏ **You will need:**
  Tag board
  Clear contact
  String
  Markers
  Scissors

GOT GOD?

❏ **To do:**
Copy and enlarge the "Got God" pattern provided. Have the children cut out and color the circle. Glue this to a larger circle or tag board and cover with contact. Punch a whole in the top of the circle and lace a string through it for hanging.

116

Grapevine Wreath ☺ ALL

Decorate the outside of your classroom door with a wreath for every season.

❑ *You will need:*
Large grapevine wreath
A variety of paper cutouts and
ornaments for each season

❑ *To do:*
With the help of the children decorate your
wreath for every season of the year. Use paper
cutouts or ornaments. For example, in
September hang apples and back to school
items. In October and November use
pumpkins and other fruits of the harvest.
Christmas ornaments in December and
snowflakes in January. In February hang hearts,
March shamrocks, and eggs and flowers in April and May. Use your imagination to fill up your
class wreath and be sure to involve the children in changing it each season.

Great Graffiti Messages ☺ ALL

Provide a place where "great" graffiti about God and God's love can be written or drawn.

❑ *You will need:*
Several sheets of large newsprint
Markers
Tape

❑ *To do:*
Tape the sheets of large newsprint together and tape them on a wall that is accessible for the
children. Encourage the children to write or draw pictures of God's goodness around them. They
might use bumper sticker sayings or add Bible verses as well.

Greet One Another ☺ PRE

Reflect God's love for each child with a personal greeting.

❑ *To do:*
As part of your gathering or opening time each day, take some time greeting one another. This
could be a very informal time where you ask the children all at once to say 'Hi" to their neighbor,
or it could be more formal. Have the children sit in a circle and take turns going around the circle
greeting one another. Each child greets the child on either side with a, "Good morning (name of
the child)." That child then says, "Good morning," back and so it goes. If a child forgets
someone's name, have him simply ask, "What is your name?" As time goes on change the
greeting to, "Good day," or "Merry Christmas" depending on the time of year.

Grid Game 😊 ALL

Classifying, color recognition, and counting are key concepts to this activity. Use these concepts to play a game while introducing some faith-filled symbols to young children.

❑ *You will need:*
Masking tape
Clear floor space to play
Empty film canisters
Small seasonal objects that have a faith-related meaning
(A sample of possible Easter objects might be jellybeans, silk flowers, and small toy bunnies.)

❑ *To do:*
Use the masking tape to lay out a 3' x 3' grid on the floor as shown in the diagram. Across the top of the grid label the columns 1, 2, and 3 using small post-it slips. Label the columns by placing a different object at the side of each row. Fill each canister with 1, 2, or 3 of the same symbolic objects. Cover the canisters with the lids. Place the filled canisters off to the side of the grid. Invite a child to take and open a canister to reveal the contents. Discuss the contents as revealing the faith symbolism. Place the object in the appropriate row (determined by the number of objects) and column (determined by which object) before opening the next canister.

❑ *More to do:*
For younger children this activity can be simplified. Give each player a symbol of the season. Place matching small objects under the empty film canister. The children take turns looking in the canister for an object that matches the one the children were given at the start of the game. The entire playing time allows for discussion of the symbols' meaning to the season.

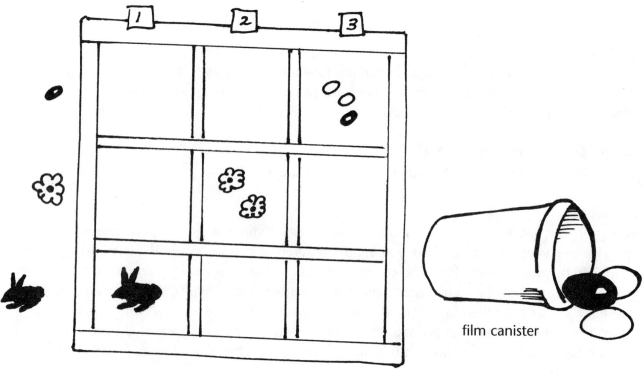

film canister

Grow Closer to God by Walking With Jesus ☺ ALL

Plant this idea early in Lent and send it home to families
as a reminder of what the season is about.

❑ *You will need:*

Clear plastic beverage cups
Small hearty plants
Potting soil
Plastic forks
3" x 5" index cards

❑ *To do:*

Early in spring help the children to plant a hearty plant with potting soil inside clear plastic cups.
Fold an index card in half. On the outside print the message, "Walking with Jesus, growing closer
to God." Preprint the inside of the card to read the blessing, "Jesus, walk with me as I grow closer
to God. Attach the card to the planter by slipping it into the prongs of the fork and burying the
handle of the fork into the soil. Send the planter home to families with a note inviting parents to
place the cup inside a shoe or boot. Encourage the families to place the shoe planter in a place
that reminds everyone that Lent is the time for growing closer to God.

Growing Easter Grass ☺ ALL

Send home this growing basket, adding an egg and a few Easter treats.

❑ *You will need:*

Wide-mouth plastic cups, margarine tubs, or yogurt cartons
Potting soil
Pebbles
Grass seed
Pipe cleaners
Stickers

❑ *To do:*

Decorate the containers with stickers. Punch a
hole on each side of the container to fasten a
pipe cleaner handle. Put pebbles in the bottom
for drainage and add dirt. Sprinkle grass seed
on top and water by lightly spraying with a
water spray bottle. Within a few days the grass
will grow. To keep it trimmed, cut it with a
scissors. Before sending the growing basket
home add an egg and a few Easter treats.

Growing Together With God   ☺ ALL

Plant an indoor class garden.

❑ *You will need:*

Several slits (small stems cut off a healthy plant)
Clear plastic cups
Large planter box
Potting soil
Pebbles
Tongue depressors or craft sticks

❑ *To do:*

Cut a slip off a healthy plant for each child in the class. Place the slip in a cup of water. Write children's names on their cups. Place in a sunny spot and within a few days roots will appear.

Transplant the rooted slips into a large planter box. To prepare the planter box place a few rocks in the bottom of the box for drainage and add potting soil. Print each child's name on tongue depressor or craft stick and place in the dirt next to each child's plant. Label the planter, "Growing Together With God."

Guessing Game   ☻ PRE

❑ *You will need:*

Small bag
Symbol of lesson topic (such as rocks, sticks, etc. for a lesson about creation)

❑ *To do:*

Place symbols from your lessons in the bag. Raise the children's curiosity about what might be in the bag. Invite one child to reach into the bag and try to guess what she has in her hand. After she has guessed, place that symbol in the middle of your group. Ask another student to do the same. Once all the symbols are out, invite the children to guess what your lesson might be about.

Gum Nature Walk 😊 ALL

Chew a piece of bubble gum and spread on a paper plate to attach nature finds.

❑ *You will need:*
Bubble gum
Paper plates

❑ *To do:*
Take a nature walk with bubble gum for all. After chewing the gum have the children stretch the gum out on a paper plate. While traveling on your nature trail have the children attach their nature finds to the gum on the plate.

Gum Wrapper Earth Mural 😊 ALL

God has given us each an important role in caring for the earth. Give children an opportunity to experience this role through a walk and mural project.

❑ *You will need:*
Butcher paper
Wrapped chewing gum
   piece for each child
Tape
Markers

❑ *To do:*
Take the children on a walk around the community noting all the color they see in nature. Following the walk, gather the children and give them each a piece of chewing gum to chew. Ask them to keep the wrapper close by. While they are chewing, talk about our role as stewards of the earth God has created. On a large butcher paper mural draw the outline of a painter's palate next to a large red circle with a red line drawn though it. As you continue to discuss our roles, title the mural "God painted our world with color, not trash and wrappers." Invite the children to use their markers to decorate the palate with colors they saw on the walk. They could also use their gum or tape to adhere their wrappers to the inside of the red circle. Display the mural to remind the children and others of the important role God has given to each of us.

❑ *More to do:*
Ask the children to collect small pieces of paper found on the playground and add them to the mural.

G

List Your Favorite Projects Here

Handle With Care ☻ PRE

Treat others the way you would like to be treated and handle with care. Make handle with care signs for the children to wear as a reminder to be kind.

❑ *You will need:*

8" x 4" pieces of construction paper
Markers
Handle with Care postage sticker
Scissors
Tape

❑ *To do:*

Talk with the children about what it means to handle with care. Suggestions include using kind words, being helpful, playing nicely together and taking turns. Look at a Handle with Care postage sticker and make some of your own. With adult help print "Handle with Care" on the paper. Decorate with pictures of kindness. Tape or pin the pictures to the shirts of the children to wear all day.

Hands to Do the Hearts Work ☺ ALL

Hands are extensions God gave people to do works of the heart. Children can discover this message as they make this card.

❑ *You will need:*

Variety of colored construction paper including flesh tones
Markers
Scissors
Brad fastener
Circles cut from poster board

❑ *To do:*

On the circle use markers to print the message, "These hands do God's work." Trace and cut out 2 hands from the flesh tone construction paper. Overlap the fingertips to the tag board circle as shown. When the hands are opened, the message on the tag board circle shows. Construction paper can be added to the hands and decorated to look like shirtsleeves.

❑ *More to do:*

Give cards to people who use their hands to make the community a more loving place.

Hanging Doorbell   ☺ ALL

Welcome all who come to the door with this musical message.

❑ *You will need:*

2 sticks
Dowels or straws (approximately 12" long)
Pellon or interfacing material (found in
   fabric stores) 8 1/2" x 12"
Masking tape
Markers
Collection of different jingle bells
Twine
Scissors

❑ *To do:*

Print a message of welcome such as, "We open our hearts and this door to all whom God sends" on the panel. Use tape to secure a stick at the top and bottom of the Pellon panel as shown. Attach a piece of twine to both ends of the top stick so the panel may be hung. Tie bells and shells to 5 pieces of twine. Use masking tape to attach the strands of bells and shells across the bottom of the panel.

Happy Parade   ☻ PRE

Use this spontaneous activity to break the tension or change the tone of the classroom. Call for a "Happy parade."

❑ *You will need:*

Tape or CD recorded marching music

❑ *To do:*

Invite the children to put on their happiest face as you put on a tape with some upbeat marching music. Tell them everybody loves a parade and it is time to put on a "Happy Parade" for God. Lead the children around the room as you chant together, "Join us as we march in God's praise."

Harvest Prayer Poem   ☺ ALL

Use this grateful poem during Thanksgiving prayer times.

Thank you, God, for all good things,
All blessings a fruitful harvest brings.
Apples, oranges, corn, potatoes,
Peas, carrots, squash, tomatoes.
For others help us to always care,
Your bountiful harvest to always share.
Thank you, God, for all good things,
All the blessings a fruitful harvest brings. Amen.

Heart   ☺ ALL

God has filled our hearts with love. Love from parents, relatives, and friends.

❑ **You will need:**
Cardstock or construction paper
Plastic mesh (found at craft stores)
  or use sections of grocery produce bags
Tape
Various lengths of colored ribbon and yarn
Scissors

❑ **To do:**
Cut out a heart in the center of the paper. Cover the cutout space with a piece of plastic mesh. Tape the mesh in place on the underside of the paper. Encourage the children to select a piece of ribbon, yarn, string, or lace for each person who loves them. Thread and weave the ribbons, yarn, string, or lace for each person who loves them. Thread and weave the ribbons and yarns in and out of the mesh heart. Remind the children that God has made these people to be an important part of our lives.

❑ **More to do:**
Add magnet strips to the back and send home for families to be reminded how important they are to the children.

Heart Basket   ☺ ALL

A fun basket to make for Valentine's Day or May Day.

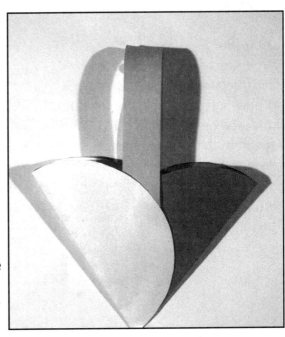

❑ **You will need:**
Construction paper (two different colors)
Glue
Stapler
Stickers
Glitter

❑ **To do:**
For each child cut two 6" circles of different colors. Fold both circles in half.
Join the circles together at the bottom, one side overlapping the other and glue in place. To make the handle cut and glue a 1" x 8" strip to the inside of where the two circles intersect. Fill with treats, flower seeds, a tea bag, etc.

Heart Cookies to Show Gratitude   ☺ALL

God has filled our world with people who love us. With these people's love and guidance we are growing. Show appreciation for these people with a plate of stained glass heart cookies.

❑ **You will need:**

Tube of pre-mixed cookie dough found in the dairy case of a grocery store
Red candy lifesavers
Paper plates
Non toxic markers

❑ **To do:**

As you prepare the cookies following the package directions, talk about how grateful we are for the people in our lives. Before baking the cookies, cut out a heart shape in the center of the cookie. Sprinkle crushed red candies into the cut away centers of the dough. Bake according to directions watching that candies don't burn. Cool cookies on cookie sheet until candy centers are firm before arranging on decorated paper plates. Encourage children to deliver the stained glass cookies to those who love them.

Heart People Deliver a Message of Love   ☺ALL

Make these delightful heart people to deliver your valentine message.

❑ **You will need:**

Heart playing cards from old decks
Glue
Red construction paper
Red pipe cleaners
Black marker
Stapler

❑ **To do:**

Cut a heart-shaped head from red construction paper and use a black marker to draw a face. Staple the heart head to the front of a heart playing card. Cut arms and legs from the pipe cleaners. Hold them in place by stapling them between the card you have and another. Cut a small heart and print, "God loves you." Poke it onto one of the pipe cleaner hands.

Heart of Hearts   🐻 PRE
A fun group project, making a heart of hearts for Valentine's Day.

❑ *You will need:*
    Poster board
    Markers
    Scissors

❑ *To do:*
Follow up your Valentine discussions by making a heart of hearts. Draw a large heart on a piece of construction paper. Inside the large heart have the children draw their own hearts. Add their names. Label the poster, "Our Heart of Hearts." Display for everyone to see.

Helicopters Floating Through the Air, Reminding Us That Jesus Is Always There   😊 ALL
Make these great helicopters to send through the air.

❑ *You will need:*
    1" x 9" strips of construction paper
    Paper clips
    Markers

❑ *To do:*
To make the helicopters fold the paper strip in half, slightly overlapping one side to the other. Next, begin an angled fold about 1 1/2" from the top of each end of the paper. Fold the ends in opposite direction. Fasten a paper clip to the bottom fold of the paper strip. With marker write a message such as "Jesus is always near" or "God bless you." Toss in the air and enjoy the flight.

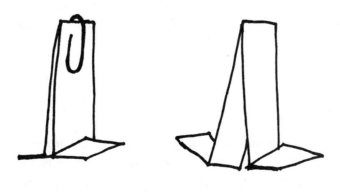

Helping Hands Cross 🖐 PRI

Following the example of Jesus, make a cross of hand cutouts.

❑ *You will need:*
   Construction paper
   Scissors
   Markers

❑ *To do:*
Have the children trace both hands, write their names on them and cut them out. Glue the hands to a paper cross and label it. "Helping others, following Jesus."

Hibernating Animals Awaken as We Celebrate Easter 🙂 PRE

Hibernating animals rest in winter to awaken refreshed and ready for the new spring. Like the hibernating animals during Lent, we rest and reflect on our faith. Then when Easter arrives we are renewed and ready to celebrate the Resurrection of Christ.

❑ *To do:*
Invite the children to use their imaginations to pretend to be various hibernating animals resting as they wait for spring.
Bears crawling on all fours into a dark cave.
Turtles pulling in their legs and arms, then hiding under mud.
Snakes slithering on their tummies into the sand.
Toads swimming to the bottom of the pond and wiggling deep down into the mud.
Tell the children while the animals sleep, we will rest, pray, and learn more about God's love for us through the life of Jesus.

Hidden in Our Hearts 🙂 ALL

Help children learn that God's Word is the best thing we can have in our hearts.

❑ *You will need:*
   Candy hearts
   Prepared muffin mix
   Paper baking cups
   Muffin tray
   Spoons

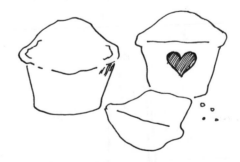

❑ *To do:*
Remind the children that God tells us how to live and care for other people. God wants us to keep His words close to our hearts. Have the children use spoons to put muffin mix in a cup. Then have them push a candy heart down into the batter in the cup. Bake all of the muffins. When the muffins come out remind the children that we are to take God's Words to heart and use them in our lives.

Hidden Message ☺ ALL

Even though we cannot see Jesus, we know he lives in our hearts. Sometimes we let things in our lives keep Jesus from others.

❑ *You will need:*
   Red paper
   Black felt marker
   Black crayon
   Coin

❑ *To do:*
Cut a large heart from red paper as you are talking to the children. Tell the children how our hearts are filled with the love of Jesus as you print the word "Jesus" on the heart with a black felt tip. Talk about how some of our actions hide Jesus, keeping others from seeing that love that lives within us. As you share specific examples of these actions, such as looking the other way when someone needs our help, use a black crayon to scribble with heavy pressure over the word. Give the children time to discuss actions that come to mind each time scribbling over the word Jesus with the crayon. After some discussion, talk about the ways we can reveal that Jesus' love fills our hearts. As suggestions are made use the coin to scrape away the black crayon once again revealing "Jesus."

Holiday Holly ☺ ALL

An ancient symbol of good fortune. Make a holly wreath to bring home.

❑ *You will need:*
   Construction paper
   Large paper plates
   Red beads
   Jingle bells
   Ribbon
   Paper punch
   Fishing line

❑ *To do:*
Cut out the center of the paper plate. Using the pattern provided trace and cut out enough holly leaves to cover the edges of the paper plate. Glue the leaves to the plate as well as the beads for berries. Add a ribbon to the top or bottom of the wreath.   With fishing line hang a jingle bell from the top center of the opening of the plate.

❑ *More to do:*
For a different look do not cut the center of the plate. Glue an old Christmas card picture to the center of the plate and add the holly around it.

Holy Family Picture 😊 ALL

How about your family as the Holy Family? Set up a photography station in your classroom and take pictures of the families in your program dressed as the Holy Family.

❑ **You will need:**
Polaroid camera and film
Dress up clothes such as bath robes, belts, dish towels, etc.
Props such as a manger or basket, bale of hay, etc.
Construction paper

❑ **To do:**
Set up a corner of your classroom for the pictures. If possible set out a few props. Have the children and their families dress up as Mary, Joseph, Jesus, shepherds, angels, and kings. Take an instant picture and glue it to a piece of construction paper to take home.

Holy Ground 😊 ALL

Declare your space a place of holy works. Make a Holy Ground doormat to remind all who enter of the good work happening in your classroom.

❑ **You will need:**
Poster board
Holy Ground letter cutouts
Glue
Clear contact
Markers

❑ **To do:**
Glue the letters Holy Ground to the poster board. Place the poster on the floor on the doorway to your room and cover it with clear contact. Be sure the contact is larger than the poster so that it sticks to the floor and holds it in place.

❑ **More to do:**
Have the children sign their names to the poster. Make a poster for each family and send home a sheet of contact for them to fasten it to their front step.

Holy Spirit 😊 ALL

The Holy Spirit brings comfort and guidance to our lives. Make this reminder of the presence of the Spirit that we know is there even if we cannot see it.

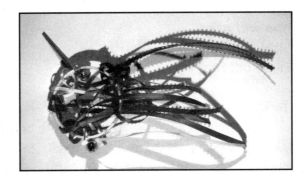

❑ *You will need:*

Felt
Mayonnaise jar lids
Glue
Variety of ribbons 1/2" x 12"
Wide rubber bands
Scissors

❑ *To do:*

Trace and cut the felt so that it fits the top of the lid. Glue in place. Place a rubber band around the lid and make sure it is a tight fit. Gently pull the pieces of ribbon through the rubber band. Adjust the ribbons so that they are different lengths. To make a hanger pull a 28" piece of ribbon through the rubber bands one on each side. Hang on a branch outside and watch as the wind moves it.

Hopes and Dreams ✋ PRI

Goal setting for a new season of growing in faith formation.
At the beginning of the year plan a bulletin board or poster that will bring together everyone's hopes and dreams for the year. Try to use a space that can accommodate it all year long.

❑ *You will need:*

Poster board or bulletin board
Hopes and Dreams letter cutouts
Colored star cutouts
Stapler
Fine point marker

❑ *To do:*

Staple the letters, "Hopes and Dreams" to the top of the bulletin board. With adult help have the children write down their, "Hopes and Dreams" for the year ahead on the star cutouts. Examples include getting along with others, praying more, learning about God, etc. After everyone has written down his or her "Hopes and Dreams," discuss what people wrote. Talk about some ways you can all accomplish your goals. Refer to the, "Hopes and Dreams" board throughout the year as a reminder of where you are headed as a group.

Hopscotch Fun   ☺ ALL

Hop, hop-play, play-skip, skip-pray, pray.
Play a game of hopscotch to stimulate lots of prayerful thoughts.

❏ *You will need:*
Sidewalk chalk
Large buttons

❏ *To do:*
Draw hopscotch on a sidewalk or substitute construction paper squares for indoor hopscotch. In each square write a phrase as listed below. Take turns tossing a large button on the square and the children complete the phrase the button lands on.

God loves me because…
Thank you, God, for…
I pray for…
Who prays for me?
God made…
God's with me when…
God's like…
God gives me…
God loves…
I like to pray when…

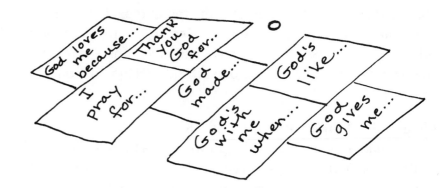

Hosanna Banner   ☺ ALL

Recognize Passion Sunday by making a Hosanna banner with the children.

❏ *You will need:*
Flat twin bed sheet
A permanent wide black marker
Green tempera paint
Palm branches (or stencils of palm branches)
Note: Palm branches should be available from the local florist if ordered ahead of time.
Do not confuse these palms with the reed variety most churches distribute on Passion Sunday.

❏ *To do:*
Use the black marker to print the message, "Hosanna! Blessed is He who comes in the name of the Lord" on the sheet. Then pour green paint into pie tins and place on newspaper covered tables. Supervise as the children lay the palms in the paint. Then again as they lift the palms off the sheet leaving a print. Hang this banner in an entryway for the Passion service.

Hosanna Palms   ☺ ALL

When Jesus rode into Jerusalem, the people waved palm branches and shouted words of praise. We too should greet Jesus with words of thanks and praise.

❑ *You will need:*
   Green poster board
   Green construction paper
   Markers
   Glue

❑ *To do:*

Cut a 12" strip of poster board for each child. Have the children trace several hands including their own. Then cut out the hands and glue onto the strip of poster board.

Hot Air Balloon   🐨 PRE

Up, up and away with the love of God.

❑ *You will need:*
   Colored construction paper
   String
   Paper cup
   Newspaper
   Stapler

❑ *To do:*

Enlarge and copy the pattern provided and cut two hot air balloons from brightly colored paper. Crumble up a piece of newspaper and put it between the two balloon cutouts. Staple them together. Leave the bottom neck of the balloons free. Punch 2 holes on each side of the neck and tie a 12" string to each. Next punch 4 holes equally spaced around the top of the cup. Tie the 4 strings from the balloon to the cup. Write, "Up, up and away with God," on the balloon.

Hug From Me to You   ☺ ALL

Greet one another with a holy "hug" – Romans 16:16

Hugs warm the hearts of everyone. Use these hugs to warm the hearts of shut-ins or anyone needing some heart warming.

❑ *You will need:*

Paper plates
3" x 12" strips of tag board
Yarn
Markers
Construction paper
Glue
Masking tape
Paper clips

❑ *To do:*

Make facial features on the paper plate using the markers. Glue on yarn for hair.
Cover the tag board with decorative contact paper or fabric and glue in place. Make a collar cut from fabric or construction paper. Trace each child's hands and cut out to be attached to each end of the covered tag board. Tape open paper clips to the back of each hand for easy hanging. Print across the arm span, "A hug from me to you!"

Hugs and Kisses   ☺ ALL

A Valentine idea that is just too cute not to use throughout the year.

Celebrate the love God has for us by sharing that love with others. Our ideas include a sweet, little gift and poem for the children to give to their families.

❑ *You will need:*

Nylon net
Hugs and Kisses chocolate
Ribbon
Copies of the poem provided below

❑ *To do:*

Wrap a few, "Hugs and Kisses," chocolates in an 8" circle of nylon net. Gather the sides of netting and tie it with a ribbon. Add a card with the following poem.

Hugs and kisses, hugs and kisses,
We grow in love each day, it's true.
Hugs and kisses, hugs and kisses,
A special gift from me to you.
God blesses our family!

Hula Hoop Mobile 😊 ALL

A great hanging-around idea for your room.
Use a hula hoop to display artwork or reinforce a unit you are working on.

❑ *You will need:*
    Hula hoop
    Yarn
    Construction paper
    Scissors
    Paper punch

❑ *To do:*
Tie 6 long pieces of yarn (spacing them evenly) to the hoop. Join the ends of the yarn together and tie a knot. Hang the hoop at the eye level of the children. Tie artwork or the characters from a story or pictures from a unit you are working on to the hoop. Punch a hole in the top of the picture or cut out and lace a piece of string through it for hanging.

Hum-Along 😊 ALL

Instead of singing the Lord's praises, why not hum the Lord's praises?

❑ *You will need:*
    Paper towel tube
    Tissue paper
    Rubber band
    Large nail
    Marker
    Colored tape

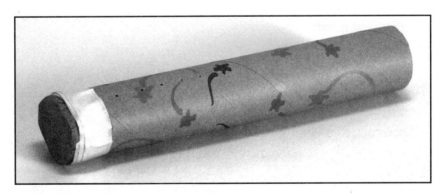

❑ *To do:*
Use the markers to decorate the tube. Cover one end of the tube with tissue paper and use a rubber band to hold in place. Cover the ends of the tissue paper and rubber band with tape. Put tape at the other end of the tube as well. Punch six holes about one inch from the covered end. You are ready to hum-along into the open end of the tube.

Humming Bird Feeder 😊 ALL

A unique way to care for our feathered friends.
Make a little nectar feeder that attaches to a tree for a humming bird.

❑ *You will need:*

Small, narrow plastic cups
1 cup sugar
2 cups water
Pan
Red silk flowers
Twine
Nectar

❑ *To do:*

To make the nectar, boil 2 cups water and 1 cup sugar. Allow to cool.
Tie or glue the red flower to the front of the cup. Punch two holes to the top of the cup on the side opposite the flower. Lace the string through these holes and tie to a tree branch. When the cup is secure pour in the nectar and enjoy the show!

Hunt for Matches 🐱 PRE

God has placed many things in our world that come in pairs. As a group brainstorm and hunt for items that are found in pairs.

❑ *You will need:*

Brown paper grocery bag
Markers
Paper

❑ *To do:*

Make a large grocery bag ark by rolling the top of the bag, from the inside out, down to a height of about 5" to 6". Invite children to search for things that are in pairs such as shoes, pant legs, mittens, etc. Provide paper and markers for children to make a drawing of pairs that are too large to fit in the bag or just cannot be brought to the bag, such as twin children.

I am the Good Shepherd Picture ☺ ALL

Remind the children that Jesus is with them always, just as the shepherd is with his sheep, by helping them create this picture and frame.

❏ *You will need:*

9" metal or aluminum pie tins
Pelon or interfacing material that is found in a fabric store
Glue
Scissors
Patterns
Markers or crayons

❏ *To do:*

Using the patterns, cut out a Jesus and child figure out of pelon. Invite the children to add color to the pattern of Jesus and to make the child-figures look as much like themselves as possible. Glue the figures on the inside of the pie tin.

❏ *More to do*:

Tape a paper clip or small hook to the back of the pie tin so that the children can hang their pictures on their wall at home.
Add the phrase, "I am the Good Shepherd" above the figures.
Glue ribbon around the edge of the pie tin to decorate the "frame."

I

I Can 👹 PRE

Teach this fun action song when your children need to stretch. After you have led a couple of verses, invite some of the children to offer their ideas and actions.

❏ **To do:**

Sing to the tune of "Did You Ever See a Lassie."

> I can clap my hands, my hands, my hands
>   (Clap hands…)
> I can clap my hands, with God at my side.
>   (Clap hands)
> Clap this way and that way and
> that way and this way.
> I can clap my hands with God at my side.
> I can climb mountains, mountains, mountains.
>   (Pretend to climb a mountain)
> I can climb mountains with God at my side.
>   (Pretend to climb a mountain)
> Climb this way and that way and
> that way and this way.
> I can climb mountains with God at my side.

Other ideas include:

Snap my fingers

Swim through oceans

Walk in space

"I" Collage ☺ ALL

Make an all-about-me collage for each child in your group.

❏ **You will need:**

Large sheets of construction paper

Magazines

Glue

Markers

Scissors

Photographs of each child

❏ **To do:**

Enlarge, trace, and cut out the "I" pattern provided. Have the children think about their favorite things, foods, toys, etc. and then look for pictures of these in the magazines. If possible put a photo of each child on his or her poster.

I

I Love You ☺ ALL
Use the sign of love to send a very special Valentine.

❏ *You will need:*
  Construction paper
  Markers
  Scissors
  Glue
  Large doilies

❏ *To do:*
Have the children trace one of their hands. Glue the palm only of the hand cutout to a large heart. Fold the ring and middle finger down to make the sign of love (in sign language). With adult help write, "I love you." Mount this to a large doily.

I Spy God ☺ ALL
God touches our world in so many ways, colors, sizes, shapes, and textures.

❏ *To do:*
Invite the children to view God's work as you play "I spy." Narrowing the game by suggesting a category such as shape, size, color, etc., will help focus younger children. A leader starts the play with the statement "I spy…" and continues to describe an object. From the clues the leader provides, the other players try to identify the object.

Ice and Snow Snack ☺ ALL
Warm up the cold days of winter with this cool tasty snack.

❏ *You will need:*
  Blue Jell-O® Jigglers
  Whipped cream

❏ *To do:*
Make a pan of blue jigglers according to box directions. Give each child a square of Jell-O and a spoon of whipped cream. Using a craft stick as a knife have the children frost their Jell-O with whipped cream.

Ice Cream Friends 🖐 PRI

Make 2 servings of ice cream treats as a community-building experience.

❑ *You will need:*
1 of each, a pint and a gallon sized zip lock freezer bags
1/2 cup milk
Ice
1 tablespoon sugar
1/4 teaspoon vanilla (or substitute milk, vanilla, and sugar for a package
  of instant pudding mixed according to manufacturer's directions).

❑ *To do:*
Mix the milk, sugar, and vanilla into the pint-size freezer bag. Place this bag inside the gallon size bag and fill with ice. Here is where the fun begins. Invite the children to work in pairs shaking the bag back and forth — the milk mixture must be kept moving while in the freezing process. Serve the ice cream to the pairs who worked together.

Ice Cream, Ice Cream. We All Scream for Ice Cream. ☺ ALL

Try these fun ice cream ideas to cool off the warm months of summer.

❑ *You will need:*
Brown burlap
Construction paper
Glue
Scissors

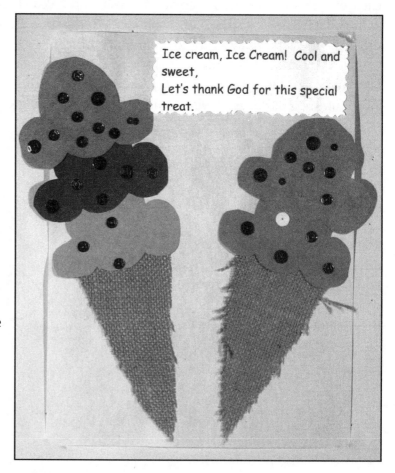

Ice cream, Ice Cream! Cool and sweet,
Let's thank God for this special treat.

❑ *To do:*
Using the pattern provided cut out a cone from burlap for each child. Also cut out several colored circles for the children to glue on the cone.   To add toppings, glue sequins or buttons to the paper circles.
Ice cream, ice cream! Cool and sweet,
Let's thank God for this special treat.

❑ *More to do:*
Put small, mini marshmallows in bugle cones for a fun treat.   Serve instant pudding in ice cream cones.

Icicles   ☺ ALL

Enjoy the beauty of winter without the cold in the classroom.

❑ *You will need:*

White and silver long pipe cleaners

❑ *To do:*

Whenever the children have a little extra time and are looking for a project have them make icicles by twisting three or four pipe cleaners together. Show the children the basic icicle shape but remind them that no two are exactly alike. That is one of the reasons they are so beautiful. Hang the icicles up in your room for a bit of winter delight!

ID Bracelet   ☺ ALL

Identification bracelets make learning a child's name easy. But these bracelets go beyond the name game by identifying the child as a member of the group.

❑ *You will need:*

   Glue
   Wallet-size photograph of each child
   Tag board
   Marker
   Ribbon
   Wooden or plastic bead
   Laminating materials (or clear contact)

❑ *To do:*

Using glue, mount each child's picture to a piece of tag board the same size as the picture. On the back of the tag board invite the child to print her/his name. Laminate or clear contact the mounted picture and punch a hole at the top. Thread a 10" piece of ribbon through the hole. Slide a bead onto the ribbon at each side of the picture. Each time you meet with the group tie each child's ID bracelet to his/her wrist or ankle and welcome them to the group.

Idea Can ☺ ALL

Conversation starters will warm your group up immediately.

Make a decorated can to hold ideas for starting conversation during your gather time. Ideas are printed on the strips of paper in the can. Each day a different child randomly chooses a strip, thus a topic for sharing that day.

❑ **You will need:**
> Pringles® chip can
> Contact paper
> 1 1/2" x 11" strips of paper

❑ **To do:**
Cover the can with contact paper and label it, "Our Idea Place." On the strips of paper write out questions or statements that follow a theme or the unit that you are working on. Ideas include, "All About Me," "How Do I Feel," "I'm Thankful for," "Songs We Know," or "Act It Out."

Idea File ☺ ALL

Share and exchange faith ideas with others in your ministry. This is a great way to spread the faith.

❑ **You will need:**
> Index cards
> Pen
> Ring fastener

❑ **To do:**
Record your ideas for sharing faith with children on index cards. Each time you find a new idea make a new card. Other ideas can be found in magazines. Clip the ideas and tape them to an index card. Keep the collection of your favorite ideas together on a ring.

❑ **More to do:**
Bring index cards to record ideas you may hear at in-services you attend throughout the year. Set up a monthly exchange of ideas with others who share your ministry. Trade idea cards.

Imagination   ☺ ALL

If we look around our world, we can see that God has an amazing imagination. Imagine designing all those stripes on a zebra's back or creating the countless number of shapes found in the clouds scattered across the sky. To appreciate God's imagination we must learn to use our own imaginations and creativity. Help children explore their imaginations with a few of these ideas. Then stretch your creative mind to come up with your own ideas for using the great gift of imaginations.

Ice skating without the ice
Enjoy winter fun without the cold.

❑ **You will need:**
2 sheets of paper
A carpeted surface

❑ **To do:**
Pretend to lace up a pair of ice skates. Don't forget to wipe the blades. Then with the sheets of paper on the carpet, place feet on the paper, and begin sliding feet across the carpet. Imagine skating on an ice-covered pond in the middle of winter.

Jesus story box

❑ **You will need:**
Cardboard box

❑ **To do:**
Invite the children to use their imaginations to recreate stories of Jesus. Use an empty cardboard box to serve as a boat rocking on rough waters. Or ask the children to imagine what it must have been like to be baptized in the river by John the Baptist and discuss their thoughts.

Drifting on the clouds

❑ **To do:**
On a partly cloudy day go outside to drift from cloud to cloud. While lying on your backs, ask the children to find a special cloud in the sky. Encourage them to imagine they are standing in the cloud. Ask them to describe what they would be doing there.

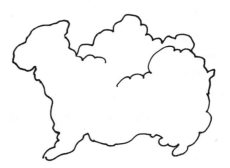

Inchworm ☺ ALL

"Inchworm, inchworm along the way, taking time out to enjoy the day."
Remember the little things in life with this fun and easy inchworm.

❑ *You will need:*

   12" x 18" construction paper
   Scissors (with decorative edges if available)

❑ *To do:*

Cut the construction paper into strips about 4" wide and 18" long. Fold
the strips the long way as you would a paper fan, making the folds
about 3" wide. Round off the four corners of the folded paper and cut
with pinking shears or other decorative edge scissors. Be careful not to
cut the folds. Open the folded inchworm and draw a cute face on one
end of the worm. Decorate with more drawing. Attach the little quote
from above to the inchworm.

Individual Snowflake ☺ ALL

Just as every snowflake is different, so are we.
Celebrate the special gift of our uniqueness with this snowflake project.

❑ *You will need:*

   White copy paper
   Blue construction paper
   Photo of each child
   Iridescent ribbon
   Pencil
   Scissors
   Glue
   Stapler

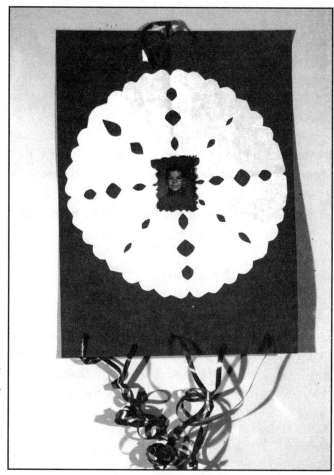

❑ *To do:*

Fold the white paper into eighths. Snip the
edges and angles into the folds to make a
snowflake. Younger children may need to
have lines drawn for them to cut. Unfold the
snowflakes and glue to the blue paper. If
time allows have the children make two
snowflakes, one for each side of the paper.
Glue a picture of the child to the center of the
snowflake. Staple several iridescent ribbons to
the bottom of the snowflake. Add ribbon to
the top for hanging.

Ingredients for a Faith-Filled Classroom  ☺ ALL

Sharing faith with young children requires a few basic ingredients.

❑ **To do:**

Mix all of the following with a faithful teacher.

Concrete experiences — Young children need lots of experience in the concrete before understanding the abstract.

Many joyful songs — Even the task of putting toys away can become a joy when you turn it into a song.

A variety of prayer — Prayer can be spontaneous and can happen anywhere. Take time to be thankful and invite Jesus to be a part of the activities.

Lots of one-of-a-kind individuals — Recognize and be sensitive to the variety of learning styles, family make-ups, and needs the children possess.

Teacher who models God's love, forgiveness and acceptance — Actions speak louder than voices.

Many playful games and fingerplays — These activities keep the children's short attention spans actively involved.

Opportunities for discovery — Remember God's great love is "caught not taught." The children will learn more by the experiences than by what is told to them.

Props — Support storytelling and role playing with pictures, puppets, and props.

Serve in a non-threatening loving environment — Establish and maintain an environment where the children feel safe to share thoughts and feelings without negative criticism.

Don't forget to cool with reflection — Take time to reflect on your role as the instrument that opens a window for children to learn about God.

Imagination Station ☺ ALL

A place to go to dress up for dramatic play.

❏ *You will need:*

Grocery boxes with handles
Markers
Pictures or drawings of Bible story characters
Bathrobes, belts, dish towels, sandals, crowns, long dresses, etc., for dress up
Wall mirror

❏ *To do:*

Label the boxes, "Imagination Station." Fill them with dress up clothes and leave in a space that is easily accessible to the children. Hang up a wall mirror that is at child level so that they can see themselves all dressed up.

Ink Prints ✋ PRI

Ink prints are a creative way to teach children about religious symbols.

❏ *You will need:*

Stamping inkpad
Paper
Pencil
Scissors
Construction paper

❏ *To do:*

Lay the papers face down on the inkpad. With a pencil make the outline of the symbol you wish to emphasize. Trim away excess paper and mount the symbol on construction paper. A collection of symbols may be used to make a collage for a particular liturgical season such as Easter, Lent, Advent, or Christmas.

❏ *More to do:*

After introducing these symbols to young children, provide the materials needed to make their own ink prints to share at home.

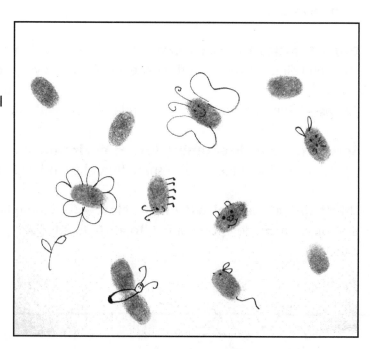

In the Bag With Grab Bag Ideas ☺ALL

Mary Poppins always brought the magic in her carpetbag with her wherever she ventured. Tuck God in your bag whenever you go with this bag of ideas. Always fit God into the laughter, play, prayer, and fun you share with the children in your care using items as simple as an egg carton, jump rope, handkerchief, suntan lotion, snack, hand mirror, and spray bottle.

❑ *You will need:*
Egg carton
Jump rope
Handkerchief
Suntan lotion
Snack
Hand Mirror
Spray bottle

❑ *To do:*

Count God's blessings with an egg carton.

Keep an empty egg carton handy for a nature walk. Ask the children to walk with you as you look for twelve things God has blessed our world with. Look for tokens that will fill in empty spaces in the carton. Once the carton is filled, sit together to count and thank God for the many blessings that fill the carton.

Fill a jump rope circle full of God's blessings.

While outside make a circle on the ground with a jump rope. Ask the children to stand outside the circle. Encourage them to take turns sharing what they know to be God's blessings. Each time someone identifies a blessing, he gets to jump inside the circle. Children inside the circle get to help children outside the circle to think of blessings, too. When the circle is full, invite the children to go out and share God's blessings with others.

Create with God's creation on a handkerchief.

Take a group of children outside. Spread a handkerchief on the ground. As the children walk around the yard and collect treasures to place on the cloth, work together to arrange the treasures in such a manner that will form a picture of God's creation.

Feel the warmth of God's sunshine coated with sunscreen.

On a warm sunny day, spread God a blanket on the lawn. Apply sunscreen on children as you bless them with these words: "God, You send the sun rays to kiss the earth, making our days warm and bright."

Compare, classify, and share a snack with the friends God has given us.

Here is a way to pass a day with small friends. Collect rocks and pebbles from your play yard. Compare the findings, classifying them from smallest to largest. Use the pebbles, stones, and rocks to make a trail for the children to follow. At the end of the trail hide a snack for the children to share, celebrating their friendship.

Look in a mirror to see God's great blessing.

At a special moment pull a hand mirror from your bag. Sit with the children examining the mirror. Let the children take turns looking at their reflections. Talk about what a blessing they each are to the lives of others. Invite them to fill in the blank of this rhyme with something God has given to them: "When I look in the mirror, what do I see? A _____ that God has given to me!"

Use a spray bottle filled with water to splash an abundance of blessings.

Fill a plastic spray bottle with water. (For safety's sake, label as water.) Sprinkle a few pieces of plastic heart confetti inside the bottle.

Inn Keeper Game 😊 ALL

Similar to "Doggie, Doggie Where's Your Bone," the Innkeeper Game is a fun one for Christmas time.

❑ *You will need:*

  8" tag board key

❑ *To do:*

Have the children sit in a circle. Chose two children, Mary and Joseph, to leave the room. While they are gone give one child in the circle (the innkeepers) the key to the inn to hide in her or his lap. Ask Mary and Joseph to come back. They then go around the circle asking an Innkeeper if there is room in the inn, "Inn Keeper, Inn Keeper do you have room?" The Inn Keeper then responds, "No sir, no sir, I have no room." If the innkeeper with the key is chosen, he or she responds, "Yes sir, yes sir, I have room." The key is then turned over to Mary and Joseph. The person who had the key is the new Mary or Joseph. That person also chooses another person to join him or her in leaving the room while the key is hidden again.

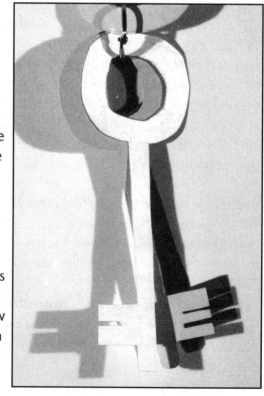

Inside-Out Fan ✋ PRI

Beat the summer heat with a fan that carries this cool fan fare message, "God loves us inside and out!"

❏ *You will need:*
Flat craft sticks or tongue depressors
Strips of paper 3 1/2" x 8 1/2"
or strips cut to approximately 3 1/2" x 17")
Markers
Stapler
Tape

❏ *To do:*
Tape the two strips together, if using smaller strips. Use markers to decorate the paper lengthwise with hearts and the message "God loves us inside and out." Fan fold the whole strip starting at the smaller edge. Keep the fan fold together by stapling one end. Tape the edges of the fan to the craft sticks so the stapled end of the fan meets the top of the sticks. Open the fan by bringing the handles together as shown.

Inside Out Upside-Down ☺ ALL

Plan a wacky inside out, upside down day.
Remind the children that God loves us no matter what. Whether we are inside out or upside down or backwards.

❏ *You will need:*
Construction paper
Markers
Shoe box cover

❏ *To do:*
Have the children dress with their clothes inside out or upside down or backwards. Put shoes on the wrong feet and wear paper or plastic glasses on the back of the head instead of the front. Plan your day a little differently. Have snack at gym time and take rests at circle time, sit back wards in chairs, etc. Mix up the day. Make upside down pictures. Cut out the construction paper to fit the inside of the shoe box cover. Have the children draw an upside down picture and mount it to the box cover.

Introduce Yourself With the M&M® game.    PRI

Get to know each other the first week of class with the M&M game.

❑ **You will need:**
Large bag of M&M's
Paper napkins.

❑ **To do:**
Tell the children you are going to play a special game. Everyone is going to take some M&M's from the bag. Tell the children they may not eat the M&M's until it is their turn in the game. After everyone has their candy, tell the children that they have to say one thing about themselves for each piece of candy they took. Those who took lots of candy will do lots of talking. Those who took less will need to say less. The children may eat their M&M's after they have had their turn to talk. It would probably be helpful for the teacher to go first to demonstrate the sharing part.

Instruments to Make Music   ☺ ALL

The music ministry in any church is a very important part of our worship. Provide homemade instruments for young children to use in praising God.

Bongo drums

❑ **You will need:**
Two empty 3 lb. coffee cans with lids
2 extra wide long rubber bands

❑ **To do:**
With lids on, join two cans together by wrapping the two rubber bands around the cans. The cans may be decorated with contact paper or shapes cut from contact paper. Children will delight in the opportunity to beat drums. Use these as part of a praise celebration.

Rubber band guitar

❑ **You will need:**
6 rubber bands
Frozen pizza box
Yardstick
Masking tape

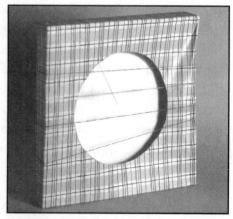

❑ **To do:**
Cut away a hole from the center of the pizza box. Then wrap the rubber bands around the frozen pizza box to make the strings of the guitar. Sliding the yardstick through the inside of the box and securing it in place with the masking tape makes the neck of the guitar. Strum the strings.

Jingle bell ringer

❑ *You will need:*

Scissors
Plastic butter tub lid
3-4 jingle bells
Yarn

❑ *To do:*

To form a handle for this instrument cut away half the lid leaving the rim intact. Use the yarn to hang the bells from the rim. Holding the solid half of the lid, jingle away.

Inventions   ☺ ALL

This is a fun game to get the children's creative juices flowing.

❑ *You will need:*

A variety of familiar objects such as toothbrush, book, or rock. Remind them who the greatest inventor is – God.

❑ *To do:*

Pass the objects around to various children and ask them to create a new use for that item. Be sure to give them a bit of time and a little help if they need it.

Invisible Ink   ☺ ALL

Write secret God messages that will disappear.

❑ *You will need:*

Lemon juice
White paper
Fine tip paint brushes

❑ *To do:*

Have the children paint a picture using the lemon juice as paint. With adult help write a message of faith, such as God's love is forever. When the picture dries the drawing will disappear. To see the picture after it has dried hold it up to a bright light.

Invite God Into Your Heart ☺ ALL

Through prayer and acts of kindness we express our love for God and others.
Make a heart mobile to remind the children of the ways we invite God into our heart.

❑ **You will need:**
Construction paper
Paper punch
Marker
String

❑ **To do:**
Enlarge and cut out the 4 patterns provided. With adult help write, "God is invited into my heart," on the big heart. On the folded hands write "prayer," on the flower write "good deeds," and on the smaller heart, "love." Punch 3 holes around the bottom of the heart and in the top and bottom of the praying hands and flower. Since the small heart is last, only one hole is needed. Use the string to tie the symbols together to make a mobile.
Remember to punch a hole in the top of the big heart for hanging.

Iris ☺ ALL
The Greek Word for Rainbow.
Reinforce the story of Noah and the promise God made and sealed with the rainbow by making rainbow flowers.

❑ *You will need:*
Coffee filters
4 bowls of water
4 different colors of food coloring
Construction paper
Glue
Scissors
Petal pattern pieces

❑ *To do:*
Have the children fold 2 coffee filters. Gently dip the filters into bowls of water colored with food coloring. Unfold the filters and let them dry. After drying trace and cut out 6 Iris petals. Glue these to the top third of a piece of construction paper, 3 petals going up and 3 petals facing down. Add a stem and leaves. With adult help write the words, "Iris means rainbow and rainbow means the promise of God's love."

Ivy Topiary ☺ ALL
The Ivy is an ancient symbol of love.
To celebrate Valentines Day have the children make a fun topiary to share with their families on Valentines Day.

❑ *You will need:*
3" clay flower pots
3" or 4" Styrofoam balls
Artificial ivy
Spanish moss
Glue
Ribbon

❑ *To do:*
Place the ball in the top of the pot. Push it down to secure it in place. If necessary add a bit of glue around the edge of the pot before putting the ball on it. Use a paintbrush to spread glue around the ball. Then cover as much of the ball as possible with moss. Cut the ivy leaves so that they can they can be put on the moss one a time. Allow to dry overnight.
Add a ribbon around the bottom of the pot and a little explanation.

List Your Favorite Projects Here

_____

_____

_____

_____

_____

_____

_____

_____

_____

_____

_____

_____

_____

_____

_____

_____

_____

_____

_____

_____

_____

Jam Tarts   ☺ ALL

Jesus said, "I am the bread of life. No one who comes to me shall
ever be hungry." – (Cf. John 6:35.)

❏ *You will need:*
   Jam
   Dairy case biscuits

❏ *To do:*

Give each child half an uncooked biscuit to flatten out with his or her hands. Push the flattened
dough into mini muffin pan cups, bringing dough up the sides. Instruct the children to fill the
biscuit cup with a spoonful of jam. Cook for 5-10 minutes at 425 degrees. Watch carefully as jam
burns easily. Caution: Cool completely before serving.

J.C. Pin   ☺ ALL

A reminder of Jesus Christ's constant presence in our lives.
Using craft foam have the children make pins for their jackets to remind them that Jesus
is always near.

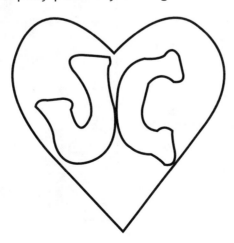

❏ *You will need:*
   Craft foam sheets
   Glue
   Scissors
   Puffy paint
   Clasp pin
   Glue gun

❏ *To do:*

Using the pattern provided, trace and cut the letters J and C from foam. Glue these to the heart
shape also provided. With adult help use a glue gun to attach the clasp pin to the back of the
diamond. Decorate the pin with puffy paint. Dry overnight.

Jean Pillows    ALL

Soft additions to your reading corner.
Make some soft but sturdy pillows for your reading corner with worn out blue jeans. (If you do not sew, check your volunteer list for help.)

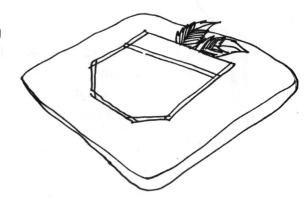

❑ *You will need:*

    Old blue jeans
    Fiber fill stuffing
    Thread

❑ *To do:*

Cut the legs out of an old pair of blue jeans. Turn inside out and sew up the leg openings. Next sew up the waist leaving an opening to put in stuffing. After stuffing the jeans, sew up the opening.

❑ *More to do:*

From time to time put secret things in the pockets of the jean pillows. A tiny book, picture, cross, heart, or toy would be fun for the children to discover as they look at books.

Jell-O® Box Puppet   ALL

Create a hand puppet using an empty box and a few craft supplies. This can be a mouthpiece for telling stories or reciting various readings.

❑ *You will need:*

    Empty gelatin or individual sized cereal box
    Construction paper
    Yarn
    Glue
    Pipe cleaner
    Pompoms
    Masking tape

❑ *To do:*

Cut the box in half through three faces of the box as shown. Do not cut through the front face. Fold the front face in half forming openings to the inside of the box for fingers and thumbs to fit. The front face of the box becomes the mouth of the puppet. Decorate the box with construction paper, markers, fabric, pipe cleaners, pompoms, etc.

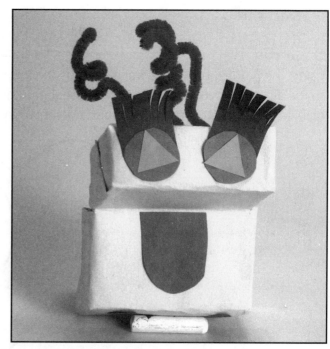

Jell-O® Cubes 😺 PRE

The bright colors of finger gelatin provide a great experience for teaching children about all the colors of God's creation. Tell the story of creation using cubes of gelatin.

❑ *You will need:*
Wooden skewers
Gelatin mix (purple, blue, yellow, green, orange, and red)
Depending on the size of your group you may want to mix
   some of the colors yourself so you don't have too much gelatin.
   Example: blue and red to make purple.

❑ *To do:*
Mix gelatin according to directions on the package for making finger gelatin. Cut the finger gelatin into 1" cubes. Mix the variety of colorful cubes into a serving bowl. Then as you tell the story of creation let the children add a cube to their skewer.
God said, "Let there be light. And God separated light from darkness (add a purple cube). God made the land and the blue sea (add a blue cube). God marked day from night with the yellow sun and the night moon (add yellow cube). Then God made people and animals of all colors to roam the earth, land, and water (add any color cube). God wanted the people and animals to have food so green plants and fruits were added to the earth (add a green cube). After working to create the world for us, God rested. Now when we see all the colors around us we can be reminded of how much God loves us to create all of this beauty around us (add a red cube)."

Jell-O® Picture 🙂 ALL

A sweet way to create!
Use powdered Jell-O to create a beautiful scene.

❑ *You will need:*
Boxes of Jell-O
Paint brushes
Small cups
Water
Paper

❑ *To do:*
Put different flavors of powdered Jell-O mix in small paper cups. Also put out paper cups with small amounts of water. Have the children paint with water on the paper. After painting with the water have the children
sprinkle Jell-O on the paper to add color to the picture. The powdered Jell-O will stick to the paper as it dries. *Be careful as the colored gelatin may stain.

Jesus Gift Boxes   ✋ PRI

Be reminded Jesus is present in every gift we give with this gift box idea.

❑ *You will need:*

Poster board or card stock paper
Sticker of Jesus
Clear tape
Markers

❑ *To do:*

Measure the poster board into a 3" x 4" grid and cut into a cross as shown. Place the Jesus sticker in the center of the cross, 2"-2" of the grid. To form the box, use square 2"-2" as the base and fold the surrounding grid squares up. Place the gift contents on the Jesus sticker. Close the box around the gift by taping square 1"-2" to 4"-2". Secure square 2"-1" and 2"-3" to 4"-2" with the tape. Decorate the box with markers.

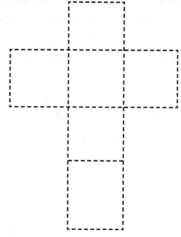

Jesus Loves Me Chain   ☺ ALL

Use the pattern provided to make a Jesus love necklace.

❑ *You will need:*

Enlarge and copy the pattern provided on white paper
Red construction paper
Glue
Ribbon
Scissors
Paper punch

❑ *To do:*

Have the children color the heart picture. Next, cut the white hearts out and glue them to bigger red hearts. For added support put a piece of tape on the top back of the heart and put the paper punch hole there. Lace a ribbon through the hole for hanging.

Jesus Pennant   😊 ALL

Make a reminder of the most important message of Jesus' ministry, Love One Another...

❑ *You will need:*
   Pelon (medium or heavy weight interfacing
      material available in fabric departments or stores)
      or tag board
   Permanent marker

❑ *To do:*
Cut the pelon or tag into triangles 12" x 24" x 24".
With adult help print, "Love One Another," on the
pennant. Have the children decorate the rest with
marker.

Jesus Poem   😊 ALL

This poem just about says it all.

❑ *To do:*
Read the poem to the children. The next time through have
the children repeat each line back to you.

Jesus loves you.

Jesus loves me.

Jesus makes us feel

Happy and free.

Jesus is gentle.

He makes me glad.

He cares for me,

When I am sad.

Thank you, Jesus,

For all that you do

To make me know

I'm loved by you.

J

Jesus Said, "Come." PRE

After telling the children the story of Jesus and the children (Matthew 19:13-15 and Luke 18:15-17) play this game to further the children's experience.

❑ *You will need:*
 Chalk
 Tape or string

❑ *To do:*
Mark off boundaries in a large open outdoor area for the children to play this game, using chalk, tape, or string. Encourage the children to run freely around the marked off area. Call out "No, don't bother Jesus today, he is too tired and busy to play." Instruct the children to run to a designated spot. The last child to the spot becomes Jesus who says, "Let the children come!" Then the group disperses. The child who was Jesus taps someone on the shoulder to be the person to say, "No, don't bother…" and that child indicates a new meeting spot. The play continues until every child has had the opportunity to be Jesus.

Jewels That Reflect God's Love PRI

Take time to look for the light of Jesus in your classroom. Then encourage the children to continue to share it by making sparkling reflectors.

❑ *You will need:*
 Heavy paper such as colored construction paper
 Patterns such as snowflakes, flowers, or jewel shapes
 Glitter
 Scissors
 Glue
 Paper punch

❑ *To do:*
Cut the paper into interesting shapes (you may want to use shapes that reflect the season you are in, i.e. winter – snowflakes). Have the children dot the shapes with glue and sprinkle them with glitter. Place two similar shapes together, and using a paper punch, make a number of holes in each. Place colored tissue paper between them and glue together. Use your paper punch to make a hole for a piece of yarn for hanging the jewel reflector. Hang your "light" around the room or send them home to remind the children to be reflectors of God's love.

Jigsaw Puzzles   ☺ ALL

What to do with those puzzles that are missing pieces? Try these fun ideas.

❑ ***You will need:***
> Puzzle pieces
> Glue
> Construction paper

❑ ***To do:***
Give each child 3 puzzle pieces. Ask them to glue the puzzle pieces to the paper to make a fun picture. Encourage the children to draw around the piece to finish their picture.

Jingle Bell Bracelets   ☺ ALL

Make a joyful noise unto the Lord!
Try these little bell bracelets to ring in the joy of the season – whatever that might be!

❑ ***You will need:***
> Ribbon
> Jingle bells
> Beads
> Scissors

❑ ***To do:***
Cut lengths of ribbon long enough to tie and comfortably fit the wrists of the children. Have the children string one bell and any combination of beads on to the ribbon. With adult help tie the ribbon to the wrists of the children and make a joyful noise!

Job chart   ☺ ALL

Participating community members feel as though they belong when they are given an active role. Provide small jobs that allow the children to feel they are important participants in the classroom community.

❑ ***You will need:***
> Spring clothes pins
> Circle cut from poster board
> Markers

❑ ***To do:***
Print each child's name on a clothespin. On the poster board, print a list of classroom jobs that the children can do by themselves. Clip the clothespin to the job assigned to that individual child. Change the tasks frequently by reassigning the clothespins, allowing all the children the opportunity to do a variety of jobs.

Jointed Me Puppet  PRI

Psalm 139:13 reads, "I give thanks that I am wonderfully made." Making this delightful puppet will remind the children that they truly are wonderfully made.

❑ **You will need:**
Brads
Tongue depressors or straws
Construction paper
Patterns
Markers

❑ **To do:**
Using brads, have the children connect a head, arms, and legs to a body and let them color their puppets to look like themselves. Glue a tongue depressor or straw to the back of the puppet. Let the children make their puppets jump, dance, turn around and hop.

Jolly Jointed Puppet ☺ ALL

Use up your leftovers to make this jumping puppet.

❑ *You will need:*

1 empty soap bottle
4-5 feet of twine
6 large empty spools of thread
   (could substitute with large beads)
Margarine tub
2 18" wooden dowels
8 beads or large buttons
Markers
Glue
Scissors
Leftover ribbon, fabric, felt, etc.

❑ *To do:*

Fold the piece of twine in half and about 8" from the fold tape to the top of one of the dowels. There should be at least a 6" loop at the top of the dowel with the ends of the twine loose. Punch a hole in the bottom of the margarine tub and thread the top loop through it and secure in place with a knot. Thread the empty spools on the free ends of twine, alternating beads and buttons. Knot one end of the twine. Knot the other end of the twine around the second dowel. To make the body punch a hole in the bottom of the dish soap bottle and secure with masking tape. Decorate the body and face of the puppet with marker and leftover craft materials.

Journal Roll ✋ PRI

Use this journal to sketch the wonder of all God has created.

❑ *You will need:*

Empty toilet paper tubes
Hole punch
Cording
Short pencil
Two 8 1/2" x 11" sheets of paper
Stapler

❑ *To do:*

Punch hole in the tube and thread cording through it to make wrist tie. Cut the paper into 4 1/4" x 11" strips of paper and staple together in a tablet. Roll the tablet together with the pencil and slide inside the tube. Tie tube to wrist. While out on a walk observe all God's glory. Use the journal to record observations.

J

Joyful In God Are We!   PRE

Remind the children that we have wonderful experiences to be grateful for every day. God has blessed us with a lot and God finds happiness in our joy.

❏ *To Sing:*

Sing to the tune of "The Old Gray Mare."
Make up new verse and actions to use. Repeat words in ( ) three times.

> Verse 1:   *The sun is out and (shining bright today)*
> *The sun is out and shining bright today.*
> *Joyful God are we!*
>
> Verse 2:   *The baby bird flies (out of the nest today)*
> *The baby bird flies out of the nest today.*
> *Joyful God are we!*
>
> Verse 3:   *The fish swim up to (take the worm from me)*
> *The fish swim up to take the worm from me.*
> *Joyful God are we!*

Joyful Shout   ALL

Psalm 47 reads, "All you people, clap your hands; raise a joyful shout to God." Don't forget to give a joyful shout in your classroom from time to time. Try this one.

❏ *To shout:*

Spilt the group into two and have one side begin this cheer while clapping. The other side will respond with the same words until the last time.

We've got joy, yes we do.

Clap.

We've got joy, how about you?

Clap... point.

The cheer goes back and forth a few times, until the group

that started ends with... We've got joy, yes we do.

Clap.

We've got joy, because God loves you!

Clap ... point.

The other group responds with the same words and actions.

Juice Can Lid Charm ALL
Use saved up juice can lids to make a Bible story necklace.

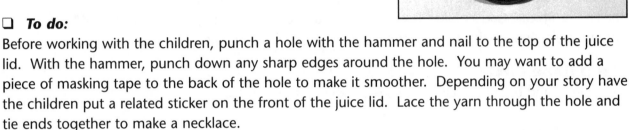

❑ **You will need:**
Juice lids
Hammer
Large nail
Stickers
Heavy yarn

❑ **To do:**
Before working with the children, punch a hole with the hammer and nail to the top of the juice lid. With the hammer, punch down any sharp edges around the hole. You may want to add a piece of masking tape to the back of the hole to make it smoother. Depending on your story have the children put a related sticker on the front of the juice lid. Lace the yarn through the hole and tie ends together to make a necklace.

❑ **More to do:**
Older children would enjoy using puffy paint to make their own design on the juice lid.

Juice Can Lids, 1-2-3 ALL
Collect juice can lids for a variety of two to three step activities.

❑ **You will need:**
Metal juice can lids
Nail
Hammer
Yarn
Fabric paints
Permanent markers
Stickers
Wooden dowel
Classmates photos
Clear contact

❑ **To do:**
1. With a nail and hammer punch a hole in the lid. String a piece of yarn through the hole and make the start of a necklace or pendant. Decorate with fabric paints, permanent markers, sticker, etc.

2. Make a class wind chime using the same hole-punched lids. Hang at varied lengths from a thick wooden dowel.

3. Keep lids handy for prayer tokens. Decorate the lids with stickers or photographs of classmates. Secure photographs to the lids by covering the picture with a circle of clear contact.

Jump Jive and Jingle   😀 PRE

When we do good for others, we are ringing praise for God and bringing joy to others. This simple activity will give young children time to practice and share kind actions.

❑ *You will need:*
Hand bell

❑ *To do:*
Sitting in a circle, talk about how our actions can bring joy to others and how when we do this we are praising God. After some discussion, play this simple game to practice bringing joy to others. Begin by demonstrating how to JUMP up with an idea for sharing joy with others. Ring the bell to JINGLE God's praise. Then explain your idea for sharing JOY with others. When someone else has an idea they do the same – Jump, jive and jingle!

Jump Rope Circle   😀 PRE

Jumping in and out of the circle helps share the blessings of God.

❑ *You will need:*
Jump rope

❑ *To do:*
Lay a jump rope on the ground in the shape of a circle. Have the children stand outside the rope. Encourage the children to take turns sharing what they know to be God's blessings. Each time someone identifies a blessing, they get to jump inside the circle. Children inside the circle can help children outside the circle think of blessings too. When the circle is full, invite all of the children to go out and share God's blessings with others.

Jump Rope Rhyme   😀 PRE

For outside fun!
Play a follow-the-leader game with this little rhyme.

❑ *You will need:*
Jump rope

❑ *To do:*
Lay the rope on the ground for the children to jump over as they recite this rhyme.
Follow a leader back and forth.
Didder, didder, dee,
Chitter, chitter, chat.
God loves you and God loves me.
Didder, didder, dee,
Chitter chitter chat.
Be my friend and follow me.
Didder, didder, dee,
Chitter, chitter chat,
Children of God all are we.

Jump Up Puppet   ☺ ALL

Add some giggles and fun to your next story with a pop-up puppet.

❑ *You will need:*

1 empty egg cup from an egg carton
Unsharpened pencil
Paper cup (7 oz. size or larger)
Masking tape
Yarn
Markers
Scissors

❑ *To do:*

Punch a hole in the bottom of the paper cup big enough for the pencil to go through. With the open end down, decorate the egg cup with a face and hair using yarn and markers. Tape the egg cup to the unsharpened end of the pencil. Place the pencil with the eraser down into the cup and push it up and down to make it move.

❑ *More to do:*

Glue a small paper cup to the end of the pencil for the head instead of the egg cup.

Jumpin' Jonah and the Whale   ✋ PRI

Retell the story of Jonah and the whale, with Jonah looking to God for forgiveness and God saving him from the stomach of a whale.

❑ *You will need:*

Plastic gallon milk jug

❑ *To do:*

Cut the jug into the shape of an opened-mouth whale. The bottom is cut away to make the mouth and the handle makes the tail of the whale. Use permanent markers to draw in details such as eyes and fins.

❑ *More to do:*

Play the game by tossing beanbags into the mouth of the whale. Each time the beanbag lands in the whale's mouth the children can say this chant:

Jonah, Jonah why are you in the mouth?
You must ask God to help you out.
1-2-3 days in. Out, out, out you spin!
The beanbags are dumped out and given to another child to try.

Jungle Praise Book　　🐨 PRE

A Jungle Praise book.

Make, "My Jungle Praise Book," to help tell the following story.

> The monkey praises God with an O-O-O!
> The lion praises God with a loud strong roar!
> The hippo praises God with a great big splash!
> The toucan praises God with a caw! Caw! Caw!
> The elephant praises God as he lifts his big trunk.
> The tiger praises God with a loud, loud growl.
> The crocodile praises God with a quick, sharp snap!
> I praise God with a shout hurray, in all I do and say, every single day.

❑ *You will need:*

White copy paper
Construction paper
Markers
Stapler
Glue

❑ *To do:*

Enlarge and copy the praise book patterns provided on next page. Have the children color the animals before cutting out the squares. Be sure they draw a picture of themselves in the last square. With adult help put the animal pages in the same order as the story. Glue the palm tree to a piece of construction paper cut in half the long way. Next staple the pages to the bottom of the palm tree and enjoy.

Junk Art　　😊 ALL

"One person's junk is another person's treasure."

Let the children have at it with a bag of junk and their creative energies.

❑ *You will need:*

Brown lunch bags
Paper plates
Glue
Lots of left over craft materials, (foams, packing peanuts, beads, and nuts, buttons, bows, fabric, macaroni, rocks, and small pieces of wood.)

❑ *To do:*

Put equal amounts of leftovers in a lunch bag for each child and close them up. Give each child a paper plate. Tell the children that they are to make a creation using everything in the brown bag on the paper plate. When everyone is done share the finished products.

My Jungle Praise Book

STAPLE PAGES HERE

I Praise God

J

List Your Favorite Projects Here

_____

_____

_____

_____

_____

_____

_____

_____

_____

_____

_____

_____

_____

_____

_____

_____

_____

_____

_____

_____

_____

Kaleidoscope of Color 😺 PRE

Celebrate the color in our lives with this kaleidoscope project.

❑ *You will need:*

Toilet tissue tubes
Wax paper
Mylar pieces (found at a craft store)
Rubber bands
Ribbon

❑ *To do:*

For each kaleidoscope you will need two 6" circles of wax paper. Lay one circle on the table and put a spoonful of Mylar in the middle of it. Lay the next circle of wax paper on top of the first one. Place the toilet tissue tube on top of the wax paper circles centering the Mylar in the middle of the tube. Carefully gather up the edges of the wax paper circles around the end of the tube. Secure in place with a rubber band. Give the tube a little shake to loosen up the Mylar. Tie a couple of ribbons around the tube for decoration.
Look through the open end towards natural light and enjoy all God's colors.

Keep the Teaching Fire Burning, Reflection 😊 ALL

Reflect on your exciting role as a religious educator of young children. As a person who fosters the faith development of children, you are kindling the presence of our Christian faith in the future.

❑ *For Reflection:*

The flame of enthusiasm I have for teaching extends
The love of Jesus to all those around me.
I am reminded that my attitudes are reflected
In how I react to different situations.
If I ever feel my flame begin to flicker, I will trust that God
Will be there to strengthen me with love, patience, and perseverance.
So as I look into the little smiling faces and twinkling
Eyes of the children I teach, I will remember that I am
An example of God's love to each of them.
I trust that God's flame will continue to glow throughout their lives.

Keepers of the Earth ✋ PRI

God loved us enough to gift us with beautiful surroundings. To show our love and thanks to God, we can care for the earth. Here is a board game that will reveal ways for children to respect and care for the world we live in.

❑ *You will need:*

Coin

Game board copied from book and laminated

❑ *To do:*

Toss a coin to move around the board. When heads is turned up, the player moves ahead one space. When tails is turned up, the player moves ahead two spaces.

Board reads:

Start

Watch a nesting bird from afar without disturbing it

Use both sides of drawing paper

Lead a can drive at your school, take stairs to move ahead three spaces

(Picture of the earth with a ribbon on it)

Show you care about God's world by reusing plastic bottle to make a drinking bottle
 – move ahead one space

Celebrate earth day with an outdoor prayer service

Littered on the beach — slide back to earth keeper's school

Water thirsty plants — move ahead 2 spaces

Stay here until you toss heads because you need to learn more about recycling

(Picture of sun)

Reduce waste by sharing your magazines and books with friends

Keeping Shelf ☺ ALL

A special place for special things.
This idea comes from an early American tradition of having a special room or shelf in the home for special family heirlooms, photos, etc. Create a special place in your classroom for mementos of your class and the time you spend together.

❑ *You will need:*
Paper
Markers
Shelf

❑ *To do:*
Clear off a shelf or bulletin board to use. Cut out letters or write, "Our Keeping Shelf." Suggestions for items to place on the shelf include a picture of the class, unique nature finds, mementos of a field trip, a special cross or statue, favorite books or toys.

Keepsakes ☺ ALL

Keepsakes are tokens used to remind us of an event. Sharing with others the significance of a particular keepsake is a way of sharing who we are and what we value. Through our actions we keep Jesus alive and share his memory with those around us. Christ lives on in each of us. Here are a few ideas to remind children of events and times they have shared. Memories of picnics, field trips, and vacations can all be made into keepsakes with these ideas.

Picnic Tablecloth

❑ *You will need:*
Sturdy vinyl cotton-backed tablecloth
Markers

❑ *To do:*
Each time the family or class gathers for a picnic or cookout, write something about the occasion on the tablecloth with the permanent markers. Younger children can write their message in drawing form. Even spilled food stains may tell a story someday.

Car pillow

❑ *You will need:*
Canvas-covered pillow
Permanent markers

❑ *To do:*
Turn the pillow into a travel log. Keep track of places traveled by jotting down the dates and places on the pillow with permanent markers. Each individual may be given his/her own special marker to be used each time a notation is made.

Vacation ball

❏ **You will need:**

Ball (soccer, volleyball, nerf, softball etc.)
Permanent markers

❏ **To do:**

Not only is this useful for tossing around and burning off energy, it also may be used to record events of a trip. Throughout the trip invite various group members to write a highlight of the trip on the ball. Later, after the trip has passed, the highlights will not be so easy to forget.

T-shirts

❏ **You will need:**

Tee shirt per child
Fabric or laundry markers

❏ **To do:**

Some schools wear special tee shirts on outings to identify their group. These or any other shirt may be used to keep track of where the group has been together. Use the fabric or laundry marker to write the place and date on the back of the shirt. Children may also want to make a drawing of a highlight of the outing.

Key to Your Heart   ☺ ALL

The key to life is to keep God in your heart. This end-of-the-year gift may be made with the help of the children.

❏ **You will need:**

Plastic lacing
Plastic margarine tub lids
Hole punch
Permanent marker or puffy paint
Small chain or key ring

❏ **To do:**

Cut heart shapes from the lids. Write the message "Give God the key to your heart." Hole punch around the edge of the heart. Give the children plastic lacing to sew in and out of the holes. Add a small chain or key ring to the heart. Sign and date the back of the heart key chain. As you present this end-of or beginning-of-the-year gift to children, remind them that even when you are not near they will be in your heart.

Kick the Ball With a Twist ☺ ALL

Here is an energy releaser that will identify and celebrate the many ways we can move our bodies.

❑ *You will need:*
Rubber ball
Two orange cones to serve as goal post markers

❑ *To do:*
Depending on the age and skills of the children, stand the goal markers about four feet apart. Invite a child to kick the ball at the goal starting 20 feet away. If the child misses, he or she moves a few feet closer to the goal until the goal is made. When the ball goes through the markers, the child making the goal shouts out:

I've got energy, yes I do.
I've got energy, so do you.

Then the child points to a new child to attempt to score.

After all the children have made the goal, close with a short prayer.

God, We've got energy, yes we do.
We've got energy because of you.

Kicking Off to a New Year ☺ ALL

Try these fun soccer ideas to get everyone excited about a new beginning.

❑ *Soccer cheer*

Hello friends, we're glad you're here!

Kicking off our class to a brand new year.

Our parents and teachers love us a lot,

With God's blessing, they'll give us all they've got!

Playing and working and praying together,

We'll be true to God in any type of weather.

With friends by our side and God in our hearts,

We're sure to be off to a real good start!

We've got a lot to do so don't be slow,

Put on your soccer feet and let's go, go, go!

Kick-Off Games ☺ ALL

Guaranteed to burn off excess energy of little ones.

Try these fun games with your soccer kick-off. Adapt them to other activities or units that might come along.

❑ *You will need:*
  Soccer balls
  Orange sport cones
  Music

❑ *To do:*

Soccer Relay Games

Have the children line up in two or three lines depending on how many you have in your class. Give the first person in each line a small sports cone with a soccer ball on the end. The object is to run with the ball in the cone to the end of the field or room, bring it back, and hand it off to the next person.

Other relay games include holding the ball and running, or dribbling the ball with the feet, or using a shorter distance and having the children roll the ball with their noses. Set out the soccer net and have the children kick the ball into the net and then pick it up and carry it to the next person in line.

Pass the Ball

Play pass the ball, a combination of musical chairs and hot potato. Have the children sit in a circle and when the music starts, they pass the ball around the circle. The person left holding the ball when the music stops sits in the center or circle. Begin the music again and pass the ball. The new person left holding the ball gets to be in the center and the first person rejoins the circle.

Kid Catchers – Classroom Rituals ☺ ALL

Children like to know what is happening and in what order. They like to be warned of transitions. And they are very curious creatures. With these ideas in mind here are a few ideas for catching the children's eyes and keeping their attention.

❑ *To do:*

Element of surprise – Bring something for the day's lesson gift-wrapped and reveal it as part of the lesson.

Flick the lights – Turn the lights on and off to call for their attention.

Tame them with tunes – Play a short tune on the piano, harmonica, horn, etc. to bring the children's focus to you.

Pass the squeeze – Before you start a quiet lesson or prayer, send a settling squeeze around a circle of sitting children. Use a squishy ball for the messenger.

Kid Gloves ☺ ALL

The expression "handle with kid gloves" came from a time when fine expensive gloves were made from goatskin. These gloves were fine and required special care. Children are precious and require this same kind of respect and special care.

❑ *You will need:*
Inexpensive gloves (a pair for each child)
Markers or fabric paints

❑ *To do:*
Direct children to use the markers to decorate the palms of the gloves. Be sure they print their name or initials on one palm. Once the gloves have dried place them in a pile in the center of the floor. Gather the children around the pile to play a matching game. Pull one glove from the heap and encourage a child to find the match, naming the owner of the gloves.
When all the children have been reunited with their pair, talk about how important it is to take care of something special. This is true for each of us. God made each one of us and we should all be treated with care and respect. Join gloved hands to say this prayer of thanks:

> God, you made each of us so special
> Because you love us.
> We will treat each other special
> Because we love you.
> Making others to feel happy
> Is how we say thank you.
> Laughing, playing, singing, praying,
> Showing our thanks in all we do.

Kidney Bean Scene ☺ ALL

Make mosaic type pictures with the children using a variety of dry beans.

❑ *You will need:*
Square pieces of heavy cardboard
A variety of dry beans such as kidney,
     pinto, lima, black-eyed peas, etc.
Clear drying glue
Markers

❑ *To do:*
Have the children draw a simple picture on the cardboard. Invite them to use a variety of beans to fill in the spaces of the pictures they have created. Let them know that they need to be a bit generous with the glue, which will dry clear. After drying the pictures, spray them with clear shellac.

K

Kid's Picnic 😺 PRE

Build community with this idea for a kid's picnic your children will love.

❑ *You will need:*
Egg cartons
Bowls of finger foods
Colored wooden toothpicks

❑ *To do:*
Put finger foods such as carrots, cheese cubes, fruit, crackers, lunch meats, hard boiled eggs, celery and peanut butter, etc. in bowls with a spoon or fork. Invite the children to fill their picnic carton with these foods. Give them each a toothpick, and you are ready for a great picnic indoors or out.

Kind King, May I 😊 ALL

Children always enjoy this old game with a new twist.

❑ *You will need:*
Bathrobe
Paper crown
Fake jewels or scepter

❑ *To do:*
Have one of the children dress up like a king or queen. Send the king or queen to one end of the room to sit up on his or her throne. Have the other children line up along the wall at the other end. Allow the children to ask the queen or king for permission to move closer by moving to another area of the room. The queen/king may answer telling them how many and what kinds of steps he or she may take to try to get there. An example would be, "Kind king, may I move to my desk?" "Yes, but take three baby steps, two large and four hops." The first person to actually reach the throne becomes the new queen or king.

King, Martin Luther ☺ ALL

A day to celebrate hope and love.
Remember the good works of Martin Luther King with this bulletin board activity.

❑ *You will need:*
Bulletin board or large piece of construction poster board
Assorted colors of construction paper including white
Markers
Scissors
Stapler

❑ *To do:*
Make a rainbow on a large bulletin board or poster board.
Using the dove (a symbol of peace) pattern provided, trace
and cut out white doves. As a group discuss with the
children what it means to love one another and the hopes
and dreams they have for all people. With adult help write
these on the doves. Staple the doves to the rainbow.

❑ *More to do:*
Using the pattern provided, make a badge or medallion for the
children to wear to witness to others the message of Jesus and
Dr. King. Color the picture, cut it out, and glue it to heavy
cardboard. Punch a hole on the top for lacing a ribbon
through for hanging.

Kings and Epiphany ✋ PRI

Remind children that the celebration of Christmas doesn't end
with Christmas but continues with this
Epiphany banner.

❑ *You will need:*
Black or blue felt square for each child
Pieces of red, green, and purple felt
Pieces of three different skin colors of felt
(examples are, light pink, light brown, dark brown)
Scissors
Glue
Sequins
Ribbon or cording
Fine-point dark colored marker
A variety of yarn

❏ *To do:*

Make the bodies of the three kings by cutting triangles from red, green, and purple felt. Cut a head for each of the kings with the skin-colored felt. Arrange and glue the triangles on the black or blue piece of felt. Glue the heads in place and draw a face on each one using marker. (Younger children will need help with this.)

Older children may want to cut small pieces of yarn to make hair and beards for the wise men; markers can be used to do the same. Cut crowns from foil or leftover pieces of felt. Use the ribbon and sequins to decorate the king's crowns and robes. Fold the top of the banner over and tape or glue the edge to the back of the banner. Insert a thin wooden dowel and attach ribbon to both ends to hang.

Kings' Cake ☺ ALL

An Epiphany cake full of surprises.

To celebrate the visit of the three kings to the manger, people hide coins or other treasures in a cake. The person who finds the treasure is king for the day. Try these new ideas to make an Epiphany cake full of surprises.

❏ *You will need:*

    Layer cake or cupcakes
    Recipe cards
    Aluminum foil
    Ribbon
    Stapler

❏ *To do:*

Cut the recipe cards to a size of 1" x 3." On each card write a blessing such as "May the dear Lord always be in your heart," or "Be happy with Jesus in your heart," or "Jesus bless you." Punch a hole in the end of the cards and tie the end of a ribbon to the hole. Cover each card with aluminum foil or plastic wrap and tape to hold in place. Gently slide the card with the long end of the ribbon out into the center of the cake. Space the ribbons equally around the cake. After all of ribbons are in place, have the children pull them out one at a time to receive their blessings. Be sure to start with an explanation of the kings' cake tradition and the visit of the three kings.

❏ *More to do:*

Make paper crowns for each of the children to wear. Decorate them with Mylar, glitter, or leftover beads and buttons.

Kings' Crowns 🙂 ALL

These crowns are not only fun to make but also a terrific way to teach children that their family members are jewels!

❑ *You will need:*

2" x 20" pieces of construction paper
Glitter glue
Colored macaroni
    or fake jewels (found at craft stores)

❑ *To do:*

Remind the children that every member of his or her family is like a jewel in a crown. Each one is precious and unique. God loves each family as if it were royal. Have the children decorate their crowns with a jewel for each member of their families. Tell them to remember when they wear their crowns that every family is "royal" in God's eyes.

Kites From the Ceiling 🙂 ALL

Even though we are unable to see the Holy Spirit, we are moved by the Spirit toward God's love.

❑ *You will need:*

Manila file folder
Drinking straw
Markers
Construction paper
Tape
Scissors

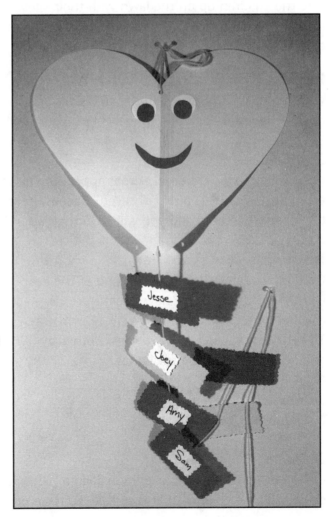

❑ *To do:*

Cut a large heart shape from a file folder. Draw eyes and a mouth on the outside of the heart. Punch a hole at the top of the heart. Tape a drinking straw to the back to act as a brace for the kite. Give each child a 3" x 5" piece of construction paper and ask that they print their name on it. Tape the name cards together in a row to make a kite tail. Tape the tail to the heart kite. Display the kite high from the ceiling.

Kites -"Lets Fly a Kite"  PRE
What would fresh warm spring air be without kites?

❑ *You will need:*
Plastic shopping bags (plain colored if possible)
Mylar strips
Stickers
String or ribbon
Tape
Permanent markers

❑ *To do:*
Collect plain-colored shopping bags from parents or a local store. With permanent markers write, "Celebrate the fresh air of spring." Have the children decorate the bag with stickers of birds, the sun, and flowers. Tape three to five Mylar strips to the outside bottom of the bag. Tie ribbon or string to each handle of the bag. Hold the ends of the strings together and it is ready to fly.

❑ *More to do:*
Line the children up on the lawn with their kites. Have them spread out, arms length apart, and run to a certain place with their kites. Split them up, boys and girls, or have them run backwards or sideways.

Knock, Knock...Who's With Me? ☺ ALL
What's a teacher to do when the children's energy level is peaking and the teacher's is not? Try this lighthearted approach to recovering your sanity and their attention.

❑ *To do:*
Keep a file of silly, clever jokes that appeal to young children handy for a moment just like this. For example, "Why is six afraid of seven? Because seven eight nine." The children will laugh even if the jokes are foolish, and you will have their attention back.

Knowing One Another ✋ PRI
Getting acquainted at the beginning of the year. Pair the children up and have them trace one another with chalk on the sidewalk or driveway. The children will get to know one another by adding facial features and clothes.

❑ *You will need:*
Sidewalk chalk

❑ *To do:*
Pair up the children and give them each a piece of chalk. Tell the children that they have to trace one

another lying down on the sidewalk. Let them know that they have to trace around arms, legs, heads, etc. After tracing one another, they can work on coloring in clothes, etc. Include names and have older children write something about their partner next to their drawing. Take time to look at everyone's work and how closely it resembles the real thing.

❑ *More to do:*
If sidewalk is unavailable, have the children trace one another on long sheets of paper and display them in your classroom.

Krazy Kritters ☺ ALL

Don't forget the smallest of God's creations when you work on your spring and creation units. Starting with eggcups from egg cartons, the children can use their own imaginations to create a variety of creepy crawly things.

❑ *You will need:*
    Paper egg cups from egg cartons
    Tempera paints
    Pipe cleaners
    Beads
    Buttons
    Movable eyes
    Glue

❑ *To do:*
Have the children paint the inside and outside of the eggcups. After they have dried, add pipe cleaner arms, legs, and antennae. Next, glue on the movable eyes and other facial features. Add beads and buttons for more decoration. Display these on a shelf or bulletin board labeled, "God Makes the Kraziest of Kritters."

Kris Kringle ☺ ALL

Secret Santa of good deeds.

Kris Kringle is a German custom in which people do good works for one another in secret. Try this with the children in your class and with your staff during the days of Advent. Simplify this project by only doing it over a week. Make a string of lights that go around the room to represent everyone's acts of kindness.

❑ **You will need:**
   Assortment of different
   colored construction paper
   Glue
   Scissors
   Ribbon
   Stapler

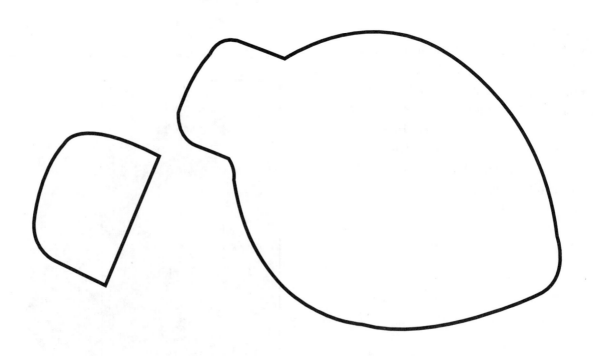

❑ **To do:**

Invite the children to be thoughtful and caring in quiet ways. Encourage them to try to do kind acts without being discovered. Each time an act of kindness is noticed, a colored bulb is hung from a string. Try not to reveal the person doing the act of kindness.

Enlarge and trace the Christmas light pattern provided. Cut and trace the lights. Hang a ribbon along a wall or a bulletin board at the child's eye level. As the children discover or witness acts of kindness they add lights to the ribbon.

Labor Day   👹 PRE

For a community to function happily, it takes the labor of many loving people. Celebrate the labors of your community workers with this activity.

❏ *You will need:*

Newspaper folded into paper hats (see below)
Markers
Paste
Magazines
Mural paper

❏ *To do:*

Give each child a newspaper hat. As you hand out the hats, ask the children to name workers who wear hats. Encourage the children to use the markers to decorate the hats representing workers in the community's workforce.

*To make hats out of newspaper, lay a sheet of newspaper with the fold at the top flat on a table. Fold both top corners to the center and crease the folds. Fold the bottom of the paper up to meet the top fold. Turn the newspaper over and fold the lower edge up to match the other side. Tape will hold the hat in place.

❏ *More to do:*

Help the children create a mural that shows the hats that represent the various occupations in your community. Cut pictures of hatted workers to glue or paste to the mural. Display this for visitors to see.

❏ *Even more to do:*

Near the Labor Day holiday, invite people from your community to join the children for a short prayer service and fellowship.

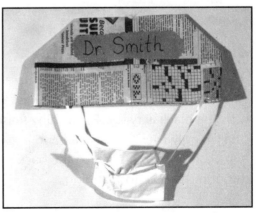

> God, thank you for the people in our community who protect and help us.
> Through their love and care we are learning to do your work, helping and protecting those around us. Amen.

Invite the children to name the jobs of people in the community that help them. Some children may need help of an adult to articulate the jobs of different people. Each time an occupation is stated, lead the children in saying "God bless (name the occupation)."

185

Ladder of Faith   ☺ ALL

Make a list on the rungs of a ladder of how we live out our love for God each and every day.

❑ *You will need:*
Cardboard cut into 1" x 8" strips
Craft sticks
Permanent marker
Stickers
Glue

❑ *To do:*
Have the children brainstorm ideas on how they can show their love for God on a daily basis. With adult help have them write one of these on a craft stick. For younger children use stickers or drawings to illustrate the words, such as a heart for love others, folded hands for cross or prayer, a flower for taking care of the earth, a smiley sticker for being kind, etc. After printing on at least six sticks, glue them to the cardboard strips to make a ladder. On the top stick print, "My Ladder of Faith." Allow glue to dry over night.

My Ladder of Faith

Lady Bug Pin   ☺ ALL

Also called the "beetle of Our Lady."
In the Middle Ages, the ladybug was dedicated to Mary and called the "beetle of our Lady." Its cute appearance and the help it gives farmers with controlling pests are probably related to the honor given its name. Try these fun ladybug ideas to welcome the warm months of summer.

❑ *You will need:*
Modeling clay that dries hard
Red and black acrylic paint
Shellac
Jewelry pin

❑ *To do:*
Have the children shape the clay into a plump, oval shape with flat bottom. Allow to dry until hard enough to paint. Paint with red acrylic and dry overnight. Next paint the spots and head with the black acrylic. For a shiny finish, spray with shellac after all of the paint has dried. Glue small wiggly eyes to the head and a jewelry pin to the back. To make a necklace instead of a pin, make a hole with a straw in the back end of the bug. After painting and shellacking, lace a ribbon through the hole for hanging.

❑ *More to do:*
Purchase round, red, fuzzy balls from a craft store and glue black felt pieces on them to make the spots, wings, and head. Put a magnet strip on the bottom and you have a fun refrigerator magnet.

Ladybug Count ☺ ALL

God has filled our world with many creatures, some of which people call "creepy crawly" things. Lead children to a greater appreciation and knowledge of the many bugs that share the world around us with this springtime activity.

❏ *You will need:*

    7" red paper plate
    7" white paper plate
    Black marker
    Brad fastener
    Construction paper
    Black pipe cleaner
    Hole punch
    Dot stickers
    Glue
    Tape

❏ *To do:*

On the serving side of the white plate (bug body), write the message; "God loves bugs!" Cut the red plate in half. Use the hole punch to punch a hole in the red halves and on the white plate as shown. Secure the red halves to the white plate using the brad fastener. Make a head for the ladybug by cutting a 2-inch semi-circle. Glue the head to the edge of the bug body. Tape pipe cleaner antenna to the head.

Every occasion the child finds a bug crawling about, encourage the child to place a dot sticker on the back of his or her ladybug. By the end of spring, the decorated ladybugs will be a bright reminder that God loves bugs.

Lamb Handprint ☺ PRE

A fun and easy project for the many Bible stories we listen to each year.

❏ *You will need:*

    White construction paper
    Cotton balls
    Glue
    Marker

❏ *To do:*

On white construction paper have the children trace their hands with fingers and thumbs wide open and cut them out. Turn the handprint so that the fingers are down. Draw a face on the thumb and glue cotton balls to rest of the hand. Use heavier paper if you'd like your lambs to stand up.

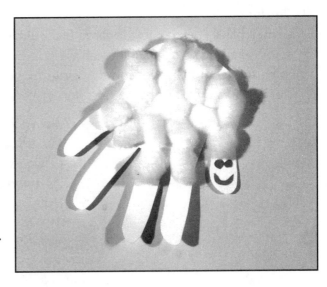

Lamb Craft ☺ ALL

After telling the story of the Good Shepherd, have the children make this lamb to hang on their wall.

❑ *You will need:*
   Flat rectangular Styrofoam tray
   Styrofoam packing peanuts
   Black construction paper
   Thin colored ribbon
   Jingle bells
   White glue
   Scissors

❑ *To do:*

Cut out a head, legs, and a tail from the black construction paper. Glue the head, legs, and tail a ribbon for hanging, on the back of the tray as shown. Use white construction paper and a black marker to make the eye. Add an ear cut from the black paper. Tie a bow around the lamb's neck with a jingle bell attached. Cover the tray with glue and stick Styrofoam packing peanuts all over to make the lamb's coat.

Lapel Ladybug ✋ PRI

These are lapel button covers that may be used at the end of a bug unit for a blessing.

❑ *You will need:*
   (Body) 2-inch wide circle of black felt
   (Wings) 2 inch wide circle of red felt
   (Head) 3/4 inch wide circle of black felt
   Tiny dots of black felt
   Glue

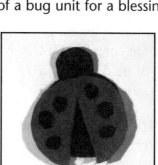

❑ *To do:*

Glue small black (head) circle to large black circle on the underside of the body. Cut a buttonhole slit across the body circle. Hold each wing in place at the base of the head with a drop of glue. Use glue to attach black dots on the wings. Once glue has dried completely, button ladybug to a shirt or sweater through the slit as a sign of new life.

Ladybug, ladybug
With a spotted wing.
God sent you
As a sign of spring.
Ladybug, ladybug
With a spotted wing
The sight of you
Makes me want to sing,
Thank you, God, for everything!

Leaf Rubbing ☺ALL

Another fabulous fall idea.

❏ *You will need:*

A collection of leaves found outside
Construction paper
Glue
Crayons
Markers

❏ *To do:*

Take a nature walk and have the children pick up three leaves each. When you return have the children place a leaf under a light colored piece of construction paper. With one hand holding the paper have the children color gently over the whole leaf. Within a few minutes the shape of the leaf will appear in the coloring. Have them place 2 or 3 leaves under the paper to get an interesting picture. Mount the pictures to a contrasting color of paper. Older children will enjoy making leaf people by adding arms, legs, and faces to the leaves with marker.

Leaf Rubbing Mural ☺ALL

After a fall walk to collect fallen autumn leaves, make a class mural to show how diverse God's world really is. Use this activity to show how diverse God has made each of us.

❏ *You will need:*

Chalk or crayons
Paper
Leaves
Scissors
Mural paper
Glue

❏ *To do:*

Provide children with crayons or chalk in a variety of colors. Demonstrate how to make a leaf rubbing by laying a leaf on a hard surface and covering it with the sheet of paper. Rub the paper with a crayon or chalk making an imprint of the leaf. Point out the variety of colors, textures, and shapes of the leaves.

While the children are working on their rubbings, make a mural that reads "God has filled our world with so many…" Draw the outline of a large tree below the text. Instruct the children to cut out their leaf rubbings and invite them to glue the leaves to the tree mural.

As the mural comes together point out that just how no two leaf rubbings are exactly alike, no two people are exactly alike either.

Leaf Wreath   ☺ ALL

Make a wreath of colored leaf cutouts and nature finds.

❑ *You will need:*

A variety of colors of construction paper
Glue
Scissors
Raffia
Small pine cones and acorns
8" or 9" paper plates

❑ *To do:*

Cut out the center of the paper plates. Enlarge and
trace the leaf patterns provided here on the
construction paper. Cut out the leaves and glue
them to the edges of the paper plate. Overlap the
leaves so that the white of the plate does not show.
Add a few pinecones or acorns to the top of the leaves and a raffia bow. For best results dry over
night and then add a piece of raffia for hanging the wreath of leaves.

Leftover Soup Gorp 😊 ALL

A dry soup that is always fun!
Clean out your snack cupboards with this snack that is always a big hit.

❑ *You will need:*

   Paper cups
   Leftover cereals, raisins, mini-crackers,
   pretzels, marshmallows

❑ *To do:*

Mix up all leftovers in a large bowl. Have the children take turns stirring.
To serve, put the soup in paper cups and enjoy.

Lending Library 😊 ALL

Children's books, puzzles, and videos are great tools to reinforce faith-sharing themes. Not every program can afford to buy every title so here is an idea for sharing books.

❑ *To do:*

Early in the year, invite program participants (parents, volunteers, teachers, etc.) to make a list of materials they would be willing to share with the program volunteers and leadership. Organize the lists by theme, title, author, and names of material owners. Ask that request for these materials be made a week in advance to allow time to collect them.

Lenten Cross With a Simple Message 😊 ALL

Remind children to think about Jesus and pray often throughout Lent.

❑ *To do:*

Help the children cut out a cross from 8" x 11" rough sand paper. Punch a hole in the top and run a piece of twine through it. Invite the children to attach the cross to their backpacks or desk. Ask them to say a prayer every time they notice it. Give them some ideas for prayer, such as asking God to help them think more about God or to fill them with enthusiasm for their faith or to help them reach out in kindness to others.

❑ *More to do:*

The last week of Lent invite the children to add spices to their crosses. Help them sprinkle spices over glue such as ginger, nutmeg, or allspice. Explain that the women who went to the tomb where Jesus' body was took sweet-smelling spices to put on Jesus' body.
Easter week, invite the children to decorate their crosses with glitter and construction paper flowers that they have made.

Lenten Candle   😊 ALL

A take-home project for the six weeks of Lent.

Make a kit containing seven symbols and a candle for families to use to observe Lent at home.
We have included symbol ideas as well as a prayer for each week. We suggest you begin
accumulating items early and take a couple of sittings to complete the symbols.

❑ *You will need:*
   Construction paper
   Markers
   Paper punch
   Cotton balls
   Glitter
   Stickers
   Small tree branches
   Large pretzels (traditional shape; not stick pretzels
   Silk flowers
   Gallon size zip plastic bags
   Ribbon
   White candles about 8" - 10" high and 2" - 3" wide
   (We use votive candle inserts that come in a plastic liner.
   Check with your local church supply store, they run about $1 each.)

❑ *To do:*
Enlarge and copy the four symbols on page 194. Have the children color them and cut them out.
Punch a hole in the top of each and lace a ribbon through them for tying to the candle. Enhance
the symbols by gluing cotton balls to the lamb, glitter to the butterfly, and stickers to the heart.
Gather a silk flower, pretzel, and branch for each child. Place these along with the paper symbols
and a copy of the prayers in a plastic bag for home.

❑ *Week 1*
Heart. A simple symbol of love that reminds us that God loves us so much that he sent us
his son, Jesus.

Prayer 1
   Dear God, thank you for loving us so much that you sent us your son, Jesus.
   Be with us during Lent and help us grow closer to you. Amen.

❑ *Week 2*
Pretzel. Early Christians baked pretzel breads during Lent as a symbol of prayer.

Prayer 2
   Dear God, thank you for being with us when we pray. Help us to remember to pray
   every day. We ask you to bless our parents and brothers and sisters. Amen.

❏ *Week 3*

Lamb. A soft warm lamb reminds us of the gentleness and patience of Jesus.

Prayer 3

Dear God, thank you for the people in our lives that care for us. With their patience and gentleness we will grow up to be safe and happy. Help us to always be kind and gentle with others. Amen.

❏ *Week 4*

Cross. The cross reminds us of the sacrifice Jesus made for us. What a great gift of love!

Prayer 4

Dear God, thank you for being with us and in our hearts when we are alone or scared. Today we pray that you are in the hearts of those who are sick or afraid. Amen.

❏ *Week 5*

Flower. A beautiful, living flower is always a sign of new growth, new life, and new beginnings. A sure sign of spring!

Prayer 5

Dear God, thank you for all of the beautiful flowers and trees you have put on this earth. Help us to remember to take good care of the plants, animals, and water of our earth. Amen.

❏ *Week 6*

Tree branch. As Jesus rode to Jerusalem on Palm Sunday, people proclaimed him their long-awaited Messiah or King. They honored him by throwing their coats and branches along the road for him to walk on.

Prayer 6

Dear God, thank you for sending Jesus to show us how to be truly happy. We ask that you help us to do what is right and good each day as we learn and play. Amen.

❏ *Week 7 Easter*

Butterfly. The butterfly has long been an Easter symbol of new life. Just as the beautiful butterfly emerges from a dark cocoon, we renew our hearts and become filled with the newness of life. Jesus fills our hearts with joy!

Prayer for Easter Week

Dear God, we thank you for being with us as we celebrate the risen Jesus. Our hearts are full of joy and hope. Be with us today and always. Amen.

Licorice Necklace   🐼 PRE

Edible and fun.
A great party snack the children make themselves.

❏ *You will need:*
  Licorice whips
  Cereals such as Cheerios®,
  Fruit Loops®, or Honey Combs®

❏ *To do:*
The children string the cereal onto the licorice.
Leave about 4" on each end to tie off the necklace.

Life Seeking   🙂 ALL

Sometimes we can forget the special gift of life, especially during what seems to be the life-less months of winter. January, February, and March are the months that outdoor life can be pretty hidden and go unnoticed. This is the very time to take a "Life Seeking" walk.

❏ *You will need:*
  Lifesaver candies

❏ *To do:*
As you take a winter walk, talk about how life exists outdoors, even when we cannot see it. Animals are keeping warm underground. Trees are resting and waiting to grow new leaves in spring. Outside surrounded by the wonder of winter life, gather in a circle for this short prayer.

God, be with us as we look for signs of your life giving presence. In the trees, in the animals, and in each of us, you are living, life-giving, and life-saving. Thank you, God.

As the children leave you for the day give them a lifesaver candy as you bless them saying, *Thank you, God, for (name of child) and bless her life this day.*

Lift our Hearts   🐼 PRE

God's presence in our lives lifts our hearts.

❏ *You will need:*
  Helium-filled balloon attached to a string or ribbon
  Construction paper heart
  Permanent marker

❏ *To do:*
Write the word "GOD" on the balloon using the marker as you tell the children God is like the air in the balloon. We cannot see or feel God, but we know God is there. Ask each of the children to print his/her name on the heart. Tie the heart to the string and watch how the balloon lifts the heart. Keep the balloon floating around the room as a reminder of God's lifting presence in our lives.

Light the World 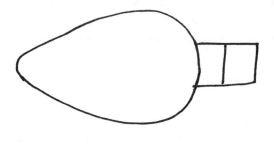 PRI

God sent his Son to be the light for the world.
Children can also act as lights in a dark world.

❑ *You will need:*
   Globe
   Color construction paper
   Tape
   Scissors

❑ *To do:*

Cut Christmas light bulb shapes from the colored construction
paper. Place in a basket near the globe. Encourage the children
during Advent to look for kind actions taking place around them.
Each time a kind act is noticed, ask a child to print the name of
the person performing the kind act onto a construction paper
light bulb. Tape the bulb to the globe and talk about how we
can light up the world with kind acts.

Lighthouse ALL

Jesus lights our way.
Make a lighthouse and discuss how Jesus lights the way for us in life. Fill the lighthouse with ways
the family can grow closer in faith.

❑ *You will need:*
   Pringles® can
   Tape
   Markers
   Enlarged and printed lighthouse copy
   Yellow paper

❑ *To do:*

Have the children cut out the lighthouse and color it. Next
tape it around the Pringles can. On yellow paper strips, print
out the following suggestions for families. Inviting them to
take one idea a week from the lighthouse and work on it
together.
Read a Bible story together right after supper or at bedtime.
Take a walk and talk about the wonder of God's creation.
Begin recycling something you have not yet started to recycle.
Clean out your closets and drawers and take a trip to the
Goodwill.
Bake cookies together and give some of them away.

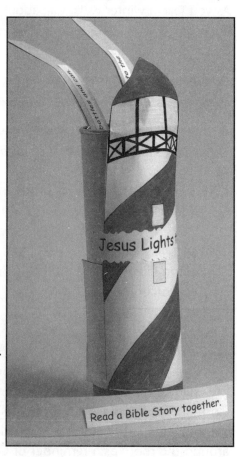

❑ **More to do:**

Wrap and tape a smaller copy of the lighthouse to a flashlight.

Sing, "this Little Light of Mine," or the following song to the tune of, "I'm a Little Teapot."

I'm a little lighthouse tall and bright,
Standing through the darkness always spreading light.
When the ships float by me they will see,
That my light is always shining faithfully.
Jesus is my brother always near,
When He's standing by me I have nothing to fear.
Keeping me safe both day and night,
His love is forever shining bright.

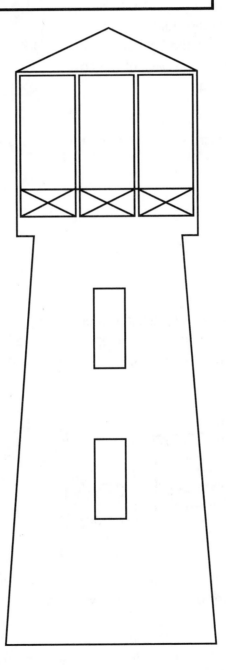

Light Switch Cover   ☺ ALL

A gift to light the way. Decorating a light switch cover is a great gift for the children to make all by themselves and give away.

❑ *You will need:*
Plastic light switch covers (May be purchased at hardware or discount stores.)
Fine-point permanent markers

❑ *To do:*
Talk with the children about whom the gift is for. If it is for Mother's Day, ask the children to think about Mom's favorite things to do or the things she likes to do for her family. On a sheet of paper have the children do a practice drawing before drawing on the light switch.
Write the child's name and date on the back of the cover.
Allow them to dry before wrapping.

Line-Up of Good Work   ☺ ALL

Hang a clothesline up in your classroom to "line up" the hard work of your students.

❑ *You will need:*
Clothesline
Clothespins
Poster board
Markers

❑ *To do:*
Hang the clothesline along a wall in your classroom or along the ceiling out of reach of the children or head bumping of the adults. On one end of the line hang a poster that reads, "Our Line Up of Good Work." With the clothespins, hang up the drawings and projects of the children.

❑ *More to do:*
During Lent or Advent use the clothesline to hang numbers to count down to the holiday. Write good deeds your class is doing for others or hang collection items such as socks or mittens from the clothesline.

Linking to God in Prayer   PRI

Uniting with God in prayer is not something we can see with our eyes. Nor is it limited to a particular form. Make connecting to God in prayer concrete with these linking ideas. Leading the children in prayer frequently, creatively, and in a variety of ways will help enrich their prayer lives as well as yours.

❑ *You will need:*

Anything that can be linked together:
Phone receivers (see pattern)
Paper clips
Safety pins
Band-Aids®
Gum wrappers
Fallen leaves.
The ideas are endless.

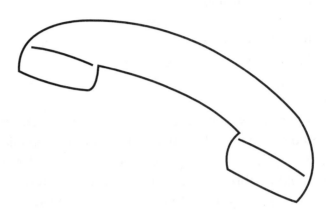

❑ *To do:*

Lead the children in prayer activities using tokens as starting off points. Give each child a token and after the prayer experience link the tokens together. The chain of prayer tokens will serve as a reminder of the power of prayer.

Telephone – Just chatting with God. Take time to check in and express to God how things are going in life.

Paper clips – Attaching to the life Jesus taught us. Take time to reflect on how we can be more connected to a life with Jesus.

Safety pins – Keeping loved ones safe. Invite each child to pray for the safe keeping of a loved one. Remind the children that sometimes this means joining God in heaven.

Band-Aids – Mending a hurt. Ask for God's forgiveness for a time that we have caused others hurt.

Gum wrappers – Celebrating the blessings in our lives. Reflect on the many blessings in our lives.

Fallen leaves – Giving thanks for natural surroundings.

L

Listening to God   🐰 PRE

Listening to God takes practice, as does developing listening skills. Here is a game that encourages listening.

❏ *You will need:*
   Key chain of keys
   Bell
   Baby rattle
   Box of pasta

❏ *To do:*

Place the items before the child. Show how each item makes a unique sound when lifted. Blindfold a child and ask him or her to listen carefully as you remove an object from the grouping. Ask the child to identify the objected that was moved. If needed allow the child to remove the blindfold to obtain a visual prompt as to which object was removed.

Use this listening game to discuss how we need to use more than just our hearing to learn God's message.

Liturgical Calendar   ✋ PRI

Teaching children about the church year can be confusing. Use this simple idea to make the seasons easy to see and understand.

❏ *You will need:*
   Markers
   Enlarge copies of the blank
      pattern provided
   Magazines
   Old Christmas and Easter cards
   Scissors
   Glue

❏ *To do:*

Give each child a copy of the liturgical calendar pattern. Discuss each season and some of the symbols that represent that season as shown on the sample. Have the children cut out pictures of symbols to glue on or draw liturgical signs on the calendar.

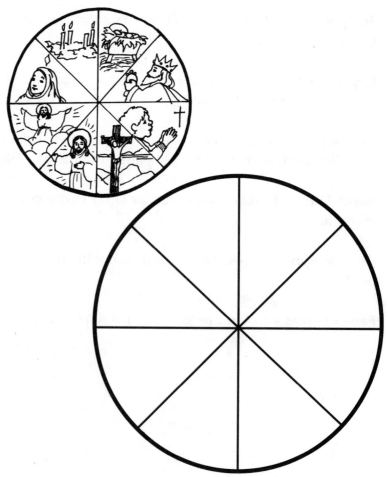

Loaves and Fishes   ☺ ALL

In the Bible story of the loaves and fishes, Jesus shows us how to share and care for others. The little boy provides a small amount of food that Jesus uses to feed thousands. Do you think it was hard for the boy to share his food? How do you think he felt after he shared with all those people?

❑ *To do:*

Invite children to bring in their favorite foods for a food drive. Keep in mind that food pantries and shelves run low in the months following the Christmas holidays and the summer months when children are out of school. As the food begins coming in discuss who will benefit from the food drive and why is it important to share with others. Before delivering the collected foods gather the children around the food for a blessing. With hands held out over the food offer this prayer,

> *Dear God,*
> *Be with the people who will receive this food. May they always know the touch of your love.*
> *And may their hearts be filled with the warmth of your love. Amen.*

Allow the children the opportunity to help bag up the food for transporting.

Lollipop Puppets   ☺ ALL

A sweet way to tell the story. Add a face to a lollipop and bring a story to life.

❑ *You will need:*
    Lollipops
    Construction paper
    Wiggly eyes
    Tape
    Glue

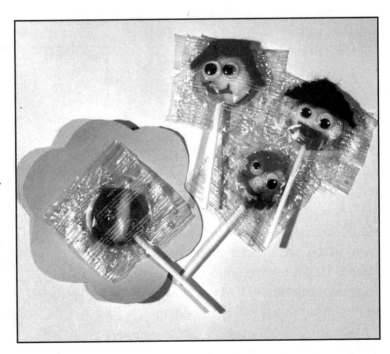

❑ *To do:*

Glue eyes and other facial features to the lollipop. Tape hair or hats on also. To make a flower puppet, tape the lollipop to a flower cutout and add a leaf to the stick.

Look and You Will See  PRI

Sometimes it is not enough just to look at the surface for something. Sometimes we must work at finding the message.

❑ *You will need:*
White paper
White crayon
Paint brush
Watercolor paints

❑ *To do:*
Prepare the white paper for the children ahead of time. Use the white crayon to write the message "Look and you will see" on the paper.
Distribute the paper to the children and talk about how we must often look deeper than the surface to get the entire message. Ask the children to read the message written on their papers. Instruct them to use the watercolor paints to paint over the paper revealing the message. At times we may not understand what God is trying to tell us until we work at it.

Look Out Glasses 😊 PRE

Keeping an eye out for God! Make a pair of, "Look Out Glasses" to look out for God in the world around us.

❑ *You will need:*
2 eggcups cut out together from an egg carton
Thin elastic
Hole puncher
Scissors
Small stickers

❑ *To do:*
Have an adult cut out 2 eggcups together from an egg carton as well as the bottom of each cup. Punch a hole at each end of the cups. Tie a piece of thin elastic to each hole adjusting it to fit comfortably around the child's head. Have the children decorate their glasses with small stickers. Take a walk around the inside or outside of the building looking for God. Hint: God can be found in the air, the flowers, a friendly smile, a handshake, a pretty picture, etc.

Lost Coin   ☺ ALL

Have you ever lost something that was very dear to you? What did you do to find it? In the parable of the "Lost Coin" found in Luke 15, Jesus relays an important message. Each and every one of us are very important to God. God will not give up on us.

❏ ***You will need:***
   Small tokens to hide
   Coin
   Crayon
   Any of snack options listed below

❏ ***To do:***

Activity

Hide "Lost Coins" for the children to search for and find. In a dry open outside area, hide coins, wrapped candy, wooden nickels, coat buttons or other small trinkets in grass clippings, straw, sand, or Styrofoam packing peanuts. Encourage the children to look for the hidden prizes in the pile.

Craft

Make a copy of the coloring picture below for each child.
Give each child a coin. Place the coin on a hard surface and lay the coloring picture face up over the coin. Rub a crayon over the paper to make the coin visible.

Snack

Serve a snack of "coins." Possible circle coin-like treats might be round mini crackers, steamed or raw carrot circles, sliced bananas, chocolate coins, candied gummy coins, etc.

Lost Glove Puppets ☺ ALL

A great way to rid the lost and found of those lonely lost gloves. Make some fun puppets to tell the great stories of our faith by using gloves from the lost and found.

❑ *You will need:*
   Gloves from the lost and found
   Wiggly eyes
   Felt scraps
   Pompoms
   Ribbon
   Tacky fabric glue

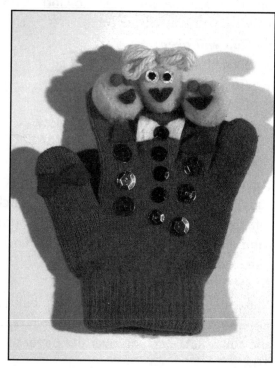

❑ *To do:*
Use the wiggly eyes and felt scraps to make the faces on the top of the fingers of the glove. Experiment with the fingers of the glove and their positions to make a head or arms, etc. Glue them together or at an angle or cut some of them off. Glue pompoms on for hair and tie ribbons around the fingers to make belts or ties. Have the children take turns retelling the stories you share with one another.

❑ *More to do:*
Make the characters for one whole story on one glove. For example, make the three pigs, the mother pig and the wolf, one per finger.

Lost Sheep ☺ PRE

Encourage the children to use their imaginations to play this game of lost and found. Remind the children that God never wants any of us to be lost. God will always find us.

❑ *You will need:*
   Poster board
   Lamb
   Shepherd stickers (or cotton balls and marker)
   Masking tape

❑ *To do:*
Form a crown for each child by cutting a 2" wide band of poster board long enough to fit around his or her head. Place a sticker of a shepherd (or draw a staff to represent a shepherd) on the front of one of the crowns. Place a lamb sticker (or cotton ball to represent a lamb) on the front of all the remaining crowns. Secure crowns with a piece of masking tape.
Distribute the crowns. The child who receives the shepherd crown is asked to count the sheep in

the "Flock" and then turns around so the other children may hide out of sight. The group hides in an obvious place. One child in the group is invited to hide in a different hiding place away from the rest of the group. The shepherd is then asked to return to find the "flock," counting to be sure everyone is in the group. If the shepherd notices one missing, a search begins until all the sheep are gathered back together again.

Ask the children to imagine what it would be like to be lost or to be looking for someone who is lost.

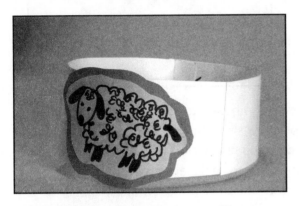

Lotto Game Cards   ☺ ALL

Creating experiences for children to explore stories about Scripture and God's love happen in a variety of ways. One way for children to further experience these stories is to play this lotto game.

❑ **You will need:**

Matching pairs of colorful, interesting greeting card pictures
Scissors
Clear contact paper
Marker

❑ **To do:**

These are the instructions for preparing one game card set. Cover the matching pair of greeting card pictures with clear contact. One card is to be used as the lotto card.

Use the marker to draw a 9-16" square grid, depending on the skills of the children, on one of the clear contact covered cards. Cut this card apart along the marked lines to make the lotto cover cards.

❑ **To play the lotto game:**

A game card set is needed for each child. The children take turns selecting a cover card from a face-down pile, seeking a cover card that matches his or her game card. As the pieces are found they are placed on their game card. The first person to completely cover their game card with the matching cover cards wins.

Love Bugs 🖐 PRI

Share these love bugs that carry a note of love.

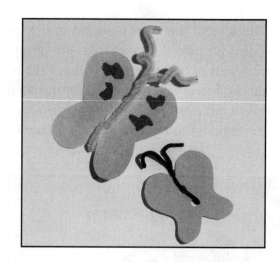

❑ *You will need:*
Construction paper
Markers
Paints
Brightly colored pipe cleaners
Embroidery thread
Paper hole reinforcers

❑ *To do:*
Cut paper hearts from the construction paper. Decorate the hearts to look like wings. Punch a hole at the top and bottom of the wings, making a place to slide the pipecleaner body through, as shown in the picture. To make the bug's body, fold a pipe cleaner in half and twist the ends together. Slip embroidery floss through the fold of the body to make antennae.
Print little messages of love on the back of the wings and share it with loved ones.

Love Is In the Air ☺ ALL

Add some balloon excitement to your class. Try this great discussion starter during your gather times.

❑ *You will need:*
Large balloon

❑ *To do:*
Bring an un-inflated balloon to your circle. Ask children to think of ways their family members make them feel loved. You may need to give them suggestions like, "My sister reads to me before bed," or "Mom makes my favorite cookies." Each time the children identify a way that love is shown, blow a breath of air in the balloon. Do not tie the balloon; just hold the air in the balloon by pinching the opening together. When the balloon is filled up with air, let go of the opening and allow the balloon to fly around the room. Explain that the air in the balloon is like the love in the world, it is everywhere.   Adapt this idea to other topics you are working on.

Lucia – The Saint of Light   ☺ ALL

During Advent spend some time learning about Saint Lucia who is the patron of the "light of the body," the eyes. Christian people pray to her when they have problems with their eyes and are in danger of going blind. Because of her name many ancient customs with light and fire became associated with her day, December 13. In Scandinavian countries it is still customary for the oldest daughter in the family to dress in white with a wreath of leaves and candles on her head on St. Lucia Day. She then awakens the household to coffee and cakes. Saint Lucia reminds us that her own light is only a reflection of the great "Light of the World – Jesus."

Make a candle wreath for the children to wear on their heads as a reminder of the coming of Jesus, the "Light of the World."

❑ *You will need:*

Green, white, red, and yellow construction paper
Glue
Stapler

❑ *To do:*

Enlarge, trace, and cut out 4 of the candle patterns shown here. Make the candles white and the flames yellow. To make the headband crown, cut strips of green paper 2" x 12". Staple 2 pieces together and have the children glue 4 candles to the green strip. Glue green holly cutouts and red berries to the green headband. After the glue has dried, adjust and staple the wreath to fit the child's head. At snack have the children take turns wearing their wreaths and serving the food.

Luminaries   PRI

God led shepherds and the Magi to Jesus with the light of the night stars. Light a starry path for your Advent program visitors with these children-made luminaries.

❏ *You will need:*
   Paper lunch bags
   Scissors
   Tea candles
   Sand

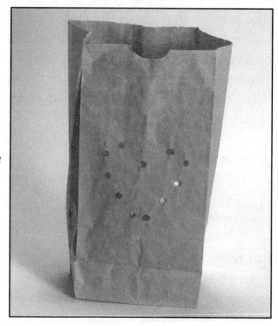

❏ *To do:*
With the bag folded flat as it is when purchased, ask the children to make small cuts into the bags. Then show the children how to fold back the cuts as shown in the diagram.
The evening of the program, place the bags around the entryway. Pour a small scoop of sand in the bottom of each bag to help weight the bags. Place lit tea candles inside the bag on the sand piles. See how the path becomes brightly lit.

Lunch Bucket Picnic   ALL

Welcome the children to your group with a picnic lunch packed in a bucket.

❏ *You will need:*
   Ice-cream bucket with lid
   Invitation

❏ *To do:*
Make up little invitations inviting the children to have a special lunch at school. Tell them to pack their lunch in the bucket and bring it to school. Send the invitations home inside an ice-cream bucket with lid. On picnic day sit inside or out on blankets and simply enjoy one another's company.

Mail Box   ☺ ALL

A fun way to spread the news in the classroom.

Use a regular postal mailbox in your classroom to receive notes from parents or staff. Use it as a suggestion box or as a way of introducing a new topic or toy.

❑ **You will need:**

Mailbox
Acrylic paint
Misc. items to decorate the mailbox

❑ **To do:**

Decorate the mailbox in any way you wish. Paint with bright colors and add the symbols of our faith such as a heart star or cross. If you use a rural mailbox with a red flag, tape a cardboard cross to it or a sign that reads, "Mail for Mrs. Green's Class" or "New Notes." Encourage parents and children to put notes, etc. for you in the mailbox. Use the mailbox to introduce a new topic or unit. For example, if you are going to be working on spring or new life, put an egg or flower in the mailbox. Give the children a few clues about what is in the box and then ask them to guess.

Manger for Baby Jesus   ☺ ALL

The children will love filling their mangers full of hay in preparation for the Baby Jesus.

❑ **You will need:**

Brown construction paper
Light-blue construction paper
Yellow yarn
Stickers or cutouts of Baby Jesus
Scissors
Glue

❑ **To do:**

Have the children cut out a manger and glue it to a piece of blue construction paper. Leave the top of the manger open, forming a pocket. Cut out small tufts of hay from yarn. Give each child enough pieces of yarn for each day of Advent. Tell the children Advent is the time of year we prepare for Jesus' coming. They can do this by helping out at home, being kind to one another, and praying for others. Every day of Advent, they should do something in preparation and then place a piece of yarn in the crib pocket. Close to Christmas, send

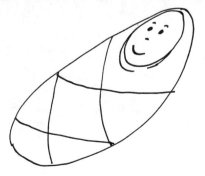

home a sticker or cutout of the Baby Jesus to place in the manger they have prepared for him.

Manger Mobile   ☺ ALL

Use this manager mobile to retell the Christmas story.

❑ *You will need:*
    Poster board
    Patterns (Mary, Joseph, Baby Jesus, Shepherd, sheep, star, 3 Kings)
    Stiff paper
    Scissors
    Markers or crayons
    Hole puncher
    Stapler
    Yarn or string

❑ *To do*:

Copy patterns onto stiff paper. Cut out and decorate with markers or crayons. Punch hole at top of each picture.

Cut a strip of tag board. Staple ends together to form the ring. Use string or yarn to hang decorated pictures from a tag board ring.

210

Mapping the Way ☺ ALL

While on earth, Jesus mapped out a way for us to find God in our lives. With Jesus in our lives, we never need to be lost.

❏ *You will need:*
   A map cut into small 1 1/2" pieces

❏ *To do:*
As children leave you, carefully give each a piece of a map to slip into his or her shoe as a reminder to follow Jesus to God.

Marble Painting ☺ ALL

Interest your children in the art of painting with this unique painting activity.

❏ *You will need:*
   Construction paper
   Box lids (big enough to lay the paper in)
   Marbles
   Tempera paint
   Pie tins

❏ *To do:*
Lay the paper in the box cover. Pour a small amount of paint in the pie tin and carefully roll the marble in the paint until it is covered. Place the marble in the box and gently tip the box so that the marble moves around and makes a neat design.

May Day Baskets ✋ PRI

May is the month of Mary. Many parishes adorn Mary's altar with baskets of spring flowers. Surprise neighbors and relatives with these little baskets.

❏ *You will need:*
   Half eggshells
   Silk flowers
   Ribbon
   Glue
   Prewritten May Day notes.

❏ *To do:*
Make an eggshell basket by gluing ribbon to the bottom of the eggshell as shown. Place a small ball of playdough or clay in the bottom of the shell basket. Poke the stems of the silk flowers into the playdough. Attach a note to the ribbon, "Many blessings to you as we begin Mary's month of May." Tie the ends of the ribbon together and hang from a neighbor's or relative's doorknob.

May Day Give Away ☺ ALL

Use a juice can to make a simple May Day basket for the children to give away.

❑ *You will need:*
Juice cans
Construction paper
Glue
Pipe cleaners

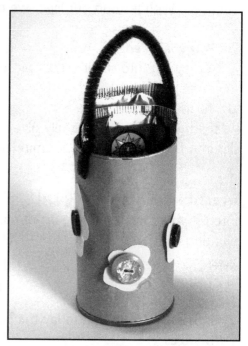

❑ *To do:*
Cover the juice can with construction paper. Punch a hole in each side of the can to tie a handle. Use ribbon, pipe cleaners, or florists' wire for the handle. Have the children trace and cut the flower patterns provided and glue them to the sides of the can. Glue buttons to the center of the flowers. Fill the baskets with candy, a package of flower seeds, tea bag, or May Day Blessing. Encourage the children to give the basket to a neighbor or friend. Remember to leave the basket, ring the doorbell, and run.

May Day Blessing ☺ ALL

Attach this wonderful blessing to May Day crafts.

❑ *To do:*
God's blessing to you,
With warm wishes from me
To brighten your way,
On this first day in May.

❑ *More to do:*
To make a bigger basket, staple two paper cups together. Punch one hole in the outside edge of each cup for the handle. Decorate with stickers and glitter paint.

May Pole   😊 ALL
Dance of spring.
Plan a little song and dance time to celebrate the warmth of spring.

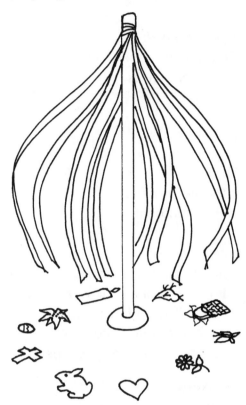

❑ *You will need:*
    Crepe paper
    Balloons
    Pole
    Tape

❑ *To do:*
If possible, use a pole on your playground for the May Day pole. Poles of a basketball hoop, light, or playground equipment would work well. Be sure there is enough room to dance around the pole safely. When you have found a pole, decorate it with the children using crepe paper and balloons. Hang one long piece of crepe paper for each child (to hang on to for the dance) from higher up on the pole. Have the children hang onto their piece of crepe as they sing favorite songs and skip, walk, or hop around the maypole.

Me Bag   😊 ALL
Use this activity to discuss the individuality of each child and celebrate his or her uniqueness.

❑ *You will need:*
    Paper bags
    Markers or crayons
    Items from each child's home

❑ *To do:*
Invite each child to bring 3-5 of their favorite items from home, (examples: food, toy, book, clothing, picture, etc). Place the child's items into a paper bag decorated by the child. For a get acquainted activity, as a group look at the items and try to guess whom the bag belongs to.

Me Book ☺ ALL

Begin a "Me Book" for each child at the beginning of the year. Periodically add pages to the book that show the growth of the child and some of the activities and projects you have worked on throughout the year.

❑ *You will need:*
Construction paper
Metal paper rings
Markers
Paint
Glue

❑ *To do:*
Ideas for the year are...
Handprint, footprint
Age
Favorite foods
Self portrait and name writing in the fall and in the spring
Class photo and/or a page with everyone's signature
Magazine collage of favorite things
Favorite prayer or Bible story
Photo or drawing of family and pets

Me Wheel ☺ ALL

Sharing things about ourselves with others.
When starting out the year with a new group of children, try making a "Me Wheel" to help you and the children in your group become more acquainted.

❑ *You will need:*
2 sturdy paper plates
Metal paper fastener
Construction paper
Magazine pictures that illustrate
various families, pets, foods, and colors
Glue

❑ *To do:*
Make a spinning wheel by dividing a paper plate into four sections. Glue magazine pictures to illustrate one of the following four categories: foods, families, pets, and colors in each section. Cut out a ¼ section of the second plate. Place this on top of the first plate and stick a paper fastener through the middle of both plates to make the wheel. Have the children take turns spinning the wheel and talk in turn about the categories.

❑ *More to do:*
Add your own categories or make two or three different wheels to help you learn more about one another.

Measuring God's Love   🙂 ALL

Teach children that God's love is so enormous that it cannot be measured!
Understanding the idea that God's love is immeasurable is difficult to understand and comprehend. Try the following ideas to get the children thinking about how much God does love us and how big that love is.

❏ *To do:*

Take a nature walk and ask the question, how much does God love us? Begin a chorus of answers as you point out the leaves in the trees or sand on the beach or grass on the ground. "God loves us more than all of the leaves in the trees in all the lands of the world." "God loves us more than all of the sand in the oceans, rivers, and lakes in the whole wide world." "God loves us more than all of the grass that grows in the ground of the whole wide world." Remind the children that God's love for us goes on and on and on. It never ends!

❏ *More to do:*

God's love for each of us cannot be measured. Understanding the idea of how immeasurable God's love is would be difficult to comprehend without first experiencing the concept of measurement. Here are a few activities that will encourage preschoolers to count, measure, and compare.

Calendar countdown

To do:

Life is full of events and activities we look forward to each month. Using a sticker or colored marker, highlight an upcoming event on the calendar for the child to see. Each day, help the children to count down the days to that particular event.

Counting Walk

❏ *You will need:*
    Lacing
    Beads or buttons

❏ *To do:*

Take the preschoolers on an outdoor walk. Before departing, tell the children they will be counting a particular object, such as cars or people. While on the walk, have the children thread a bead or button each time they count a car. When the children tire of this activity and are ready for a new challenge, divide the group into two teams. One team will count the objects on the left side and the other team will count the objects on the right side. Each team will keep track of the items counted on their side. When they return from their walk the groups may want to compare the beads or buttons they have strung.

Bubble counting

❑ *You will need:*
Bubble solution
Bubble wand

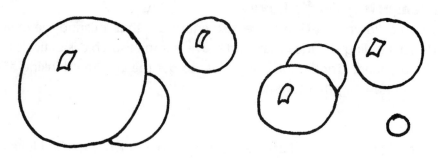

❑ *To do:*
While playing outside, the children will enjoy trying to count something that is rather difficult to hold – bubbles! Blow bubbles and have the children try counting them before they pop or disappear.

Counters and containers

❑ *You will need:*
Containers
Counters

❑ *To do:*
Encourage vocabulary to describe amounts using all kinds of containers and a variety of objects. Collect objects to use as counters, such as extra large buttons, juice can lids, crayons, etc. Place 1-5 objects in any combination into each container. Invite the children to choose a container. As a group, count the objects in the selected container. Next, ask the group to select a container that has more (or less) objects than their first selection. Count those items and compare them to their first container.

Growing ball of string

This experience works best if used as two separate activities.

❑ *You will need:*
String

❑ *To do:*
Measuring — Using string to measure, cut the length to match the height of the child. Ideally, each length of string will vary just a tiny bit. Mix all the pieces of string together in a pile. Take a string from the pile and wind it into a ball. Invite the children to add a piece of string from the pile to the ball. Watch the ball grow in size.

Comparing – Invite a child to unwind a piece of string from the ball. Ask the children, judging from the length of the string, to try to guess whose height will match. Then compare the length to the child they guessed it will fit. Keep comparing the length to whomever the children suggest until they find the correct match.

Bucket of Comparison

❏ *You will need:*

Container filled with various lengths of ribbon
String
Cording
Rope
Yarn

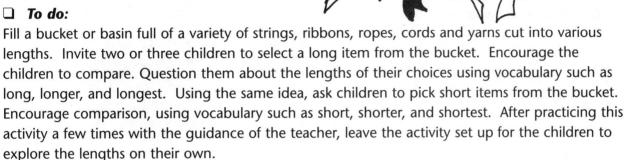

❏ *To do:*

Fill a bucket or basin full of a variety of strings, ribbons, ropes, cords and yarns cut into various lengths. Invite two or three children to select a long item from the bucket. Encourage the children to compare. Question them about the lengths of their choices using vocabulary such as long, longer, and longest. Using the same idea, ask children to pick short items from the bucket. Encourage comparison, using vocabulary such as short, shorter, and shortest. After practicing this activity a few times with the guidance of the teacher, leave the activity set up for the children to explore the lengths on their own.

As a child's experience with measurement grows, so will their ability to understand how God's love is immeasurable.

Medallions From Juice Can Lids ☺ ALL

Here is an idea for recognizing the accomplishment of children in your class. Maybe it is an award for being kind on the playground or for helping another child learn to tie her/his shoes. Maybe it is to recognize a birthday child. Whatever the reason, this is a way to acknowledge the achievement.

❏ *You will need:*

Small juice can lids
Paper clips
Masking tape
Ribbon
Permanent markers

❏ *To do:*

Using masking tape, secure a paper clip to the back of a juice can lid. Write an award-winning message on the front of the lid using the markers. String ribbon through the paper clip. Award the medallion to the child with fan fare as you hang it around his/her neck.

Megaphone ☺ ALL

Make a sturdy, reusable megaphone from plastic bottles.

❑ *These may be used:*

To repeat the responsorial
  phrase from the Sunday gospel.
To shout out thanks
To lead a cheer of praise
To call children by name

❑ *You will need:*

Plastic 2-liter pop bottles
Masking tape
Scissors

❑ *To do:*

Cut the bottom 2 inches off the 2-liter bottle.
Use masking tape to tape over the sharp edge.
Shout into the bottle top.

(Variation: Handled plastic bottles also work well. Just be sure to wash out any cleaning products that were previously stored in the container.)

Megaphone Craft That Shouts the News ☺ ALL

Praise God loud and clear with this gospel megaphone.

❑ *You will need:*

Construction paper
Craft stick
Tape
Responsorial phrase written on a strip of paper.

❑ *To do:*

Discuss the Sunday gospel with the children. Invite them to make a picture of the story they heard on a quarter sheet of construction paper. Use that decorated construction paper to make a cone shape. Secure the cone in place with tape. Attach the craft stick to the cone using the tape. Tape the responsorial strip of paper from the end of the megaphone. Send this home early in the week as a reminder for the family to live the gospel.

Memory Wall   ☺ ALL

This is an idea to use when a child in the class expresses a loss she has experienced. Start a memory wall. Provide opportunities for children to talk about the death of someone near to them.

❏ *You will need:*
   Area to display pictures
   Poster-board-size heart shape

❏ *To do:*

Post pictures of people or pets the children want to remember. Sometimes this memory is not expressed until another child talks about a recent death in the family. Help the children understand that when a death occurs, we do not erase that person from our hearts but they continue to live within each of us with the stories we tell and the memories we share. Display the pictures on a large heart. Whenever a child wants to display a photo or drawing, provide them the opportunity to talk about the pictured person or pet. Let them share their stories and memories with the class. Take time to pray for each of the pictured people by name trusting that they are happy and safe with God and asking that their families feel the comfort knowing this.

Understand this is a very sensitive topic for those suffering from the loss of a loved one, but it is an important part of our faith that is passed to the children.

Message Board for God Messages   ☺ ALL

A place for encouragement and prayer.
Make a special message board near the entrance of your room for sharing cute kid stories, a cartoon, a prayer intention from someone in the program, etc. (Be sure to receive permission if names are used.)

❏ *You will need:*
   White board or chalkboard
   Erasable markers or chalk
   "God Messages" sign with short explanation

❏ *To do:*
Place the board in a visible spot near the entrance of your classroom. Make a sign that says, "God Messages," for the top of it. To start off find a cute cartoon or story to share. Try to change or add to the board each week. People will stop looking at it if it doesn't change once in a while.

Message Tubes 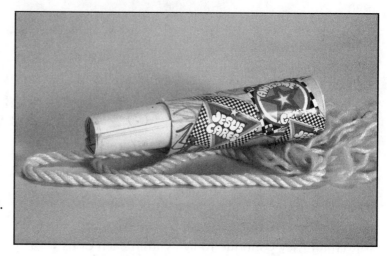 PRE

Keeping communication open between classroom and family is very important to the success of a program. Here is an idea for sending notes between home and school.

❑ **You will need:**
  Toilet paper tube
  24" – 28" of cording
  Markers
  Paints
  Stickers

❑ **To do:**
Invite children to decorate the paper tube using markers, paints, and stickers. Run the cord through the tube and tie the ends together in a knot.

When an important note needs to be sent home, roll it into the tube and place it around the child's neck.

If you are planning to reuse the message tube, be sure to make a note on it that reads, "Please return to school."

Miniature Tree ALL

The children will be amazed as they see their trees bud before their very eyes.

❑ **You will need:**
  Pinecone
  Grass seed
  A shallow pan
  Scissors

❑ **To do:**
Soak the pinecones in water overnight before taking them to class. Let the children sprinkle the wet cones with grass seed and stand upright in a shallow pan of water. Put the pan on a table near a window. The grass will begin to grow and the children will enjoy using scissors to trim their cones into tree shapes.

Mirror, Mirror on the Wall ☺ ALL

Whose love always touches us all!
Make a little frame for a mirror to remind the children that they
are very special people, loved by God.

❑ **You will need:**
Transparency paper
Permanent markers
Enlarged copy of the frame below

❑ **To do:**

As always remind the children that they are unique, wonderful people and God loves them.
Enlarge and copy on transparency film the frame shown here. Have the children wear paint shirts
to color in the designs on the frame. Ask the children to put the frame on a mirror in their home
that they use often. Let them know that the frame is a reminder of how special they are. Attach
this little poem.

Mirror, Mirror on the wall,
Whether I'm short,
Or whether I'm tall.
I can plainly see,
God made the greatest me!

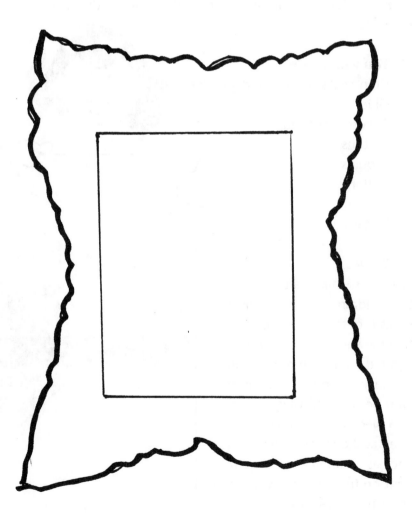

Mirror Moments   PRE

Each of us is a reflection of God's love to others. Our actions are reflected to others to see and follow. This activity with mirror play opens the door for a conversation about how we reflect God's love to others.

❑ *You will need:*
   Wall mounted mirror
   Hand mirrors

❑ *To do:*
With a child stand in front of a wall-mounted mirror and talk about each other's reflection. Mimic the movements of each other. Introduce a hand mirror and how you can look through the hand mirror to see over your shoulder into the wall-mounted mirror. Have different children try this while talking about how we each reflect God's love to others.

Mirror to Go   PRI

Make this fun little mirror to remind the children that God made each one to be wonderful and different.

❑ *You will need:*
   Craft sticks or tongue depressors
   Glue
   A variety of beads
   Buttons
   Sequins
   Glitter
   Confetti
   Metallic paper

❑ *To do:*
Give each child craft sticks. Help the children glue their individual sticks together to create a triangle square, or rectangle. Invite the children to decorate the sticks (frame of the mirror) with beads, etc. Glue the frame to a piece of the metallic paper. Then add one more stick to the back as a handle for the mirror. Print on the handle, a verse such as, "Created by God" or "Created in God's image."

Mitten Bookmark ☺ ALL

A cute gift made to mark the page.
Make a warm mitten bookmark by gluing felt mittens to the sides of a clothespin.

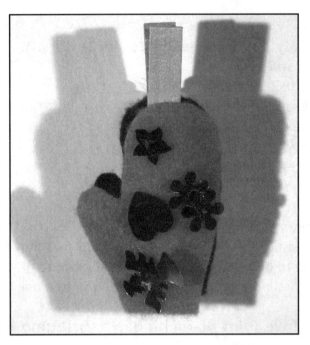

❑ *You will need:*

Felt
Glue
Spring clothes pins
Sequins
Beads

❑ *To do:*

Using the pattern provided, cut 2 mittens of the same size from felt. With tacky glue decorate the mittens with sequins or beads. Matching the thumbs, glue the mittens to each side of the clothespin. Attach to a special recipe card or book.

Mobiles ALL

Mobiles are a great way to encourage children to look all around, to look beyond their own level. Here are two mobile ideas that will encourage children to look further around for God's presence in their life.

The Holy Spirit moves us to do God's will

❑ *You will need:*

Plastic 2-liter bottle

Scissors

Glue

Paint

Glitter

String

❑ *To do:*

Cut a plastic 2-liter bottle into one long strip as shown. Provide paint, glitter, and glue for the children to decorate it. Punch a hole at one end of the strip and run a string through it. Hang the decorated strip outside by the string from a tree branch where the wind makes it spin.

God's love rains down on earth, bringing forth new life

❑ *You will need:*

Colored construction paper

Cotton

Glue

Foil

Yarn

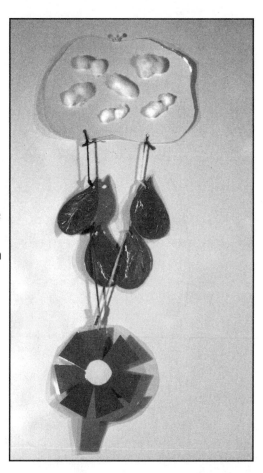

❑ *To do:*

Cut out patterns from the construction paper as follows: white clouds, blue raindrops, green flower stems, multicolor flowers. Use glue to adhere cotton to the clouds and foil to the raindrops. Tape the patterns to the yarn in the following order top to bottom – cloud, raindrops, flower, and stem. Hang the mobile in an open window so it will move with the wind.

Mosaics   🤚 PRI

Symbols are an important part of our faith. Give children some experience with symbols to represent reality in this art activity.

❏ *You will need:*

Small ceramic tile pieces (or any combination of
   small shells, marbles, pebbles, stones, or beads)
Plaster of paris (available at hardware stores)
Mixing container
Large mixing spoon
Plastic planter saucers

❏ *To do:*

Since plaster dries rather quickly, encourage the children to plan out their mosaic by laying the tiles onto a hard surface in the design they desire. Keep designs very simple by providing a limited number of tiles to each child.

Mix plaster according to the directions on the package. Pour into plastic saucer. Set tiles onto the poured plaster. Allow time to dry, usually 30 minutes depending on humidity and temperature.

(Note: Work with very small numbers of children at a time since plaster dries quickly and is not as forgiving as other mediums.)

Mothers Day Gift   ☺ ALL

A special planter.
Make a special cross planter for Mom's Day.

❏ *You will need:*

2-quart paper milk carton
Contact or wrapping paper
Potting soil
Green plant
Scissors

❏ *To do:*

Cut all but 3" off the top of 3 sides of the milk carton. On the fourth, and long side, cut out a cross measuring 4 1/2" high x 3 3/4" wide. The slats of the cross are 1 1/2". Cover the bottom of the carton and cross with contact or wrapping paper. Put potting soil in the pot and plant a green or bedded plant. Add a card that says, "God, bless my Mom."

Mother's Day Soap   ☺ ALL

This is a wonderful gift for mom! The recipe makes 30-40 small soaps.

❑ *You will need:*
   Heavy saucepan
   Grater
   Metal spoon
   Mixing bowl
   8 3 1/2 oz bars of white soap
   1 cup water
   Food coloring
   Non-stick spray
   Cookie cutters or molds
   Spatula

❑ *To do:*

Grate the bars of soap into flakes. Mix water and food coloring, bring to boil. Add the grated soap flakes. Lower heat for 2 minutes while stirring rapidly. Remove, cool, and with hands form into small balls. Allow to dry.

If shaped soaps are desired, spray mold with non-stick spray. Press soap dough into mold, trimming excess. Cool one hour. Carefully pry soap out of mold using paring knife.

To use cookie cutters, spray the cutters, spatula, and flat surface with non-stick spray. Roll out warm soap dough to 1/2 inch thickness. Press cookie cutters into soap dough, trim, and lift off surface using spatula. After soap balls or molds are completely dry, wrap in colorful tissue paper.

Mud Drawings   ☺ PRE

Spring rains bring flowers and plants to life. The wet sloppy mud helps bring spring to life too so why not let the children explore in it. Use this activity to talk about all the life God has created on the earth.

❑ *You will need:*
   Mud
   Pie tins
   Popsicle sticks or twigs

❑ *To do:*

After a wet rainy period, collect about an inch of mud in the bottom of pie tins. Provide Popsicle sticks or twigs for the children to use as drawing instruments.

Invite the children to draw anything that God has created. After some time is given to sketching in the mud, place the creations in the sun to dry. Once dry, remove the mud pies from tins. Arrange around the play yard forming a path of mud pie art. After a few days the mud pies will crumble and return to the ground.

❑ *More to do:* Too wet to play outside? Why not bring some of the outside in? Let the mud pies dry inside and on the first dry day make the mud pie path outside.

Mustard Seed Ornament   ☺ ALL

Growing big and strong in faith. Read the story of the mustard seed and discuss how our faith starts small and grows big and strong.

❑ *You will need:*
   Clear plastic Christmas balls
   Ribbon
   Mustard seeds
   Note card

❑ *To do:*
Read the story of the mustard seed, Matthew 13: 31-32. Discuss with the children how our faith begins small and then grows to be stronger just as we grow to be stronger. Give each child an ornament and have him/her put a few mustard seeds in it. Put the top on the ornament and tie a ribbon to the hanger. Attach the Bible verse, "Our faith in God is like a mustard seed that someone planted in the field. Even though it is the smallest of seeds it grows to be the largest of plants."

❑ *More to do:*
This is an excellent gift to thank teachers for sowing the seeds of faith with the children of your program.

Mystery Bag   ☺ ALL

A way to spark curiosity and wonder.

❑ *You will need:*
   A brightly colored fabric bag

❑ *To do:*
Purchase or make a brightly colored fabric bag. On the outside of the bag write, "Our Mystery Bag." Use it at circle time to introduce a new unit, story, or activity. Place a storybook, puppet, nature find, craft project, photo or magazine picture, etc. related to the topic in the bag. Spark the curiosity of the children by giving them a few clues or by passing the bag around for them to feel.

Mystery puzzle   ☺ ALL

Capture the attention of your children with a mystery puzzle that introduces or expands on your topic.

❏ **You will need:**

Large magazine pictures
Poster board
Double-stick tape
Glue
Easel or chalk board
Scissors

❏ **To do:**

Mount the picture or pictures on a poster board. Cut each into five pieces. Place rolled double-stick tape on the back of each puzzle piece. Attach one piece of the puzzle to the easel board. Attach one piece at a time encouraging the child to guess what the picture is following each piece. Talk about all the clues and how they finally guessed it.

List Your Favorite Projects Here

Name Book ☺ ALL

Create this star-studded book as a group. Then use the creation to say a prayer of thanksgiving for all of the children.

God counts the number of stars and calls each by name. Psalm 147:4

❑ *You will need:*
3-ring binder
Self-sticking stars
Markers
Dark construction paper
Hole punch

❑ *To do:*

With a permanent marker, print each child's name on the cover of the binder. Invite the children to put a star sticker next to their printed name. Using the marker print each child's name on a sheet of construction paper. Provide star stickers for the children to use to cover the letters of their name. Collect the finished names and punch to keep in the three-ring binder. Write the verse from Psalm 147: 4, "God counts the number of stars and calls each by name" on the inside cover of the binder. From time to time bring out the book and read the Psalm. Then flip the pages of the binder where the children can see the names and read with you each name.

Name Day ✋ PRI

Celebrate the day a child was named. We often celebrate the day a child was born. Why not celebrate the day they were named by having a NAME DAY. Instead of focusing on the birth of the child, focus on the naming of the child. Connect each child's name to the name of a saint. The Church honors each saint with a day to celebrate his/her life devoted to God. This will encourage the children to take a closer look at the lives of saints. If a child's first name is not related to that of a saint, use their middle name or encourage the child to choose a saint to adopt as his patron saint.

❑ *You will need:*
Books about saints
Black marker
Glitter
Glue
Self-sticking stars
Construction paper
Tag board

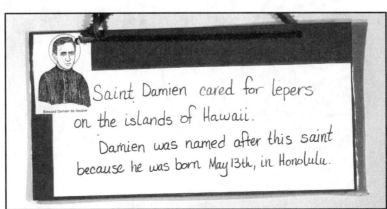

Saint Damien cared for lepers on the islands of Hawaii.
Damien was named after this saint because he was born May 13th, in Honolulu.

231

❑ *To do:*

Celebrate each child's name on the child's birthday. Recognize the day by making a nameplate. With a black marker print the child's name on a 4 1/4" x 11" piece of paper or tag board. Mount the name on a colored piece of construction paper. On the opposite side of the paper print a saint's name connected to that child's name. If available, mount a picture of the saint next to the saint's name. Help the child decorate his or her name using glitter and glue or by covering the lines of the letters with self sticking stars. Punch holes in the top so a ribbon may be used to hang the nameplate from a door at home.

Name Poster   ☺ ALL

What's in a name? Celebrate the gift of names.

❑ *You will need:*

12" x 18" construction paper
Markers
Pencil

❑ *To do:*

Trace the name of each child in large balloon letters on a large sheet of construction paper. Have the children use markers to color in each letter. Encourage older children to color designs or patterns in each letter. Laminate the name posters or cover with clear contact. Display them in your room all year.

❑ *More to do:*

Instead of coloring the letters of the name, glue packing peanuts, sequins, paper scraps, cereals, etc. to each letter.

Name Sash   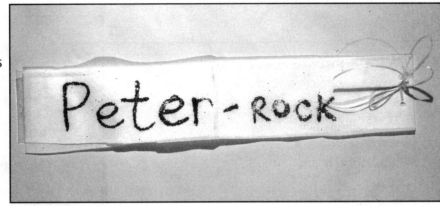 PRE

All Saints is a good time to discuss our own call to follow God. With young children we explain that people are often named after saints and that every name has a special meaning. Talk about how important names are and discuss with the children who they were named after and what their name means.

❑ *You will need:*
   Book of saints names
   Pelon or interfacing strips
      4" wide by 36" long
   Markers
   Glitter
   Glue
   Paper punch
   Ribbon

❑ *To do:*

Print each child's name across the pelon sash. If you know the meaning of the name, add that too. Have the children decorate the sash with drawings and glitter. Punch two holes on each end of the sash and lace ribbons through them. Drape the sashes over the right shoulder and fasten at the right hip.

Natural Necklace   PRE

Make sure the children keep one to hang around their necks, tie to their backpacks or belts and one to give away.

❑ *You will need:*
   Yarn
   Pine cones

❑ *To do:*

Wind a piece of yarn around a pine cone and tie the ends to make a necklace or chain. Once the children do this, they will come up with all kinds of outdoor gems to use for making necklaces.

Nature Collection   ☺ ALL

Before taking the children on a nature walk, talk about the many gifts God provides us with in nature. Help the children list a few ideas. Tell the children you will be taking them on a walk to collect some of these gifts. Set a few ground rules – leave all living creatures untouched, bring back only what you can carry, look high and low, etc.

Provide each child with a collecting container.

Here are two ideas.

Belted milk jug

(One for the whole class to share or one per child
   depending on the purpose of the walk)

❏ *You will need:*

   1/2 gallon milk jug
   Scissors
   Belt or rope

❏ *To do:*

Cut away an opening of the milk jug leaving the handle intact. Thread a belt or rope through the handle so that the container may easily be attached to any child's waist.

Paper Plate and Gum

❏ *You will need:*

   Chewing gum
   Paper plate

❏ *To do:*

Give each child a piece of gum to chew on the walk. Encourage the children to attach their found nature items to the paper plate using a small piece of the gum they are chewing.

❏ *More to do:*

When the group returns from the walk, make a class mural or mosaic with the found items.
Display the finished product as a reminder of God's gift of nature to us.

Nature Walk, I Spy God's Creation   😊 PRE

Play "I spy" while enjoying the wonder of God's creation.

❏ **To do:**

Notice the birds, squirrels, trees, flowers, etc. as you walk. Tell the children that as they see something they should say, "I spy a red flower," or "I spy a Blue Jay."

❏ **More to do:**

Give each child a piece of colored paper. As you walk ask the children to look for that color.

Nature Wreath   😊 ALL

Collect items to make a nature wreath.

Give each child a brown lunch bag to collect items such as pine cones, acorns, leaves, twigs, rocks, etc. for a nature wreath.

❏ **You will need:**

Brown lunch bags
Heavy paper plates
Glue
Paper punch
Ribbon

❏ **To do:**

Go on a nature walk with the children and ask them to collect pine cones, twigs, leaves, acorns, small rocks, etc. Cut out the center of a heavy paper plate. Punch a hole in the top of the plate and lace a piece of raffia or ribbon through it for hanging. Glue the items the children found on their walk onto the plate. Dry overnight.

Nest   ☺ ALL

A clay nest to remind us of the gift of new life.

❑ *You will need*:
Clay recipe
2 cups flour
1 cup salt
2 cups water
2 teaspoons cream of tarter
1 tablespoon vegetable oil
Food coloring
Straw or raffia
Plastic covers

❑ *To do*:

Combine all ingredients (except straw or raffia and plastic covers) in a pan and stir over medium heat on the stove. Stir constantly until the mixture becomes stiff. Cool. Have the children shape a nest using brown or green coloring on the plastic cover and add a few pieces of straw or raffia to the clay so that it looks more like a nest. Use blue or white coloring to make eggs for the nest. Store in an airtight container to use again.

Nest Building Snack   ☺ ALL

This recipe makes six nests.

Create these bird nest snacks as part of a unit about birds. As the nests are being made, community is being built. With the help of an adult the children can assist in preparing this snack.

❑ *You will need*:
Muffin tin
Paper liners
Mixing bowl
1/4 cup coconut flakes
1 tablespoon brown sugar
1/4 cup melted butter or margarine
2 full-size shredded wheat cereals.

❑ *To do*:

Crush or break up shredded wheat cereals in a mixing bowl. Add coconut flakes, butter and brown sugar. Pat mixture into the lined muffin tins covering the bottom and bringing up the sides. Bake at 350 degrees for 10 minutes or until crunchy. Serve when cooled. The nest may be filled with a scoop of pudding, yogurt, ice cream, jellybeans, or fruit.

Nest Cookies   ☺ ALL

Make these fun nest cookies for Earth Day or other celebrations of spring.

❑ *You will need:*

White almond bark
Chow mein noodles
Jelly beans
Microwave
Cooking bowl and spoons
Wax paper

❑ *To do:*

Melt the white bark in the microwave. Add chow mein noodles and stir until they are covered with the melted bark. Drop by tablespoon onto wax paper and add a jelly bean egg to the center. Refrigerate for an hour and enjoy.

New Year Crackers   ☺ ALL

Parade in the New Year with crackers for the children. Traditionally, this is a very adult holiday but it can easily be transformed into a child's celebration.
Invite God to be a part of the New Year celebration by tucking a message of God's love inside these New Year Crackers.

❑ *You will need:*

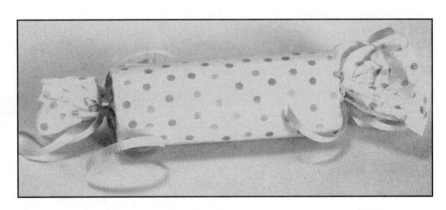

Toilet paper tube
Ribbon
Heart-shaped pony bead
Note paper
Markers
Tissue paper
Star or heart stickers

❑ *To do:*

Write a New Year's message such as "God loves you throughout this New Year." Slide the heart pony bead through the ribbon. Roll the message into a scroll and tie in place using the beaded ribbon. Tuck the scroll into the empty tube. Cover the tube with brightly colored tissue paper and hold tissue paper in place with a heart or star sticker. Twist the tissue paper closed at each end of the tube.

❑ *More to do:*

Play some marching band music for the children to parade around the classroom. Decorate cardboard boxes with silk and tissue paper flowers. Invite children to ride inside the boxes pretending to be in New Year's Day parade floats. Give each participant a New Year's Cracker.

Newsletter   ☺ ALL

Reach out and stay in touch.

Try putting together a monthly newsletter to keep parents and staff informed. You may even find that this is a useful tool in helping you plan ahead and keep the program more organized.

❑ *To do:*

Use the same color of paper and a logo each week or month so that parents recognize the notes as those from your program. Always include the names of program staff and phone numbers. Think about a few specific categories.

A calendar of "Dates to Remember." Include programs, times off, field trips, walks, parties, days specific items need to be brought in. Snack or VIP days, collection or service project items would also be appropriate to include here.

Have a, "Help Wanted" section. Provide times when extra help is needed in or out of the classroom. Let people know when you need items cut out or prepared ahead of time that they could work on at home.

For your projects and activities have a "Stuff needed" space. Make parents and volunteers aware you need specific items such as milk bottles, yarn, fabric costumes, etc. Be sure to let them know when you need it and where to put it.

"Good News" would be a great place to share successes or cute stories about the children.

Newspaper Hat   ☺ PRE

Newspaper hats are always a big hit. Make them for the 4th of July, birthdays, or any other time.

❑ *You will need:*

Newspaper
Stickers
Crepe paper
Glitter
Glue

❑ *To do:*

Lay a double thickness of newspaper on the table with centerfold up. Take the right corner and fold to the center lining up the top fold with the centerfold. Then take the left corner; bring it to the center so that the top fold is lined up on the centerfold also. Fold the bottom piece up. Turn the hat over and fold the other bottom up. To secure, tape or staple. Decorate the hats with glitter, stickers, or streamers of crepe paper hanging from the back.

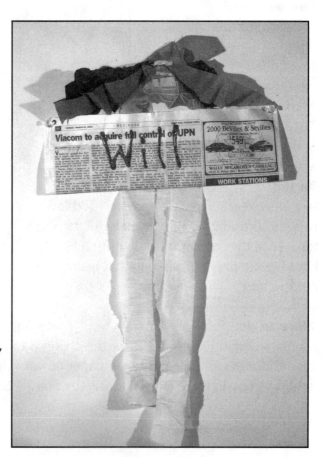

Newspaper Wand   😺 PRE

Another easy prop to make for a parade, plays, or lesson.

❏ *You will need:*
Sections of newspaper
Masking tape
Tempera paint
Strips of Mylar

❏ *To do:*

Using a whole section of newspaper fold in half. Beginning at the short end roll the newspaper keeping it tight at the bottom and a bit looser at the top. Tape the bottom of the rolled paper. Cut the top of the paper (about 6" in length) into narrow strips and fluff them out. Roll the strips on a pencil away from the center. Paint with tempera and dry. Glue or tape Mylar strips to the handle of the wand.

Noah's Ark   😺 PRE

Props for a favorite Bible story.
After reading the story of Noah, make an ark full of animals so that the children can share the story at home.

❏ *You will need:*
Paper plates
Paper punch
Animals cutouts
   (patterns provided on next page)
Markers
Yarn

❏ *To do:*

To make the ark cut a paper plate in half. Matching the sides together, punch holes around the round sides of the plate. Lace yarn through the holes and tie a knot on both ends. Using the animal patterns provided, color and cut them out in pairs. Have the children retell the story to each other before taking their arks home.

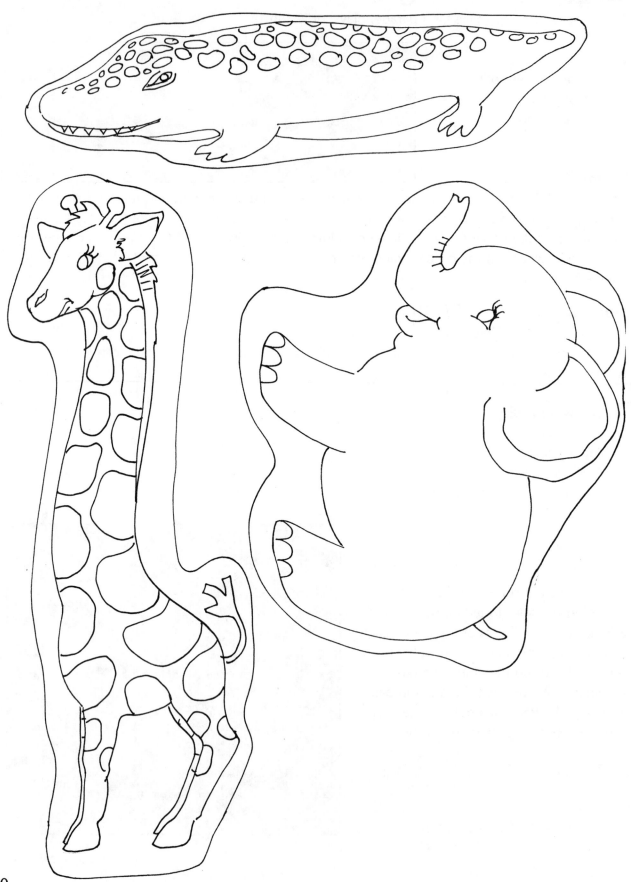

Noah's Rainbow ☺ ALL

Remind the children that the rainbow is a symbol of God's love and care for us. The rainbow reminds us that no matter what happens in our lives, God has wonderful things in store for us.

❑ **You will need:**

White construction paper or card stock
Paper punch
Ribbon
Rainbow pattern
Markers
Glitter

❑ **To do:**

Copy the pattern provided onto construction paper; then cut it out. Use markers to add color to each section of the rainbow, beginning with red on top, then orange, yellow, green, blue, and purple. Run lines of glue through the entire rainbow and sprinkle glitter over the glue. After shaking off the excess glitter, use a paper punch to make a hole at the top of the rainbow. Run a piece of ribbon through and knot at the top. Encourage the children to hang their rainbows in a place where they will see them often.

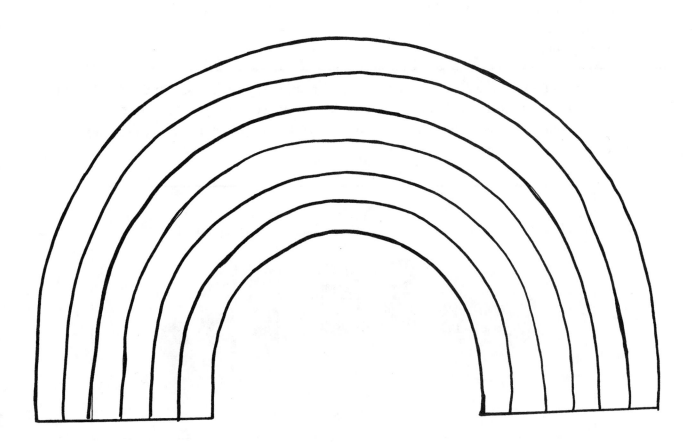

Noise Makers PRE

Praise God with some joyous noise. The laugh and giggle of young children at play can be so delightful. Here is an activity that will create this joyous noise while practicing numeral recognition. Play this game with the canisters that will mix up some fun, make some noise, and praise God.

❑ *You will need:*

Empty film canisters
Uncooked rice
Permanent black marker

❑ *To do:*

Fill the film canisters half full with the uncooked rice. Print the numbers from 1 –10 on the outside tops of the canisters. With the children sitting in a circle on the floor, distribute the canisters to the children. Help the children identify their canister number by counting from 1-10 and pointing to who is holding the number indicated. Once the children have an idea of the numbers, play the game as follows.

Sing this song to the tune of "1 little, 2 little, 3 little Indians." ♪

1 happy, 2 happy, 3 happy children,
4 happy, 5 happy, 6 happy children,
7 happy, 8 happy, 9 happy children,
10 happy children of God.

As the numbers are said, the children hold up the corresponding canisters. On the mention of 10, the canisters are all rolled to the middle of the circle and everyone takes a different canister. The play continues as other verses are added by replacing "happy" with silly, giggly, wiggly, funny, etc.

Noise Praises 😊 ALL

Use this song of praise with the children to express the children's love and gratitude to God.

❑ *To do:*

Sing to the tune of "Did you ever see a Lassie?"

Did you ever praise God, praise God, and praise God?
Did you ever praise God, with joyful noise?
With clapping and singing and singing and clapping,
Did you ever praise God with joyful noise?

Continue replacing "clapping and singing" with other actions, such as "with dancing and tapping," etc. Encourage the children to add more verses.

Noodle Art 😈 PRE

Be a wet noodle.
Make a fun picture of the nighttime sky using wet spaghetti noodles to make pictures on dark paper.

❑ *You will need:*
   Cooked, wet spaghetti noodles
   Black construction paper
   White chalk

❑ *To do:*
Cook the spaghetti noodles and cool. With chalk write "Thank you, God, for the stars and moon." Have the children use the noodles to illustrate pictures of the nighttime sky. Allow to dry flat overnight. The wet noodles will adhere to the paper as they dry.

Noodle Necklace   ⊙ PRE

Make an "I am loved" necklace by stringing a variety of uncooked pasta on yarn or ribbon. Add a special heart charm that says, "I am loved," to the center of the necklace.

❏ *You will need:*

A variety of pasta that has holes or openings
 wide enough for a preschooler to string yarn through
Yarn
Masking tape
4" hearts cut from red construction paper
Markers

❏ *To do:*

To make the charms, cut 4" hearts from red construction paper. Print, "I am loved" on one side and the child's name on the other. Punch a hole at the top of the heart for lacing. Cut the yarn into 24" lengths. Wrap masking tape tightly around one end of the yarn. This will make the yarn go through the pasta with greater ease. Have the children string the pasta to fill up about 6" of the yarn. Add the heart charm. Continue to string another 6" of pasta onto the yarn. Tie off the ends and wear.

❏ *More to do:*

Older children may enjoy painting the noodles with watercolor paints before stringing them to the yarn.

Nosegay ☺ ALL

A pretty way to say you are loved.

Make a nosegay to give away for May Day, Mother's Day, or other spring celebrations.

❏ **You will need:**

Sugar ice-cream cones
Dried flowers
Wrapped candy or potpourri
Ribbon
Nylon net

❏ **To do:**

Fill the cones with dried flowers, wrapped candy or potpourri.
(A small piece of Styrofoam in the cone will help hold the flower
stems in place.) Gather a 12" circle of nylon net around the top
of the filled cone. Tie together with ribbon and a bow. Attach a holiday blessing to the gift.

Note Cards ✋ PRI

Gifts the children can make to give to others.

Using old Christmas and birthday cards, children can make little note cards to give to their
parents or seniors in your community.

❏ **You will need:**

Used greeting cards
Scissors (decorative edges would be great also)
Ribbon or raffia
Paper punch

❏ **To do:**

Have the children help you sort out the
greeting cards. Cut the pictures along the
folds and throw out the side of the cards
with writing. Older children could use the
decorative scissors to cut around the edges
of the card. To make a gift tag, punch a
hole in a top corner of the card and lace a
ribbon or piece of raffia through it for
tying. Put these cards in sets of 4 to 6 in
plastic bags. Tie the bags with a bow.

❑ *More to do:*
Note holder

❑ *You will need:*
6″ x 12″ construction paper
Yarn
Glue
Stickers
Paper punch
Markers

❑ *To do:*
Make a pocket by folding the construction paper 3″ from the bottom and gluing or stapling along the sides. Punch a hole at the top center and hang a piece of yarn through the hole for hanging. Decorate with markers and stickers.

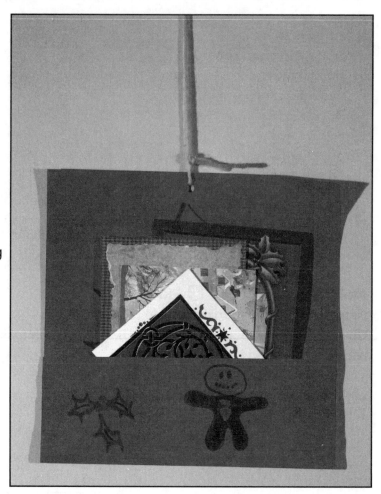

Number Game   PRI
A quick game to get your children thinking and having fun at the same time.

❑ *To do:*
Think of a number that relates to a story in the Bible and invite the children to come up with the what. Here are some examples:

Three – Three wise men or three crosses
Forty – Forty days and nights it rained or that Jesus prayed in the desert
Seven – The days in creation
Twelve – The number of disciples

Nuts to You ☺ ALL

Nutty fun with the harvest.

Think about all of the fun you can have by spending some time thinking about nuts at harvest time. Take a nature walk and collect nuts. Play a matching game or glue eyes onto them to make little critters. Make these little appreciation gifts with the children for the volunteers in your program.

❑ *You will need:*

    4" flower pot
    Permanent markers
    Salted in the shell peanuts or whole walnuts,
      almonds, pecans, or filberts
    Plastic wrap
    Ribbon or raffia

❑ *To do:*

With marker have the children decorate the pots with their drawings. Print, "We are nuts about you! Thank You for Volunteering." Fill the pots to over flowing with nuts. Center the pot on a large piece of plastic wrap and gather it at the top of the pot. Tie the gather with raffia or ribbon.

Nylon Net Christmas Ornament ☺ ALL

An easy tree ornament presentation.

❑ *You will need:*

    Styrofoam balls or clear plastic ornaments
    Variety of colors of nylon net
    (For a more festive look purchase netting
      that has glitter throughout the weave.)
    Scissors
    Ribbon

❑ *To do:*

Purchase the Styrofoam balls or plastic ornaments and netting from a craft store. Cut the net into 11" or 12" squares depending on the size of the balls. Place the ball in the center of the net and gather up all sides to the top of the ball. With ribbon tie a bow around the gathered net. Add an additional tie for hanging.   For more decoration add a jingle bell to the bow or a silk flower.

❑ *More to do:*

Use nylon netting to wrap up any small gift you are giving to the children or that the children are giving to someone else. A few candies, a ball, piece of fruit, ornament, or book wrapped in netting make a very special gift.

List Your Favorite Projects Here

Observation Station 🐻 PRE

On the lookout for the blessings of God.

Set up an observation station in your classroom complete with binoculars and telescopes. Have the children check out the room for blessings from God and point them out to one another. Make these little telescopes that will help them with their search.

❑ *You will need:*
Paper towel tubes
Stickers
Paper punch
Yarn

❑ *To do:*

Punch a hole in each side of the paper tube. Tie a piece of yarn to the two holes. With adult help write, "In search of God's blessings." Decorate the telescopes with stickers.

Observation Windows 😊 ALL

Taking a walk outside to observe nature can be very enlightening. Collecting some of the observations helps to make lasting memories. Gather a few samplings to bring back as a memory or to share at home.

❑ *You will need:*
Paper plate
Clear contact paper
Scissors

❑ *To do:*

Cut a number of 1" to 2" circles out of the center of a paper plate. Cover the inside of the plate with a square of clear contact paper, leaving clear sticky circles of the contact paper exposed on the underside of the plate. Place the protective covering on the underside of the plate to keep the sticky circles from losing their effectiveness.

Invite the children to collect samples of dirt, sand, leaves, grass clippings, etc. by peeling back the protective cover and placing the sticky side of the plate down on the object. When the plate is lifted from the object a sample is collected.

When the group returns to the classroom with samplings, talk about how the findings are just a few of the gifts God has surrounded people with.

❑ *More to do:*

Observe the findings closer with the aid of a magnifying glass or by hanging in a sunlit window.

o

Ocean Scene 🙂 ALL

And God said, "Let there be sea and plants and animals that live there." And it was so. And God said, "It is good."

As you look at the story of creation, make an ocean scene complete with blue water.

❑ *You will need:*
  Shoe box covers
  Construction paper
  Small sea shells
  Small toy fish
  Fishing line
  Sand
  Glue
  Blue plastic wrap
  Tape

❑ *To do:*
Glue blue paper to the inside cover of the box. Also glue sand and small shells to the bottom edge of the inside cover. Using the patterns provided cut out fish and plants to glue to the blue paper inside the box cover. If you have small plastic fish, hang them with fishing line from the inside top of the box. To make the blue ocean cover the box with blue plastic wrap and tape in place.

Octopus 🐯 PRE

This octopus rhyme will remind children that all of God's creations are awesome.

❑ *To do:*
  Octopus, octopus, what a creature you are!
  Swimming in the ocean you travel quite far.
  Octopus, octopus, a life full of charms,
  What a gift God gave you with all of those arms.

Odds N' Ends   ☺ ALL

Do spring-cleaning and use up the leftovers!

Give each child a paper cup full of leftover items such as pipe cleaners, ribbons and bows, sticker, fabric scrapes, Styrofoam, etc. Tell the children that they are to use up all of the items in the cup, including the cup to make an odds and ends creation.

❑ *You will need:*
    Paper cups
    Odds and ends
    Glue
    Tape
    Scissors

❑ *To do:*

Tell the children that they have to be creators using the odds and ends that they find in their cup. They may use glue and tape to fasten the items to the cup, but that is all. Be sure to take time for the children to share their creative creations with each other.

Offering Box   ☺ ALL

"It is better to give than receive."

Encourage regular giving with an offering box. Tell the children that in our Christian tradition we share what we have with others. One of the ways we do this is by giving money to church on Sundays. Talk about how this happens during your particular services or at Sunday school.

❑ *You will need:*
    Metal Band-Aid box
    Contact paper
    Magnetic strips
    Stickers

❑ *To do:*

Cover the Band-Aid box with contact paper. Decorate with stickers and the words "My Offering to God." Stick a magnetic strip to the back of the box. Tell the children to put their offering box on the refrigerator at home. Encourage them to put extra change or a portion of what they may receive as a gift into the offering box during the week. On Sundays empty out the box in the church offering.

Oil Slick Paper   ☺ ALL

Unusual and fun, this project will show the children that oil and water do not mix. However, in this case they produce some beautiful results.

❑ *You will need:*
    Cooking oil
    Light colored construction paper
    Three cups and spoons
    Powdered tempera paint, red, blue, and yellow
    Cookie sheets with edges
    Newspaper

❑ *To do:*

Spread your newspaper over your work area. Pour enough water over the bottom of a cookie sheet to cover it. Mix1/4 cup of oil and two tablespoons of powdered paint in each cup. Mix well. Pour some of each color over the cookie sheet and mix the colors together. Set a piece of construction paper down in the pan of water and colors. Then pick it up at one end and let the excess water and oil run off. Lay it on a thick pile of newspaper and plastic to dry. When dry cut into shapes such as flowers, leaves, fish, or butterflies.

Open Your Door for Jesus   ☺ ALL

An Advent activity.

Mary and Joseph heard, "There's no room," as they arrived at Bethlehem. Ask the children to, "Open their doors," and make room for Jesus in their homes and hearts during Advent.

❑ *You will need:*
    12" x 18" construction paper
    Markers
    Scissors
    Glue

❑ *To do:*

Draw a picture of a large front door on a large piece of construction paper for each child. Across the top of the door write, "Open Your Door to Jesus." Have the children draw their own front door on the copy you have made. Encourage them to add details like windows, wreaths, etc. Cut along one side and the top and bottom of the door so that it will open. Glue this sheet to another sheet of paper. Be sure not to glue the door shut. Open the door and have the children draw a picture of themselves and their family on the second sheet of paper.

Opiatek   ☺ ALL

Polish Christmas bread.

The Polish people have a Christmas custom called Opiatek (pronounced O-pot-key). The wonderful gift of Jesus' birth is celebrated by sharing a wafer of bread (usually unblessed) before the Christmas meal. After a table blessing has been said the head of the family or household breaks off a piece of bread for each person. While doing this a special blessing or sign of peace is given to each individual. After everyone has received his or her bread and blessing, the meal begins. Share this meaningful tradition with the families in your program by baking small loaves of bread with the children and sending them home with the prayer ideas for their Christmas celebrations.

❏ *You will need:*

   Small aluminum bread pans
   Frozen bread dough
   Plastic wrap
   Ribbon

❏ *To do:*

Several packages of frozen bread dough can be purchased fairly inexpensively and each loaf should yield about four small loaves of bread. Follow package directions for thawing. You may be able to thaw over night. With permanent marker, write children's names on the bottom of their aluminum pan. When the dough is thawed have the children shape their piece of dough and put it in their greased pan. Bake according to directions and cool. Wrap the bread in colored plastic wrap and tie with a ribbon. Attach the explanation for parents and prayer to a note card tied to the ribbon.

❏ *More to do:*

Make any type of bread for this prayer and involve the children in mixing the ingredients.

o

Opposites, Mary and Martha   😊 ALL

The children will love acting out this delightful story of the two sisters during a prayer time.

❑ *You will need:*

A child to play Mary
A child to play Martha
A child to play Jesus
A child to play Lazarus
Bible or story of Mary and Martha
Bathrobes, scarves, dusting cloth, and broom

❑ *To do:*

Tell the children that Jesus often stayed with Lazarus and his two sisters.

Dress two children in front of the class, one as Lazarus and one as Jesus.

The sisters were Mary and Martha, Jesus loved them both very much.

Dress up the children playing Mary and Martha with bathrobes and scarves.

Step by step have the children act out the following as you tell this simple story. Keep the story simple or add as much action as you wish.

One day Jesus met Lazarus on the road. Lazarus invited him to his family's house.

When Jesus arrived, Martha began to clean and cook for Jesus, wanting everything to be just right.

Mary and Lazarus sat down by Jesus and listened to every word he had to say.

Finally Martha was angry that no one was helping her and said, "Lord, don't you care that my sister has left me to do all the work myself?" Jesus replied, "Martha, Martha! You are worried and troubled over so many things. But just one thing is needed. Mary has chosen the right thing." (Luke 10:40-42)

Ask the children what was the right thing. Continue the discussion by sharing what this story has to do with our lives today.

Opposites, the Mary and Martha Song   🐻 PRE

Mary and Martha were opposites, and Jesus loved them both very much. This song will help the children understand what's most important.

❑ *To do:*

Sing to the tune of "Here We Go Round the Mulberry Bush."

> *This is the way Martha swept, Martha swept, Martha swept.*   🎵
> *This is the way Martha swept when Jesus came to visit.*
> Replace swept with dust, cook, and bake.
> Last verse:
> *This is the way Mary sat, Mary sat, Mary sat.*
> *This is the way Mary sat when Jesus came to visit.*
> Replace sat with listened.
> Be sure to add some fun actions.

Orange Spice Ball   ☺ ALL

A scented gift.

Orange spice balls are so easy for the children to make and they make a wonderful Thanksgiving or Christmas project.

❑ *You will need:*
    Fresh oranges
    Whole cloves
    Ribbon or raffia

❑ *To do:*

Wrap ribbon or raffia around the orange as you would a package. Tie a bow at the top. Have the children push the cloves into the orange covering the whole surface of the orange or as much as desired. Send home as gift for Mom and Dad or as a harvest table decoration.

Oreo® Cookie   ☺ ALL

A treat the children will love to help make.

After dipping whole Oreos in (melted) almond bark have the children decorate them with small candies or sugar. Serve at your programs or class parties.

❑ *You will need:*
    Oreo cookies
    White almond bark
    Microwave
    Cooking bowl, spoon and tongs
    Wax paper
    Decorating candies or sugars

❑ *To do:*

Melt the bark in a microwave safe bowl. Use the tongs to dip the cookies in the bark. Place on a piece of wax paper. As soon as the bark begins to cool have the children carefully decorate the cookies with candies and sugars. Serve at a special party or program.

Origami Sun Star   🖐 PRI

An ornament to celebrate the sun in summer or Christmas in the winter.
Make these origami sun stars with the children with a special blessing inside, to decorate the Christmas tree or your summer classroom.

❑ *You will need:*

6" or 8" squares of yellow or shiny gold paper
A large needle
Heavy thread or thin ribbon

❑ *To do:*

Print a blessing or short prayer around the edges of the paper. Fold the paper in half so that the writing is on the inside. Fold in half again. Fold a third time, matching the two folded edges to make a triangle. When you open the folded square you will have eight triangles made by folds. Next, one at a time (and unfolding in between) refold in the two long diagonals matching the corners of the square. After making the diagonal folds, lay the square flat out in front of you. Gently ease up the sides, top and middle to make the sun star. With a needle make a hole at the center point of the star. Tie a knot at the bottom of the string or ribbon and lace it through the hole. Tie another loop at the top for hanging.

❑ *More to do:*

Use a long string and make a garland of sun stars. Just tie a knot on the string as you string each one on.

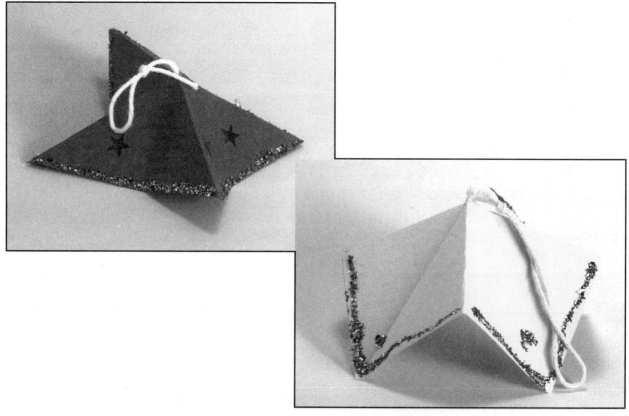

Ornaments ☺ ALL

For Christmas or any time.
Make ribbon edged ornaments for the Christmas or Easter tree, or just because.

❑ *You will need:*
Small round paper plates
Paper punch
Ribbon
Photo of the child or a holiday card picture

❑ *To do:*
Glue the picture or photo to the center of the plate. Punch holes around the outside edge of the plate. Lace the ribbon through the holes and tie a bow at the top. Attach another piece of ribbon for hanging the ornament.

Outdoor Obstacle Course ☺ ALL

Life can be an obstacle course. But with the people God has sent to guide us, we can make it past any obstacles that come our way. Setting up an obstacle course in the classroom allows a time for friends to help one another through the rough spots. Practicing with these make-believe obstacles, we can help children know God has placed people around us who can help us when needed.

❑ *You will need:*
Stepping stone
Bed sheet
Open boxes
Wooden plank
Old tire
Hanging stuffed pillowcase
Log

❑ *To do:*
Using the above-mentioned materials set up an obstacle course. Pair the children up and invite one of the pair to close his/her eyes. The open-eyed child helps to guide the other partner through the obstacle course. Stepping on each stone, crawling under the bed sheet, creeping through the boxes, walking across the plank, circling the tire, avoiding the swinging stuffed pillow and ending up sitting on the log. During the rest on the log, remind the children how thankful we can be to God for giving us so many loving and caring people in our lives who are always near to guide and lead us. After a rest and discussion, switch roles.

❑ *More to do:*
Turn the obstacle course into an adventure created around a Bible story like "Jonah and the Whale."

O

Over Five Thousand People PRE
Remind the children of the "picnic" where Jesus fed over five thousand people.

❑ *You will need:*
A storybook based on feeding the five thousand
Snack and drink that can be packed up to go
Cups and napkins
Blankets for the ground

❑ *To do:*
Tell the children that you would like to tell them a wonderful story about Jesus but first they must do some preparations for the story. Invite the children to help you pack the snack and drink, cups and napkins into some bags. Ask the children to help you carry these items to the place where you will hear this wonderful story about Jesus. Give the children clues about the story, such as – the story has to do with people wanting to hear God's Word. If the weather permits, travel outside and set up your picnic. After giving several clues, give the children an opportunity to guess the story. Read the story, share snack, and close with the scripture reading (Matthew 14: 13-21 or Mark 6:30-44) and this prayer.
Link index fingers and pray,

Dear God,
Thank you for sending Jesus to us.
He is our friend and Savior.
Caring for our every need.
Help us to care for others as he cares for us.
Amen.

Over Five Thousand People Action Play PRE
Young children will love this finger play that will help them remember this amazing miracle.

Over five thousand people came to hear Jesus talk. (Hold up five fingers.)

As it got late, their tummies began to growl. (Rub your tummy.)

We don't have enough food, the disciples said. (Show empty hands.)

You know all we have is five loaves and two fish. (Hold up five fingers on one hand and two on the other.)

Jesus took the food and prayed. (Fold hands)

He broke the bread and the fish to give away. (Pretend to give away to others.)

Wow, five thousand were fed with five loaves and two fish. (Hold up five fingers and then two.)

Overflowing With Joy ☺ ALL

God fills us with joy. The joy of God flows from within each of us. We can be outwardly thankful for God's presence in our lives by sharing this joy with others.

❑ *You will need:*
    One empty 2-liter plastic bottle
    Scissors
    Purchased bubble solution
    Shallow saucer

❑ *To do:*

Cut the top 3" from a 2-liter plastic pop bottle as shown in diagram. Cut a notch out of the large opened end to make a place for the straw to fit under. With the spout up, place the larger opened end of the bottle top onto a saucer. Pour some bubble solution onto the saucer. Place a straw into the notch and blow into the bubble solution. Continue to blow until the bottle top is flowing with airy bubbles. Change straws and take turns blowing if needed. In between blows, talk about how we overflow with God's love.

Owl Book 😀 PRE

A mini-book that reminds us who God loves.

❑ *You will need:*
    Enlarge and copy the book page on page 260 back to back
    Crayons
    Scissors
    Stapler

❑ *To do:*

After enlarging and copying the pictures back to back, color the pictures and then cut the thick black line across the middle. Place pages 3 and 4 on top of pages 1 and 6. Staple on the dotted line and fold. Read the "Owl Book" together and then have the children read to one another.

O

Palm Sunday Parade   ☺ ALL

Shout Hosanna!

With the cooperation of your pastor, plan a Palm Sunday procession that includes the children in your Sunday morning program.

❑ *You will need:*
Palm branches
A Hosanna banner
Markers
Dowels or yardsticks
Tape

❑ *To do:*

Make this parade a success by making plans way ahead of time with your pastor. This parade involves the children processing through church with the pastor as the opening hymn is sung. The children follow the pastor down the middle aisles and then they return down the side aisles and walk back to their classrooms.

Make a Hosanna Banner: Print "Hosanna! Blessed Is He Who Comes in the Name of the Lord!" on a poster board. Tape dowels or yardsticks to the sides of the paper so that it is easier for the children to carry.

Paper Cup Telephone   ☺ PRE

Spreading the Good News.

Make these fun telephones to call others to tell them of the Good News of Jesus.

❑ *You will need:*
2 paper cups
3' to 5' of string
Masking tape
Stickers

❑ *To do:*

Punch a hole in the center bottom of the cup. Push one end of the string through the hole and tie a knot so that the string stays in place. Do this with the other cup and the other end of string. Secure both knots with a piece of masking tape inside the cup. Have two children talk on the phone and tell each other about the Good News of Jesus.

Paper Plate Hat 😺 PRE

No matter the season, these hats can be made to celebrate just about any reason. The example is for an Easter celebration but with a little creativity this hat can be transformed to fit any festivities.

❑ *You will need:*
   Paper plate
   Easter grass (or other seasonal decorations)
   Glue
   Pipe cleaners
   Pompoms
   Construction paper

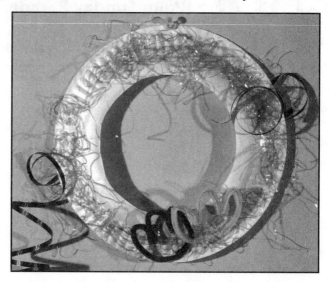

❑ *To do:*
Cut the center of a paper plate as shown. Push the plate onto the child's head to fit like a hat. Glue Easter grass around the rim of the newly formed hat.

Twist the ends of colorful pipe cleaners together to form a circle. Shape the circles into tulips. Staple the tulip shaped pipe cleaners on the points of the paper plate.

Paper Prayer Chain for the Sick ☺ ALL

When someone in our community is sick or troubled, it is often hard for children to understand praying for that person. Make a prayer chain for someone who is ill and have the children add a link to the chain every time they pray for that person.

❑ *You will need:*
   Variety of paper strips 8 1/2" x 1"
   Glue
   A paper heart

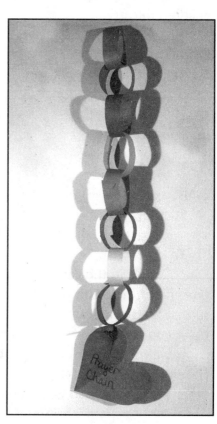

❑ *To do:*
Talk to the children about prayer and why we pray extra for people when they are sick. Let them know that as a class you will be working on a special chain that eventually will be given to the persons who are sick. Just think how good these persons will feel when they receive the prayer chain and they realize how many prayers were said for them. Cut out a large paper heart and write the name or names of the people you are praying for on it. As the children remember to say a prayer for their friend who is sick have them glue a link on the chain. You might want to set up a mini center so that the children can be independent about adding their links. Be sure to give the chain to the person for whom the chain was made. It is sure to warm his/her heart.

Paper Trail   😊 PRE

Delivering the news, Jesus Christ is Born!
Ask paper carrier for important details!

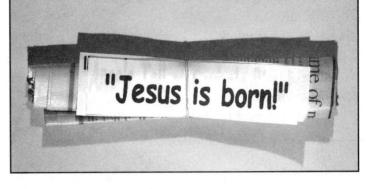

❏ *You will need:*
    Newspapers
    White paper
    Rubber bands

❏ *To do:*
Use computer letters or write your own to make a headline like, "Jesus is Born!" or "Angels Tell of Savior's Birth." Glue the headlines to the front page of a newspaper. Roll up the paper and or bag it as regular newspapers are. Have the children deliver their newspapers with good news throughout the classroom and then at home. Each time the children deliver the "Good News" to someone new, they should tell the story of Jesus' birth.

Parents' Prayer   😊 ALL

Support the parents in your program by sending home a Parents Prayer card.

❏ *You will need:*
    Card stock paper
    A cross or other religious sticker

❏ *To do:*
Enlarge and copy the prayer provided below on heavy card stock. Add a sticker or ribbon for decoration. Send the prayer cards home with parents and ask them to put it in a place where they will be able to read it often. Examples would be the bathroom mirror, kitchen cupboard, dashboard, etc.

    Parents' prayer
    Mommies are nice
    Daddies are too.
    I love you both very much,
    This is so true.
    Sharing God's love
    This I can do
    Thank you for teaching me,
    How to be true.

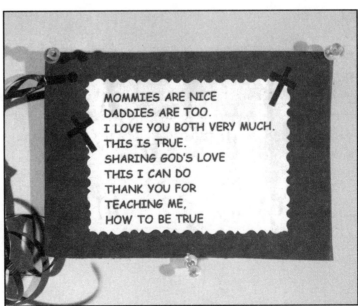

❏ *To do:*
Teach this chant to the children to say at a program or other celebration honoring parents.

Party Favor Cracker   ☺ ALL

A party surprise.

Make cracker party favors for the children for a holiday party or have the children help make them to give to a food pantry or shelf for needy families to enjoy.

❑ *You will need:*

Toilet tissue tubes
Wrapping paper (appropriate for the holiday)
Ribbon
Tape
Small toys or candies
Stickers

❑ *To do:*

Have the children decorate the tissue tubes with holiday stickers. Carefully fill the tubes with wrapped candy or small toys. Lay the tube on a 10" x 5" piece of wrapping paper. Wrap the paper around the tube being careful not to disturb the contents. Tape the paper in place. Gather the paper at the ends of the tubes and tie with a ribbon.

Pave the Way   ☺ ALL

Working together we can build the road to Jesus, a road that others may follow. In this activity the children work together to achieve a common goal, following a path they lay together.

❑ *You will need:*

Masking tape
Garden stones
Snack or treat-filled bag

❑ *To do:*

Place a bag filled with snacks, small toys, or other treats at one end of the room. Use a piece of masking tape to mark a starting point, several feet away from the bag. Hide garden stones throughout a designated area (the level of difficulty depends on the age of the children). Be sure to hide more than enough stones so that when they are placed side by side, they will reach from the tape to the bag. Encourage the children to find the garden stones, using them to make a path from the tape to the bag. Once the path of stones reaches the bag, invite the children to enjoy its contents together.

Peace Puzzle Pin   ☺ ALL

We are all part of the peace puzzle.

This is a great idea for discussing peace. Use a jigsaw puzzle of the country or world to make a peace pin or necklace.

❑ *You will need:*

1 or 2 puzzles of the world or our country
Glue
Jewelry pin

❑ *To do:*

If possible pick up 2 of the same puzzle. This will allow you to have one complete puzzle to put together and another to take pieces from. Discuss peace with the children and how we all have to work together to make this a better world. Show them the puzzle of the world. Point out your country or town and reiterate the fact that we all live on this earth and we have to work together to keep it peaceful. Do the puzzle together. If there are a lot of pieces, begin work on the puzzle early and just finish it up together. Give children a piece from the puzzle of the world and again remind them that they are a piece of peace. Make a necklace or pin with the puzzle piece.

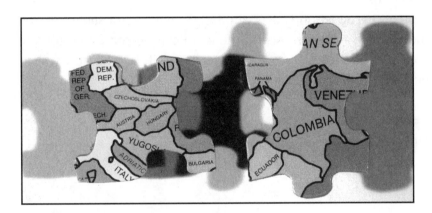

Peel and Eat Fruit   ☺ ALL

Even something as simple as sharing a piece of fruit can convey a faith-filled message. Peel, eat, and share the message.

❑ *You will need:*

Piece of fruit with a peel or rind

❑ *To do:*

Looking at the piece of fruit with the children, describe the appearance of the outside skin. As you peel back the skin of the fruit, ask the children if they can smell the fruit easier in the air. Talk about how the sweet smell is traveling around the room or building. Others know we are having a fruit snack without any word being spoken. Offer each child a taste of the fruit. Lead the children to the comparison of each of us being like the piece of fruit. When we look inside one another, we can learn about the sweetness of God's love.

Penny Walk  PRE

An Adventure.

Turn the usual summer stroll into an adventure.

❑ *You will need:*
A shiny penny

❑ *To do:*

Before taking your energetic preschoolers out for a routine walk, put a penny in your pocket. Begin the walk by following your usual route, but stop at the first crossroad or corner. Reach into your pocket and pull out the penny. Suggest to the group that the coin will decide which way to turn. Explain as the coin is tossed in the air that if it lands on the ground heads up, the walkers turn left. If it lands tails up, the walkers turn right. At each junction let a different child toss the coin and hold it until the next stop. Have fun, but be careful not to get lost!

Pentecost Mobile PRI

The Holy Spirit with us.

The spirit of Pentecost is all around us. Even though we cannot see it, we can feel it in the love we have for one another. The presence of the wind can be compared to that of the Holy Spirit. We can feel it and see its effects, but we can't really see it. On Pentecost weekend make a mobile that will be spun by the wind that we cannot see, only feel.

❑ *You will need:*
2-liter plastic bottle
Scissors
Glitter
Glue
Paint
Paper punch
String

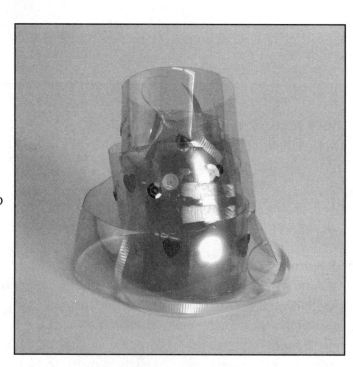

❑ *To do:*

Cut a plastic 2-liter bottle into one long strip as shown. Decorate with glitter and paint. Punch a hole in the top and lace a string through it for hanging. Hang the mobile from a tree and watch the wind spin it.

Photo Place Card   😊 ALL

Welcoming guests to the table.

A great idea for welcoming families to your programs or any dinners you might be hosting. Take an instant photo as families and individuals come in and place them at their table place for a place card.

❑ *You will need:*
   Instant camera
   Film
   Place cards

❑ *To do:*

As people arrive and register have a volunteer take their picture with an instant camera. Tape the picture to a place card that says, "We're glad you are here!" with the names of the persons added to it. Put the cards at the table or chair the guest or family of guests will be sitting.

Pickle Game   😊 ALL

A Christmas game for church or home.

Hiding the pickle is a German tradition celebrated on Christmas Eve. Parents hide a glass pickle in the Christmas tree. The child who finds the pickle gets an extra Christmas gift. Make a paper pickle to hide in your classroom or on your class tree.

❑ *You will need:*
   Tag board
   Markers
   Green glitter
   Glue
   Green pipe cleaner

❑ *To do:*

Trace and cut the pickle pattern provided. Have the children color it with green markers and add glitter. Punch a hole in the top of the pickle and make a hanger with the green pipe cleaner.

If you are making pickles for home be sure to send instructions for the game. Hide the pickle in the tree. Have the children look for it. The child who finds it gets to hide it the next time for the rest of the children and on it goes.

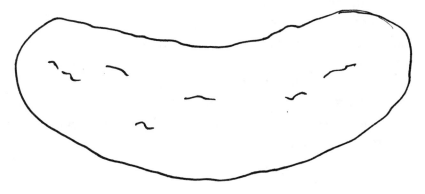

Picture Frame ☺ ALL

A cute way to frame it up.

Make a 3-dimensional picture frame using puzzle pieces, macaroni, or buttons.

❑ *You will need:*

Heavy tag board or cardboard
Glue
Puzzle pieces, macaroni, or buttons
Photos of the children

❑ *To do:*

Cut two 7" x 9" squares out of cardboard or tag. With an exacto knife cut out an inside square that is 5" x 7" from one of the pieces. This will leave you a 2" frame all the way around. Have the children glue puzzle pieces (or any of the other items suggested) on the frame. Be generous with the glue. Dry flat with a book on top to prevent curling. Be sure to wipe off excess glue before laying the book down. Tape the photo, self-portrait, or handprint facing out to the back of the frame. Tape the other piece of 7" x 9" tag to the back of the frame. Cut a 2" strip of tag and tape it into a triangle. Tape one side of the triangle to the center bottom of the back of the frame to provide support for standing. Or punch a hole in the top and lace a ribbon through it for hanging.

Pillowcase Prayers ☺ ALL

Encourage prayer with a written morning prayer and bedtime prayer on each side of a pillowcase.

❑ *You will need:*

Pre-washed, light-colored pillowcase
Permanent or fabric markers

❑ *To do:*

Place a large brown grocery bag or square of cardboard in between the fabric of the pillowcase. With adult help, have the children print a morning prayer on one side of the case and a bedtime prayer on the other. You may want to ask a volunteer to do this for you a few days before you have the children add their names and decorations. Do not stack the

colored fabrics on top of one another (as it will bleed through) until it has dried for a couple of days. Have the children add their names and drawings to the cases and again allow to dry with the grocery bag liner inside. These pillowcases may be washed normally.

Morning Prayer

Thank you, God, for this new day,
Be with me as I work, play, and pray.
Amen.

Bedtime Prayer

As I lay my head to sleep,
Good thoughts from this day I will keep.
Be with me until the morning light,
When I will greet the new day bright.
Amen.

❏ *More to do:*

Have a volunteer sew your pillowcases making one side yellow (morning) and the other side blue (bedtime). Decorate them yourself and give them to the children for an end-of-the-year or Christmas gift.

Pinch of Confetti   🙂 PRE

A pinch of confetti can communicate a faith-filled message to many. Placing this simple symbol on a child's hand will carry home a loud message that the child can share with others.

❏ *You will need:*

Small confetti shapes (available at stationery stores)
Transparent adhesive tape

❏ *To do:*

Place a small pinch of seasonal confetti on the top of the child's hand. Keep it in place with a small piece of tape. Explain to the child how the shape of the confetti symbolizes a sign of faith during the current season. Example: Heart shape — God's love is for everyone.
Star – God's love shines down on the world.

Pitch a Tent   🙂 ALL

God shelters us much as a tent provides protection from the sun, rain, and wind. Pitch a tent and share some faith or provide the opportunity to do so.

❏ *You will need:*

Small pup or domed tent

❏ *To do:*

Work together setting up a tent in an area where it can remain standing for a few days. The nylon three-man dome tents work very well to provide a safe snug surrounding. As the children work together with you to set up this shelter, talk about the many ways the tent can be used. Remind the children that God's love is like a shelter for each of us.

❑ *More to do:*

Play a game using the pitched tent. Invite the children to play this tent game showing how God's love can be shared to bring happiness to all. One child is inside the tent while the rest of the group forms a circle around the outside of the tent. As the child inside circles one way around the inside of the tent, those outside the tent circle the opposite way around the tent. The circles move singing the song below.

Sung to the tune of "Pop Goes the Weasel." 🎵
> *All around our tent we go*
> *Watching all the children play*
> *God's love is shared with everyone*
> *Come in and join us.*

Whoever is at the entryway outside the tent when the line "Come in and join us" is sung, enters the tent and helps form the inner circle. The play continues until all the children are inside the tent.

Place Mats ☺ ALL

For snack time or home.
Make place mats for the children to use during snack time or for them to take home.

❑ *You will need:*

> 12" x 18" sheets of construction paper
> Old greeting card pictures
> Glue
> Clear contact
> Copies of table prayers

❑ *To do:*

Have the children decorate their place mats with a self-portrait or cut-out pictures from greeting cards. Add a copy of a favorite table prayer and the name of the child. Cover with clear contact so that it can be wiped off.

❑ *More to do:*

Make a birthday place mat that is covered with greeting card birthday pictures.

Pocket Garden   ☺ ALL

Show love of life and appreciation for creation by planting a pocket garden.

❑ *You will need:*

Zip lock sandwich bags
Paper towels
Bean seeds

❑ *To do:*

Fold a paper towel so that it fits easily into the plastic bag. Moisten it and place it in the bag. Add 3 or 4 bean seeds. Write the child's name on the outside of the bag. Tell the children that little seeds need to receive tender loving care to grow. It is their job to see that the little seed package is kept warm and safe. During the day a good place for it would be their pocket and at night under their pillow. After about three days the bean will sprout a root and be ready to plant in the ground.

Post Card Evangelizing   ☺ ALL

Have the children color blank post cards to brighten up the day of a shut-in from your church community.

❑ *You will need:*

Blank post cards
Postage
Names and addresses of parishioners who are home-bound or ill
Markers
Stickers

❑ *To do:*

Have the children color the blank side of the post card. Encourage them to make a picture that will send happy thoughts to someone who is ill or can't get around too well.
After coloring print a note on the card that it is from their friends at church to brighten their day. Add the addresses and postage. If possible walk to the mailbox as a class to mail the cards.

Plenty of Potato Ideas   😊 ALL

Celebrate the blessing of a great harvest with the following some old, some new, "hot potato," ideas.

Growing Sweet Potato

❑ *You will need:*

Sweet potatoes
Tooth picks
Glass jar (big enough for the potato to sit in)
Water

❑ *To do:*

Place four pairs of toothpicks spaced evenly around the center of the potato. Put the potato in a jar filled about 3/4 full of water. The toothpicks will hold the potato in place. Add water when necessary. Within a few days roots will sprout from the lower part of the potato and leaves from the top.

Potato Beads

Children will enjoy wearing harvest necklaces made with potato beads that they help to create.

❑ *You will need:*

Potatoes
Bamboo wooden skewers
Block of Styrofoam or a jar to hold the skewers during the drying process

❑ *To do:*

Peel several potatoes and cut them into 1"-2" chunks. Leaving lots of space between potato chunks, stick them on wooden skewers to dry. While drying, place the skewers in a short jar or stick them into a block of Styrofoam so that air can circulate all around the potato beads. Twist the potatoes on the skewer once in a while so that they stay loose. It will take about a week for the potatoes to dry rock hard. After the potatoes have dried, have the children paint them with acrylic paints. String the beads with yarn or ribbon. For added interest uncooked macaroni pasta or plastic beads may be alternated with the potato beads.

Potato Prayer

Teach the children this finger-play prayer.

❑ *You will need:*

An uncooked potato

❑ *To do:*

To make a potato have the children make a fist tucking their thumbs inside their palms.

One potato, two potato, planted in the ground,

Three potato, four potato sunshine all around.

Five potato, six potato a part of God's great plan,

Seven potato, eight potato harvested from the land.

Nine potato, ten potato with thankful hearts we pray,

For God's blessings are received, each and every day.

As you say the poem have the children lightly pound their fists on top of the fist of another.

❑ *More to do:*

Teach the prayer to the children as they pass a real potato around a circle of children. Whoever is left holding the potato at the end of the finger play is invited to sit in the middle of the circle. The prayer is repeated as many times as the children seem interested, changing who sits in the middle at the end of each recitation.

Potato Printing

Make harvest place mats

❑ *You will need:*

Potatoes

Pairing knife

Tempera paint

12" x 18" sheets of construction paper

Clear contact (optional)

❑ *To do:*

Cut the potatoes in half. On each half carefully carve out a circle, star, triangle, apple shape, etc. Dip the ends of the potato into the tempera paint and print on the construction paper. After drying, cover with clear contact to extend its life on the table.

Vegetable Potato Heads

❑ *You will need:*

Potatoes
Carrots
Celery
Parsley
Radishes
Tooth picks

❑ *To do:*

Slice and cut the vegetables so that they can be used to make real "Mr. Potato Heads." Have the children push the vegetables into the potato with toothpicks to make facial features and hair on the potato.

Prayer Charms   ☺ ALL

Bracelets, necklaces, and charms all tell a story or have special meaning in someone's life, a meaning that is precious to the owner and to those who love them. This Lent, use any of these charm ideas to put meaning, story, and prayer into the lives of young ones.

Picture charm

❑ *To do:*

Cut out a picture of each child's face to the size a little larger than a quarter. Cut out a piece of clear vinyl the same size. Place the vinyl cutout over the face cutout. Take a 12" x 12" square of aluminum foil and keep folding it down to a 3" x 3" square. Place the picture and vinyl onto the foil square. Roll the edges of the foil toward the center forming a foil frame around the picture and holding it in place. Use a heavy object to flatten the foil edge. Punch a hole at the top of the frame so it can be strung. String the entire class onto a

long cord. At the start of each day give each child a classmate's charm to wear or keep in his or her pocket. Invite the children to pray for their classmate throughout the day. At the end of the day gather the charms together and pray for the class as a group.

Juice can lid charms

❑ *To do:*

Use a nail and hammer to punch a hole through a juice can lid. Be sure to hammer down any rough places the nail may have caused on the backside of the lid. Place a sticker of Jesus on one side of the lid and a photo of the child on the opposite side. Thread a piece of cording or leather through the hole and tie the lid to the child's backpack, belt loop etc. Remind the child that Jesus walks with us throughout life.

Pipe cleaner charm chain

❏ **To do:**

Bend a red pipe cleaner into a heart shape. Invite the child to pray for all those people in his or her heart. Later interlink a yellow pipe cleaner through the heart and bend it into a triangle shape. Invite the child to identify three people (a person for each point of the triangle) in his or her life and pray for each of them. At a later gathering, add a green pipe cleaner bent into a square. Use this shape to invite the child to pray in thanksgiving for four blessings in his or her life.

Beaded charm pin

❏ **To do:**

This season make a beaded charm by opening a large safety pin and placing a blue clear-barreled bead, a red clear heart-barreled bead and a green clear-barreled bead on it. Pin the beaded charm to a child's shoelace as you talk about how much God loves (heart bead) each one of us and surrounds us with life in the water (blue bead) and on the land (green bead).

Prayer Cloth ☺ ALL

Make a cloth for your prayer table.

❏ **You will need:**

White sheet
Fabric paint
Pie tins

❏ **To do:**

Wash and dry the sheet. Lay it flat on a large table. Pour the paint in a pie tin. Have the children press their hands in the paint to make a hand print on the sheet. With permanent marker write each child's name by her or his hand. Hang the cloth over the table and enjoy it all year.

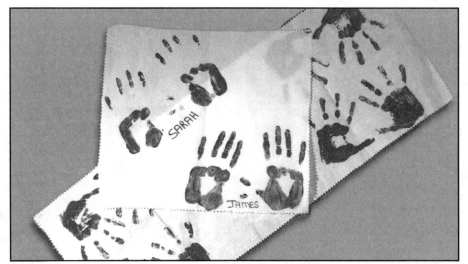

P

Prayer Rock 🖐 PRI

This little prayer rock is a great reminder to pray. Have the children make them to take home and share.

> I'm a little prayer rock,
> And this is what I'll do:
> Put me on your pillow,
> Until the day is through.
> Then turn back the covers,
> And climb into bed;
> Whack! Your little prayer rock,
> Will hit you in the head!
> You will then remember
> To fold your hands in prayer.
> Ask that God will bless you,
> And keep you in God's care.
> (Author unknown)

❑ *You will need:*

> 8" squares of cloth
> 1" x 2" rocks found on a nature walk
> Ribbon
> Copies of the prayer rock poem printed on card stock

❑ *To do:*

Take the children on a rock hunt. Tell them that that they are looking for a very special rock about 1"-2" wide. After everyone finds his rock have the children wrap their rock in a piece of fabric. Gather the edges and tie with a ribbon. Attach the prayer rock poem. Be sure to read the poem together a couple of times and discuss the importance of daily prayer.

Prayer Rug ☺ ALL

Make a little prayer rug to kneel on by the side of the bed.

❑ *You will need:*

> Carpet samples (can be purchased for about a dollar from a carpet store)
> Fabric paint
> Heart stencil
> Brushes

❑ *To do:*

Have the children decorate the rug by painting on it. With adult help print, "(Child's name)'s Prayer Rug. Dry completely before sending home.

Pretzel Log   ☺ ALL

A fun snack for any day

Make pretzel logs with the children for a special snack on an ordinary day.

❑ *You will need:*

Pretzel logs

Almond bark

Microwave

Cooking bowl and spoon

Cookie sugars

Wax paper

❑ *To do:*

Melt the almond bark in the microwave. Have the children dip the end of their pretzel in the melted bark and then in a bowl of cookie sugars. Place on a piece of wax paper to cool and harden.

Pretzel Prayer Chain   ☺ ALL

In old Germany, prayer was done with arms folded across a person's chest. That is why we use a pretzel as a reminder of praying arms.

❑ *You will need:*

Mini knot pretzels

❑ *To do:*

Gather the children in a circle. Snack on pretzels while demonstrating how a pretzel is like folded arms. When the children are finished with their pretzel snack, invite them to cross their arms and join hands with the child next to them. Take turns calling out a person the children are thankful for. After everyone has mentioned a person, close the prayer with a statement similar to the one below, while a hand squeeze is passed around the circle. This may take some patience but with practice it will get easier.

We fold our arms in prayer to thank you
for all these people we've heard of today.
Thank you, God!

❑ *More to do:*

As a follow-up activity make cards for the people the children called out to be thankful for. Preprint the phrase "Today we folded our arms in prayer for you" onto copy paper. Fold the sheets in half to make a card. Invite the children to draw a self-portrait of their face on the outside of the card. Then provide each child with a large pretzel to glue below her face, forming praying arms. Encourage the children to hand deliver their cards.

Pretzel Wreath   ☺ ALL

Make a pretzel wreath for the Christmas tree
or as a prayer reminder during Lent.

❑ *You will need:*
   Small pretzel twists
   Clear drying glue
   Ribbon
   Wax paper
   Fishing line

❑ *To do:*
Lay at least 6 pretzels in a circle on a piece of wax paper. Use generous amounts of glue to secure
the pretzels together. Allow to dry overnight. Gently remove the wax paper from the pretzels.
Lace the ribbon around the wreath through the holes of the pretzels and tie a bow at the top.
String the fishing line through a top hole for hanging. Hint: make a few extra wreaths, as they
can be a bit fragile when handling.

Psalms-a-Day   ☺ ALL

Introduce psalms, songs of praise written to God, with a psalm-a-day and corresponding booklet.
The children learn a new psalm each day and then do a page in a little booklet to take home.

❑ *You will need:*
   Construction paper
   Markers
   Glue
   Ribbon
   Paper punch
   Glitter
   Stickers
   Doilies
   Magazines
   Copy paper

❑ *To do:*
Gather the children and recite each psalm asking
them to repeat it back to you. Discuss the
meaning of the psalm and work on the
corresponding page in the book.
Print each psalm-a-day across the top of a
separate sheet of paper. Make a copy of each for every child. Each day of the week the children
will hear a new psalm and will make a new picture in the book to go with it. After all of the
pages have been done, put them together. Punch three holes along the left side of the book and
tie ribbons through them to hold it together.

Day 1 Psalm 139:14 "I give you thanks that I am wonderfully made."
Have them color a picture of themselves. Encourage them to add arms and legs, etc. and maybe a drawing of something they like to do or are good at.

Day 2 Psalm 104 "Lord you have made so many wonderful things."
On this page have the children glue leaves, twigs, flowers found on a nature walk to discover the wonderful things God has made.

Day 3 Psalm 147 "God knows the number of stars. He calls them by name."
Cut, color, and glitter paper stars for this page in the book.

Day 4 Psalm 136 "God's love will never end."
Cut out red hearts of many different sizes and decorate them with doilies for page 4.

Day 5 Psalm 100 "Praise God with harp and flute … Come before God with happy songs."
Cut out magazine pictures of instruments for page 5 or attach a small jingle bell to the page with a drawing done by the child.

Pumpkin Poem   🐻 PRE

Younger children will love acting out this rhyme during harvest time. Encourage the children to be creative with their actions. Listed below is one option.

❏ *To do:*
Pumpkin, pumpkin, orange and round.
   (Extend arms out in front, joining hands to make a circle.)
Started as a tiny seed in the ground.
   (Squat down and curl up)
God sent the sun and rain to help you grow,
   (Stand and extend arms over head, joining hands to make a sun.
    Bring arms down and make sprinkling motions with fingers.)
Oh! In the fall we love you so!
   (Arms crossed over chest)

Punched Star Ornament ☺ ALL

A shiny Christmas star for the tree.

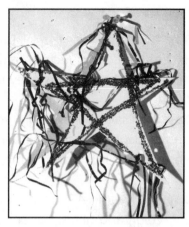

❑ *You will need:*
  Poster board
  Ribbon
  Shredded Mylar (used to stuff gift bags)
  Glitter
  Glue

❑ *To do:*

Enlarge and trace the star pattern provided. Decorate with glitter. Punch a hole in each point of the star. Thread ribbon or shredded Mylar through the holes. Thread a ribbon through the top hole for hanging.

Puzzle Collection ☺ ALL

A service project for the seniors of your community.
Many senior programs have puzzle-lending libraries and are always in need of adult puzzles.

❑ *To do:*

Plan a collection of puzzles for your area center. Always check with the center before you plan anything.

As the holidays approach, have the children collect puzzles. Puzzles are educational and because you are asking for a specific item you may get a better response.

Q-Tip Cross 😃 PRE

A simple little cross to use on cards or pictures during the Lent and the Easter seasons.

❑ *You will need:*
2 Q-tips
Ribbon
Construction paper

❑ *To do:*
Tie the two Q-tips together and tie a bow on top. Glue the cross to the front of an Easter card or picture.

Quack Quack Praise Rhyme 😃 PRE

Have fun acting out this silly rhyme and praise God at the same time.

Quack, quack says the duck,
As he paddles all around.
Singing praises to God,
What a lovely sound.
Croak, croak says the frog,
As he jumps all around.
Singing praises to God,
What a lovely sound.
Tweet, tweet says the bird,
As he flies all around.
Singing praises to God
What a lovely sound.
Bubble, bubble says the fish
As he swims all around
Singing praises to God
What a lovely sound!
Nothing says the worm
As he squirms through the ground
Singing praises to God
What a lovely sound.

Q

Share this fun praise rhyme with your children and make a paper bag puppet to go with each animal. Enlarge, color, and cut out the animal patterns below. Glue to the bag and enjoy the fun.

❑ *You will need:*
Paper lunch bags
Construction paper
Glue
Scissors
Markers or crayons

❑ *To do:*
Enlarge and copy the animals provided. Have the children color them and then cut them out. Glue to the bag and make them sing.

Quest for Peter's Faith    PRI

Jesus reached out to Peter in his search for faith. Recall the event with this creative project.

❑ *You will need:*
A paper plate with two 1/2" slits
Markers
Glue
Small construction paper boat and sail
Craft sticks

❑ *To do:*
Have the children color half of the paper plate blue, making
sure that they cover the slits.
Glue the craft stick to the back of the boat and sail. Draw eyes
and mouths on the craft sticks. Show the children how to use it to retell Peter's story.
Jesus asked the disciples to get into their boat and go to the other side of the lake, while he
prayed. In the morning Jesus decided to go to the disciples, walking on the water.
Peter wanted to go to Jesus. Jesus said, "Come to me, Peter."
The wind blew and Peter was afraid. Jesus reached out and helped Peter.
The disciples said to Jesus, "Truly you are God's son."

Question Box   ☺ ALL

"Who knows the answer? Just ask and we'll see. I'll help you and you help me."
Make a question box for reviewing ideas or concepts you have been working on. Place a box or
can in an accessible place so that whenever you have a couple of extra minutes, a child or teacher
can pull a question out of the box and answer it with the children.

❑ *You will need:*
Shoe or oatmeal box
Contact paper
Index cards for writing the questions on

❑ *To do:*
Cover the box and lid with contact paper. On the top or front write, "Our Question Box." Write
some general and specific questions on index cards for the box. Here are some suggestions.
Who always loves you?
Who is God's Son?
What is the name of God's Son?
Who made the world?
On what holiday do we celebrate Jesus' birthday?
What is Easter all about?
Whom are we supposed to share with?
When you are standing in line, eating a snack, or waiting for a transition of some kind, choose a
child to pick a card out of the box. The teacher reads the card, promotes the discussion, and puts
the card at the bottom of the pile in the box.

Quick Winter Fun   ☺ ALL

The children will be thrilled to find out that on cold days they can do winter activities inside.

❑ *You will need:*
    Paper plates
    Paper from the recycling bin

❑ *To do:*
Show the children how they may lie down and practice making snow angels. Give each child two paper plates and show him how to "ice skate" by gliding across the floor without lifting his feet. Crumble up paper and divide the children into groups. Standing several feet from one another, invite the children to have a snowball-catching game across the room.

Quiet Book   ☺ PRE

Not even a church mouse will hear.
Make a fabric Quiet Book (that doesn't make any noise when you turn the pages) with your little ones that they can read in church.

❑ *You will need:*
    Pelon or interfacing material (this works well because
      it can be drawn on with marker and it is somewhat stiff)
    Paper punch
    Ribbon
    Markers
    Felt
    Glue

❑ *To do:*
Suggestions for each page of the book will be given. The patterns can be traced and colored or cut from felt or other fabric and glued to the page. If you choose to use felt cutouts, recruit a volunteer to cut out the felt pieces ahead of time. So you and the children don't get overwhelmed with making the books, have extra help on hand or do one page a day for a week or two. If gluing, allow pages to dry separately overnight.

Below are suggestions for each page of the book. We suggest a page size of 8" by 10". Plan on about 8 to 10 pages per book. When the pages of the book are completed, put them together in order and punch three holes along the left side of the book. Lace ribbon or yarn through the holes to hold the books together.

On the front cover write, "(Name of child)'s Quiet Church Book."

Make a felt cutout of the church pattern provided. Glue to the cover. Write the name of your church on the church or somewhere else on the cover. Have the children draw flowers and a sun on next page also.

Page 1   My name is _____.
Glue a photo of the child on this page or have them draw a self-portrait. Mount the photo on a flower or heart felt cutout.

Page 2   I am (age of the child) years old.
Glue felt birthday candles to the page for the age of the child. These may also be drawn.

Page 3   I go to church with my family.
Draw the members of the child's family and write their names.

Page 4   At church I sing songs and praise God.
Glue felt cutouts or trace musical notes. Use the singing child pattern.

Page 5   When I pray I fold my hands.
Trace the child's hands with fingers together.

Page 6   I thank God for my family and friends.
Draw and color stick friends or use the cutout pattern for felt.

Page 7   I thank God for my warm home and food to eat.
Cut out a felt apple and a felt house.

Page 8   I ask God to be with me and keep me safe.
Use cutouts of the sun, stars, and moon or draw them for this page.

Page 9   When I go home, I will keep God in my heart.
A red felt heart or one traced for the children to color.

Quieting Ways   ☺ ALL

Help children relax and refocus their energy with these easy ideas.

❏ *To do:*

Tell the children that you will be explaining their next activity but they must listen very carefully or they will not hear you. Then speak very softly, moving around the room giving the children the instruction to move to another spot, being as quiet as they possibly can.

Agree on a class signal for quiet please. It might be thumbs up. Change the signal often to keep the children on their toes.

Sing the instruction. The worse you sing, the better they will listen. Pick a tune such as "Mary had a little lamb" and change the words to fit your needs. Example, "Please put all your work away, work away, work away. Please put all your work away, we're on to something else."

Stop and stretch. Tell the children that it is SST, stop and stretch time. Give them several instructions such as: Stretch your arms to the sky, stretch your fingers out wide, Stretch your legs out front, bring your feet straight up, put your feet on the ground, hands in your lap and sit up tall.

Quilt of Families   ☺ ALL

Sharing our memories and gratitude for one another.

Thanksgiving or any time is a good time to reflect on the gifts of our families. Make a quilt wall mural with the fabric and faces of the children in your community.

❏ *You will need:*

Large wall space or bulletin board.
Construction paper
8" x 8" squares or fabric brought in by the children from home.
A photo or drawing of each child's family
Pinking shears or decorative-edged scissors
Yarn
Glue markers
Stapler

❏ *To do:*

Send a note home to parents explaining your quilt project. Ask them to send in a family picture and a piece of fabric that has some history for them such as a child's costume, an old shirt, tablecloth, or curtain. Cut the fabric with pinking shears or decorative-edge scissors into 8" squares. Staple the family picture and an explanation or story about the fabric to the square. Arrange the squares in rows on a large wall or bulletin board.

With large letter cutouts title the quilt, "Our Patchwork Quilt of Families."

❑ *More to do:*
Make a Thanksgiving Quilt by having the children decorate squares of paper with things they are thankful for. Suggestions: drawings of families and friends, magazine pictures of foods, clothing, etc., paper cutouts of the sun, moon and stars.
Tie the pictures together to make a paper quilt. Punch a hole in each corner of each piece of paper. Tie the squares together with yarn to make a neat quilt to hang and enjoy.

Quotes From the Bible That Are Great for Children ✋ PRI
Always be on the lookout for great quotes to incorporate into your day, art, and discussions. Here are a few to get you started. Keep a notebook handy to jot them down when you see them.

❑ *To use:*
"Let the children come to me"… Jesus took them in his arms and blessed them.
– Mark 10:14

"Lord, you have examined me and you know me. You know everything I do; from far away you understand all my thoughts. You see me whether I am working or resting; and you know all my actions. Even before I speak, you already know what I will say. You are all around me on every side; you protect me with your power."
– Psalm 139:1-5

"As I have loved you, love one another."
– John 13:34

"Give thanks to the Lord God, because He is good; His love is eternal!"
– Psalm 107:1

"God satisfies the thirsty and the hungry are filled with good things."
– Psalm 107:9

Q

List Your Favorite Projects Here

_____

_____

_____

_____

_____

_____

_____

_____

_____

_____

_____

_____

_____

_____

_____

_____

_____

_____

_____

_____

_____

Rabbit 　　　😈 PRE

This cute little rabbit is made with paper plates and will be a favorite for years to come.

❑ *You will need:*

Small white paper plates
Large white paper plates
Metal paper fasteners
Black paintbrush bristles
Movable eyes
Construction paper
Stapler
Ribbon
Paper punch
Cotton balls
Glue

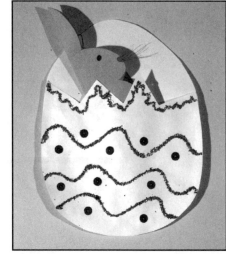

❑ *To do:*

Staple the smaller plate to the top of the larger plate. Cut another small plate in half to make the ears. Line up the ears on the head and punch a hole into the two plates and add the paper fastener. Do the same for the other ear. Glue movable eyes and a construction paper mouth to the face. Slip a few paintbrush bristles behind the cutout for the nose.
Tie the ribbon in a bow and glue under the rabbit's chin. To finish, glue a cotton ball to the back.

Rabbit and the Egg 　　　😊 ALL

Warm hearts and celebrate new life with this fun Easter card. The rabbit holds a greeting and fits into the egg of this old favorite. What a wonderful way to spread the Good News of new life at Easter.

❑ *You will need:*

White and pastel colored construction paper
Scissors
Glue
Cotton balls
Sequins
Glitter
Markers

❏ *To do:*
Enlarge the whole egg pattern so that it will fit on an 8" x 11" piece of white construction paper. Size the cracked egg so that it fits on the bottom of the whole egg. Glue the cracked egg to the bottom of the whole egg. Decorate the egg with glitter and sequins. Do not glue the top of the cracked egg so that the bunny will have an opening to fit into. Trace the rabbit and cut it out of pastel colored construction paper. Glue a cotton ball to the back of the bunny and add eye, nose, and whiskers to the face. With adult help have the children write an Easter message to the rabbit. Put the rabbit in the egg.

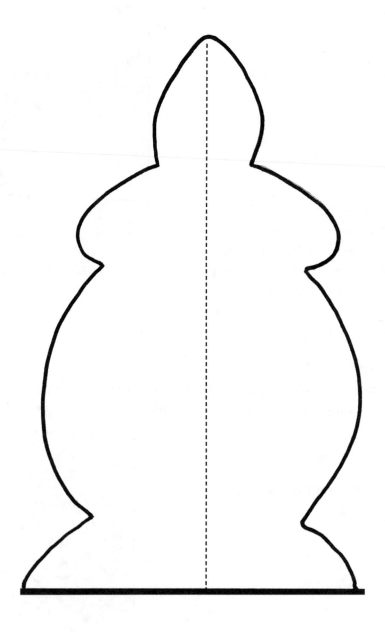

Rain Stick 😊 ALL

Add rain sticks to your rhythm band instruments or make them for each child to take home.

❏ *You will need:*
  Aluminum foil
  Pringles® can with cover
  Wrapping or contact paper
  Beans
  Masking tape

❏ *To do:*
Crinkle a piece of foil the length of the can and place it in the can with a handful of beans. Put the cover on the can and tape in place with masking tape. Cover the can with wrapping or contact paper.

Rain Wash Away 🐼 PRE

In some parts of the country rain is a welcomed sight because it serves to wash away the dust and sand that has accumulated over the winter. Use this activity to show the cleansing properties of the April showers.

❏ *You will need:*
  Large sheet of clear vinyl
  Clean empty 5-quart size ice cream bucket
  Fresh mud and rain in the forecast.

❏ *To do:*
Dig up some fresh mud and place in the empty bucket. Lay out the clear vinyl onto the floor. Scoop up some mud onto the vinyl and invite children to make a picture by spreading the mud with their fingers and hands. Give the mud painting time to set before moving the creation to be displayed. The next rainy day, hang the vinyl sheet onto an outdoor clothesline. Watch from an indoor window as the rain washes away the mud.

Rainy Day Art 😊 ALL

Use the rain to help create a rainbow or colorful designs.

❏ *You will need:*
  Chinet® paper plates
  (heavier paper plates that are not waxed on top)
  Water color markers
  A rainy day

❏ *To do:*
On a rainy day have the children draw a neat design on the paper plate. Have the children step outside the door and hold their plate in the rain. As the water hits the picture on the plate, the colors will run and make a fun design. After the plate has dried, print "A rain creation made with help from (name of the child)."

Rainy Day Tubes for God's Good News ☺ ALL

The children will look forward to bringing home bright messages on rainy days with this dry rainy day tube.

❑ **You will need:**

Cardboard tubes
Foil
Plastic wrap
Blue shelving paper
Permanent marker

❑ **To do:**

Help the children cover a cardboard tube with blue shelving paper. Cut out foil raindrops and glue them on the covered cardboard tubes. Use the permanent marker to print the name of the child and "Rainy Day News." On a day that it rains have the children roll up their papers and slip them into the decorated tubes to take home. Be sure to include a copied prayer or words of encouragement such as "God loves you!" Encourage the children to bring the tubes back to use again on the next rainy day.

Read-In Bible Stories ☺ ALL

Choose a week or month to concentrate on stories from the Bible. The children will love having new people or a person they don't usually see telling stories.

❑ **You will need:**

Weekly schedule

❑ **To do:**

Set some time aside in your schedule to have guest storytellers come in to tell their favorite Bible story. Talk to your pastor, custodian, day school teachers, directors, volunteers, and parents. Line up several people from your community to come in to share their favorite Bible story. As you schedule people, let them know that they have about ten minutes to tell the story. They may use props, costumes, picture books, or puppets. Keep track of the stories people want to tell so that you don't get the same one over and over.

Read the Room for God's Blessings   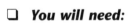 PRE

Set up a station during free time that encourages the children, with glasses and pointer, to check out the blessings of God in their classroom. Early readers in your group will really enjoy this.

❑ *You will need:*

Glasses that are minus the lenses
  (cheap sunglasses with or without the lenses would work fine, too)
A clipboard
Plastic pointer or rhythm stick
Lab coat

❑ *To do:*

Set up a center that has the glasses, clip board, pointer, and lab coat. Tell the children that during free time they have an opportunity to put on the glasses and lab coat and look for signs of God's blessings throughout the room. As they find the blessings they can point to them and pretend they are checking them off the list on their clipboard. Take time now and then to discuss the blessings that surround you in your classroom.

Reflecting God's Love   ALL

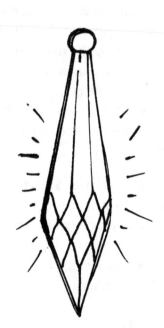

To say:

A blessing for teachers and a meeting theme.
God, Creator of heaven and earth
May your sun shine down on these teachers,
May they be rays of your love for each child,
May they warm their rooms with patience and understanding,
May your light give them guidance and energy,
And may they be a bright reflection of you.
Amen.

❑ *You will need:*

Prisms

❑ *To do:*

Use the theme "Reflecting God's Love" for one of your meetings. Reflect with the teachers on how the rays of the sun come through a prism to make the colors of the rainbow. Compare this to the children experiencing God through their teachers, parents, and friends. Not only do they hear the word; they see it in action. Our example is that action. Talk about the ways we reflect God's love at home, school, and church. During your discussions pass around a couple of prisms of different sizes and shapes. You might find these in the science department of your school or a specialty store.

Reflective Retreat Minutes ☺ ALL

These simple ideas should work any moment when a pause or reflection may be needed. Little preparation and few materials are required to provide these retreat minutes.

Daydream

❑ *To do:*

Provide a quiet time in a busy world for the children to simply daydream. This can be done standing, lying down, or just plain sitting on the floor. Daydreaming can be just the quiet time needed to hear God in our lives. Encourage the children to just let their thoughts wander wherever they may. Establish the time and environment that will allow very few distractions. Following the quiet period provide the children with crayons and paper to draw whatever came to mind. If the children are willing to share their drawings, encourage the conversation by asking, "What did you hear God say?"

Fit together

No one has it all together, but together in Christ we have it all.

❑ *You will need:*

Large floor size puzzle

❑ *To do:*

Hand out the large pieces of a floor puzzle to the children. Ask the children to sit quietly while holding the puzzle in their hands. Invite the children to close their eyes and think about all the people they are connected to. Remind them that God has given these people to us. After a few moments of quiet meditation, call the children to quietly fit their puzzle pieces together. While they are connecting the pieces to form the picture, discuss how we can live as Christ taught us, to love one another. Living the way Jesus taught us can lead us to a happy life.

Little Visits

❑ *You will need:*

Headset
Meditative music
Beanbag chair

❑ *To do:*

Set up a station in the room where children can go to sit with a headset playing soft gentle meditative music. Provide a comfortable beanbag chair for the sitting area. When the area is available for use display a sign that reads "Visiting God."

Bring God to light

❑ *You will need:*
Candle

❑ *To do:*
Invite the children, well supervised, to sit around a lit candle. As the children watch the flame, encourage the children to think about ways God is in their lives. When and where is God the brightest? Allow time for quiet meditation and a chance for the Spirit to work.
(Note: As a matter of safety, the flame of the candle should never be exposed around the children. Using a jar type candle keeps the flame from being out in the open. If you are a person who is not comfortable using a flame around young children a flashlight can be substituted for the candle.)

Reindeer   PRE

Trace the foot and handprints of the children to make a holiday reindeer.

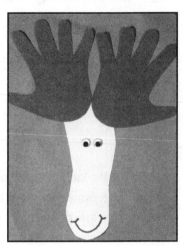

❑ *You will need:*
Construction paper
Glue
Markers
Scissors

❑ *To do:*
Trace the shoe and two handprints of each child. Cut them out and glue the handprints to the top of the foot for antlers. Add facial features and the reindeer is complete.

Relish Dish of Faith   PRI

Start a discussion with the children on how to add spice and variety to life with a relish tray of ideas.

❑ *You will need:*
 A condiment or relish tray
(To make one, staple several small boxes together.)

❑ *To do:*
In each section of the tray place pictures of happy, positive things like flowers, praying hands, a heart, sweet treats, a telephone, greeting card, someone getting a hug etc.
Explain to the children that a relish tray is something that holds a variety of items we may use to spice up our food. Relishes make our food taste better. Talk about ketchup, mustard, and pickles, etc. As Christians we are asked by God to spice up or brighten up the lives of people around us. We are called to do this every day with our families and friends. Challenge the children to think about ways you can spice up or brighten up the days of those around us. Examples include, saying please and thank you, giving someone a flower or a hug, drawing a picture, sharing a treat. From time to time have the children pull a picture from the relish tray and ask them to share the idea illustrated in the picture.

Remembering Table for All Soul's Day 😊 ALL

Explain that on All Soul's Day we remember those people who loved and served God during their lifetimes. Invite the children to bring pictures or small reminders of people they knew that they would like to remember and place it on the class-remembering table.

❏ *You will need:*

A small table near your prayer area

A cloth to put over it

A sign that says "Remembering table"

❏ *To do:*

After talking with the children about All Soul's Day invite each child to bring a picture or small reminder such as a book or favorite music of the person he or she would like to have remembered on All Soul's Day. On the feast day, say a prayer of thanksgiving for each of the people represented on the table and ask God to help us be like them in the way that they loved and served God.

Resurrection Movement 😊 PRE

Help the children to truly celebrate that Jesus is alive with this fun activity.

❏ *To do:*

Jesus died and was buried in a cave.

Squat down and wrap arms around self.

A giant rock was rolled in from of the cave.

Pretend to push very hard with both hands.

Friends were very sad that he was dead.

Make a very sad face.

On the third day, something happened—

Show three fingers

An earthquake rocked the earth.

Stomp feet and wave arms.

Mary and her friends went to the cave.

Walk in place

The stone was gone. They looked in.

Look inside with hand over eyes

A glowing angel was inside.

Shield eyes from the brightness

The angel said Jesus is alive!

Jump up and down, wave arms, and cheer.

Rock Garden  ☺ ALL

This project is a great way to see the beauty in all of God's creation, even in rocks.

❑ *You will need:*

Metal or aluminum pie tin
Small rocks
Glue
Sand

❑ *To do:*

Have the children collect a variety of rocks. Discuss the rocks with the children. Which is their favorite? Talk about the fact that even though they are all rocks, they are different colors, sizes, and shapes. Cover the bottom of the pie tin with sand. Have the children design a small rock garden in the pie tin with the rocks they found. They may glue them together. Encourage them to be creative.

❑ *More to do:*

Allow the children to use other things from nature in their gardens such as twigs. Open your craft closet and let them use a bit of glitter or some sequins.

Rubber Stamping ☺ ALL

Preschool and primary age children love to stamp. As you plan your curriculum throughout the year, provide many opportunities for the children to stamp. We hope the following ideas will help.

❑ *You will need:*

Seasonal rubber-stamps
Ink pads
Plenty of paper to stamp! Brown or white lunch bags, blank paper cut to sizes appropriate for note cards or gift tags, recipe cards, paper on rolls to use as wrapping paper, etc.
Markers
Glitter

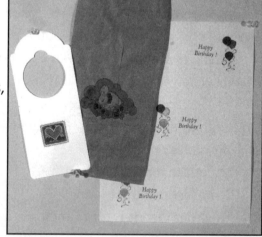

❑ *To do:*

Stamped note cards or gift tags make sweet and useful gifts for parents and volunteers. Make little gift packs tied with a bow to give to nursing home residents or shut-ins.
Whenever the children make gifts, have them stamp their own wrapping paper or gift bags. Stamp large paper grocery bags for the local food pantry or shelf. Make a party table cloth by covering the table you will be using with paper from a roll or a paper tablecloth. Have the children work together to stamp the tablecloth. If they will be attending the party, have the children decorate their own spot at the table. Lightly mark off the area with pencil and write the child's name.

Rhythm Band   PRE

Make a joyful noise unto the Lord with a happy rhythm band.

❏ *You will need:*

Rhythm band instruments (instructions below)
Bells, sticks, sand blocks, triangles, tambourines, drums, shakers

❏ *To do:*

To begin have the children sit in a circle. Tell them that when they are given their instrument, it is
to stay on the floor in front of them until it is their turn to play. Their hands must be in their laps
until it is their turn. Practice the song you will be using without the instruments. Then
demonstrate how each child should play his or her instrument and when.
Make up little songs that give every child a turn at playing an instrument. Here are a couple of
examples.

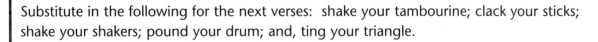

To the tune of "If You're Happy and You Know It."
If you're happy and you know it ring your bells.
If you're happy and you know it ring your bells.
If you're happy and you know then your heart will surely show it,
If you're happy and you know it ring your bells.

Substitute in the following for the next verses: shake your tambourine; clack your sticks;
shake your shakers; pound your drum; and, ting your triangle.

To the tune of "Row, Row, Row Your Boat."
Ring, ring, ring your bells,
Making a joyful noise.
Happily singing to God above,
Making a joyful noise.

Again, substitute with the following lines: shake your tambourines; clack your sticks;
shake your shakers; clack your sticks; pound your drum; and, ting your triangles.

Tambourine

❏ *You will need:*

2 small paper plates
Jingle bells
Ribbon or yarn
Stapler
Paper punch
Dry beans
Stickers
Markers

❑ *To do:*

Have the children decorate the bottoms of both plates with stickers and drawings. Lay several beans on top of the first plate and then staple the second plate on top of it. Staple close together so that the beans don't fall out between the plates. Paper punch a few holes around the edge of the plates (through both of them). Lace a ribbon through the hanger on the jingle bells and then through the holes on the edge of the plate. Let the bells hang a bit loose so that they will ring when shaken.

Drum
❑ *You will need:*

    Empty oatmeal box with cover
    Construction paper
    Glue
    Stickers
    Markers
    Yarn or rope

❑ *To do:*

Cover the oatmeal box and top with contact or construction paper. To make a strap for the drum, punch 2 holes on opposite sides of the oatmeal box. Be sure to make the holes lower than where the box cover will fit over. Lace a 16" piece of yarn or rope through the holes so that the knots are on the inside of the box. Put the cover on the oatmeal box and if necessary wrap a piece of contact around the edge to hold it in place. Decorate with stickers or drawings.

Bells
❑ *You will need:*

    4 1/2" (or bigger) jingle bells
    1/4" pieces of elastic about 8" long

❑ *To do:*

String the bells onto the strips of elastic. Match the two ends of the elastic and tie a knot.

Sticks
❑ *You will need:*

    Dowels 1/2" - 3/4" wide
    Sand paper

❑ *To do:*

Cut the dowels into 12" lengths. Sand the ends and they are ready to go.

Shakers

❏ *You will need:*

Small paper cups
Beans
Masking tape
Stickers

❏ *To do:*

Put a few beans in the bottom of a paper cup. Put a second paper cup on top of the first and tape in place. Decorate with stickers.

Rhythm Ribbons 🐨 PRE

Make rhythm ribbons to enhance your programs, parades, and sing-a-longs throughout the year. Use the ribbons for prayer, music, and movement activities. Make them with the children in the fall for use all year long.

❏ *You will need:*

3/4" elastic or plastic bracelets purchased from a variety or party store
A variety of different colored ribbons
Scissors

❏ *To do:*

Cut 3 - 5 different colored ribbons of different lengths (12" - 24"). Cut the elastic in 8" lengths. Put the two ends of the elastic together and make a knot. Tie the ribbons to the elastic band leaving long tails that will flow through the air.

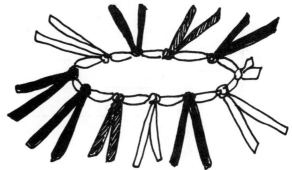

Rope Jumping ☺ ALL

An easy activity to use when things are jumping in your classroom.

❏ *You will need:*

An eight-foot rope

❏ *To do:*

Lay the rope in a straight line on the floor. Invite the children to jump back and forth over it. Jump forward, backward, sideways, and with a friend. Make different shapes, numbers, or letters and then jump through the various parts.

List Your Favorite Projects Here

Sachet   ☺ ALL

Make an easy sachet for Mom's drawers on
Mother's Day or any day.

❑ *You will need:*

    Nylon net

    Ribbon

    Potpourri

❑ *To do:*

Cut the netting into 8" circles. Put about 2 tablespoons of potpourri
in the center of the circle. Gather up the sides and tie a bow.

Safari Hat   🐨 PRE

This hat is made from a brown grocery bag and can easily be a safari hat, garden hat, or Easter
bonnet.

❑ *You will need:*

    Paper grocery bags

    Paints

    Stickers

❑ *To do:*

Open the bag. Beginning at the top of the bag, roll the edges down toward the bottom. Shape
and squeeze the paper as you go. Keep rolling until you are just about to the flat bottom of the
bag. Fold the square corners of the bottom of the bag down and tuck them into the final roll.
Use a piece of masking tape to hold in place if necessary. Decorate with paint and stickers.

Sailboat 🐷 PRE

These little boats are easy to make and a wonderful prop or reinforcement for the fishing and boating stories of Jesus.

❑ *You will need:*

Empty square juice boxes
Plastic drinking straw
Masking tape (colored if possible)
Stickers
Construction paper

❑ *To do:*

Wrap a piece of masking tape around the outside edge of the box. Try to cover the straw hole as you wrap the tape. Decorate the box with stickers. Enlarge and copy the sail pattern provided here and decorate with drawings or stickers. Punch a hole in the top and bottom of one side of the sail and slip the straw through it. Carefully punch a hole in the center of one side of the boat. Push the straw with the sail through it and you are ready to sail.

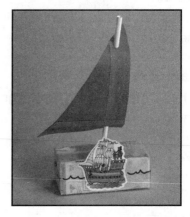

Saint Nicholas 😊 ALL

Observe the contributions of this most generous man by filling the shoes of the children and your staff with goodies on his feast day, December 6.

❑ *You will need:*

Paper cups
Shoe cutouts from pattern provided
Wrapped candy treats, prayer cards, inexpensive toys
Stapler

❑ *To do:*

Read a story about St. Nicholas and the very generous things he did for others. Tell the children how the tradition of filling shoes with goodies comes from St. Nicholas giving a poor man money to keep his daughters from becoming slaves. Nicholas left the money in the shoes of the children. Let the children know that in Holland the Dutch people leave their shoes out on December 6 for St. Nicholas to fill. Tell the children that you are going to make special shoes to leave outside your classroom door for St. Nicholas to fill.

❑ *More to do:*

Enlarge and copy the shoe pattern provided. Have the children color it and cut it out. Staple the shoe to the side of the paper cup. Leave the cups in a row outside your classroom door. Have a secret helper fill the shoes while you are busy in the classroom. Be prepared for lots of smiles and giggles when the children discover their shoes filled with goodies.

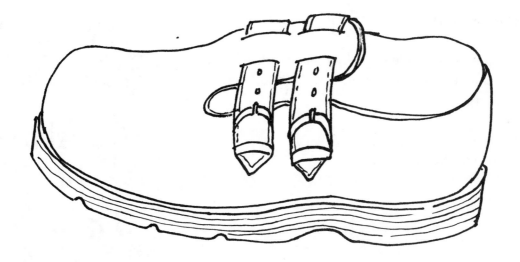

Saint Patrick's Shamrock ☺ ALL

St. Patrick was a missionary in Ireland. He used the clover or shamrock to describe the Trinity to the people he was ministering to. Make March 17 a green letter day with the following ideas.

You will need:
    Green construction paper
    Glue
    Green glitter
    Paper punch
    Scissors

To do:
Enlarge and copy the heart pattern provided. Cut out 3 hearts for each shamrock. Put the hearts together so that the bottom points overlap. Staple in place and glue to this a stem. Decorate the shamrock with glitter. Punch a hole in the top and lace a green ribbon through it for hanging.

More to do:
Serve green milk, celery, broccoli, and green mints for snack. With face paint put a green shamrock on everyone's face.

Sandwich Boards   🐨 PRE

Praise Parade Signs.

Next time you have a parade-of-praise make sandwich board signs for the children to wear to proclaim the good news of God's love for us.

❑ *You will need:*

    12" by 18" construction paper
    Yarn
    Paper punch
    Markers

❑ *To do:*

Print the message of the day on two pieces of construction paper. Examples would be, "The Light of the World Has Come," "Hosanna to Jesus," or "Give Thanks to the Lord for the Lord is Good." Have the children decorate their sandwich boards with drawings, stickers, or glitter. Punch two holes at the top of both posters. Lace yarn through the holes of both posters and tie a knot. Slip the sandwich board over the head of the child and you're ready to go.

Scarf   🙂 ALL

Children who live in all climates will enjoy spreading the message of "God's love keeps us warm," by making winter scarves.

❑ *You will need:*

    New or used thermal blanket or thermal fleece
    Fabric or permanent markers
    Scissors

❑ *To do:*

Talk with the children about how God's love for us warms our hearts. Cut the blanket into strips 6" wide x 30" long. With adult help have the children make fringes on both ends of the scarf.

With fabric or permanent markers write, "God's Love Keeps Me Warm," across the scarf. Decorate with drawings done by the children. Wear the scarf during circle time and talk about the ways God's love and the love of others warms their hearts.

Scavenger Hunt ☺ ALL

Plan a scavenger hunt for families during your beginning-of-the-year open house. Everyone will appreciate having the time and opportunity to make sure they know where things are.

❑ *You will need:*

Lists of places the children and their parents need to know.
Stickers

❑ *To do:*

Make a list of areas parents need to be familiar with. These might include rest rooms (inside and outside the classroom), kitchen area, specific places for coats, back packs, teacher notes, supplies, library, drop off and pick up areas, gymnasium, etc.

Make up a list of places you want families to visit during open house. If possible have a sticker or rubber stamp at each place so that the children can mark off the places they have been. Make it more interesting by providing a little prize for the families who complete the hunt by visiting all of the areas and turning in a completed chart.

Shake, Rattle, and Roll 🐻 PRE

Celebrate God's love with a bit of shaking, rattling, and rolling.

❑ *You will need:*

Empty margarine or Kool-Aid® canisters
Uncooked rice or pasta
Stickers
Permanent markers

❑ *To do:*

Make shaker canisters for children by pouring a small handful of uncooked pasta and/or rice into empty plastic margarine tubs or Kool-Aid canisters. These also may be decorated with stickers or permanent markers. To set up this circle prayer, pair off the children in twos. Place the pairs in a circle with the partners facing each other, as shown. Recite the phrases following these movements.

Jesus loves **me**,

(Children point to themselves on the word "me" and shake their canister.)

annnnd

(Pause.)

Jesus loves **you**.

(Children point to the person across from them on the word "you" and rattle their canister.)

Go tell a **friend**.

(The children move to a new partner by moving in the circle opposite the other circle, shaking their canisters, and stopping when the word "friend" is said.)

Continue to repeat this circle prayer until the children lose interest or have partnered with each child in the group.

Shell Charm or Pendant   ✋ PRI

Use shells to inspire prayer.

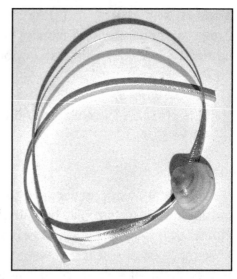

❑ *You will need:*
Medium to small sea shells
Barrel beads
Super glue
Cording

❑ *Adult preparation:*
Use super glue to attach a barrel bead to the inside or back of a shell. Let dry completely.

❑ *To do:*
Give the child a prepared shell and a piece of cording. The length of the cording depends on whether a bracelet or a necklace is to be made. Thread and pull the cording through the hole of the barrel bead.
Each week as the child adds a shell to the bracelet or necklace invite him to think about something he would like to pray for throughout the week.
For younger children, large holed buttons could be used in place of the shells and beads.

Shoe Blessing   ☺ ALL

Encourage the children as they go on their way with a different blessing every day. Use some of the blessing ideas here with the children as they come and go.

❑ *You will need:*
Heart-shaped bead
Twine

❑ *To do:*
Slip the twine through the bead and tie it to a lace on the top of the shoe closest to the toe. Be sure that the bead does not get in the way of walking. As you tie the heart to the shoe say, "May God bless you in all of your steps today" or "Walk with God."

❑ *More to do:*
Put a sticker or touch of glitter inside the shoe. With permanent marker write, "God bless," in the inside of the tongue of the shoe.

Shower Flowers ☺ ALL

On a rainy day when the children can't go out to play, make this mural for inside fun.

❏ *You will need:*

Water-filled spray bottle
Water color markers
Coffee filters
Butcher paper.

❏ *To do:*

Invite the children to color the coffee filters bright colors with the watercolor markers. Lay a sheet of butcher paper on the floor. Place the colored filters on the butcher paper. Encourage the children to lightly mist water on the colored filters so that the colors of the marker bleed onto the butcher paper mural. Lift the filter and colors from the filter should be left behind. When the colorful marks that remain have dried, turn them into flowers by adding green stems and leaves with a marker. Add a message before hanging this artistic display of spring shower flowers.

Sing and Follow ☺ ALL

This fun song will encourage children to follow Jesus.

❏ *To sing:*

Sing to the tune of the "Hokey Pokey" standing in a circle.

We put our right hands in.
(Right hand in the circle.)
We put our right hands out.
(Right hands out of the circle.)
We put our right hands in and we shake them all about.
(Right hands in the circle and shake.)
We want to follow Jesus so we turn ourselves around.
(Turn around with arms straight up.)
That's what it's all about.
(Hands at sides.)

Continue with left hand, right leg, left leg, head and whole self – just like the original song.

Smiley Face Sponge   ☺ ALL
The Yellow Smiley Face is Back!
Spread the love God has for us by making a Smiley Face sponge.

❑ **You will need:**
    Yellow kitchen sponges
    Black permanent markers

❑ **To do:**
Have the children draw happy faces on a dry yellow sponge. Use them as gifts or have the children give their smile to a special neighbor or friend.

Snow Peas   ☺ ALL
Plant new life on Good Friday.
Some European countries have a tradition of planting snow peas on Good Friday. These seeds are hardy enough to survive the cool spring weather and yet what hope and joy we receive from planting them on the most solemn of days in our Christian tradition.

You will need:
    Snow pea seeds
    3" clay flower pots
    Potting soil
    Pebbles
    Permanent markers
    Sticks
    Raffia

new life is planted here

To do:
If possible plant a few seeds outside on the grounds of your building. Be sure to provide something for the peas to eventually climb on and mark the planting area well. Make a sign that says, "New Life Is Planted Here." To plant in clay pots, add a few pebbles to the bottom of the pot and then potting soil. Fill to within about 1" from the top. Make a little hole with your finger; add a couple of seeds and then cover with dirt. Make a cross for the peas to climb on from sticks. Break off the sticks so that they are about 1/4" wide and one is 8" long and the other 5" long. Tie them together with raffia and put in the dirt. Again add a sign to the pot that says, "New Life Planted Here."

Snowflake Prayer PRE

Perfect for any winter day.

❑ **To say:**

Thank you, God, for winter fun.
And snowflakes from above.
Thank you, God, for sending me,
Your blessings and your love.
Amen.

Make a colorful snowflake to go with this prayer.

Thank you God for winter fun,
And snowflakes from above.
Thank you God for sending me,
Your blessings and your love.
Amen.

❑ **You will need:**

White paper
Water color paints
Iridescent glitter

❑ **To do:**

To make a snowflake, take a square sheet of paper. Fold one corner to the opposite corner to form a triangle. With the fold on the bottom, fold the triangle in half and fold in half again. Round the bottom of the triangle. Cut small shapes along edges and cut the tip of the triangle off. Open to reveal a snowflake!

Sparkle Star  ALL

A special star guided the Magi to Jesus. Remind children that each one of them can help direct others. They can be stars for people to follow by their actions.

❑ **You will need:**

Clear contact paper
Scissors
Star-shaped paper with child's name printed on it
Star glitter
Hole punch
Ribbon

❑ **To do:**

Cut two circles of clear contact paper a little larger than the star shaped paper. Peel away the protective cover from one circle of contact paper. Place the star on the sticky side of the contact. Lightly sprinkle star glitter around the paper star, on the exposed sticky contact. Peel away the protective cover of the other contact circle and use it to cover the star and glitter. Punch a hole in the contact paper to thread a yarn through. As you are helping children to make these sparkle stars, talk about the good actions people might witness this child doing.

❑ **More to do:**

Display these finished stars on a blue bulletin board titled "Follow the sparkling stars."

Spoon Puppets   😊 ALL

Spoon puppets are easy to make and so fun to use. Make wooden spoon puppets to become part of your permanent collection or use disposable ones for the children to take home.

- ❏ *You will need:*
    Wooden or disposable spoons
    Felt and fabric scraps
    Wiggly eyes
    Ribbon
    Scissors
    Glue
    Permanent markers

- ❏ *To do:*

Use the markers to make facial features. Older children will enjoy adding felt pieces and movable eyes also. Use the fabric scraps to make scarves, hats, shirts, etc. Just tie them around the spoon. Encourage the children to tell one another stories with the puppets they have made.

Spring Beaded Trees   ✋ PRI

Spring is the time trees radiate bright colored blossoms. Make these tree centerpieces to brighten any table.

- ❏ *You will need:*
    Barrel beads
    Brown chenille pipe cleaners
    Modeling clay

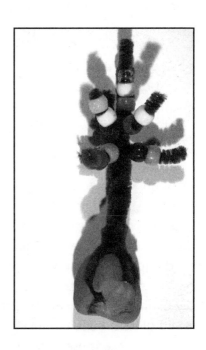

- ❏ *To do:*

Cut the brown pipe cleaners in half. Gather five halves and twist them together about a third of the way up from the bottom. Separate the pieces of the bottom third to form the roots of the tree. Separate the top half and shape the pipe cleaner pieces to look like tree branches. The trunk is formed where the pipe cleaners were twisted together. Slide a variety of bright colored barrel beads on the branches to look like the spring blossoms. If needed, shape the tree roots around a piece of modeling clay. This will help balance the weight of the beads.

- ❏ *More to do:*

Send home the tree with a spring blessing for families to keep at their dining table as a reminder of the blessings that surround our families.

Squirt Bottle Nature Walk   😺 PRE

When admiring all the beautiful gifts God has placed in the world, it can be difficult for young children to leave behind undisturbed the living creatures. Here is a simple solution to this all too common problem.

❑ *You will need:*
   Water filled squirt or misting bottle

❑ *To do:*

Before you and the children head out for an observation walk, talk about how important it is not to touch any living plants, animals, and insects. Instead of touching or taking the living life, invite the children to leave a drink of water with a small sprinkle from their bottle.

Squirt Paint Shirt   😊 ALL

This art idea will give children experience with seasonal symbols.

❑ *You will need:*
   Tee shirt
   Grocery bag
   Heart patterns cut from paper
   Eggs
   Butterflies
   Flowers
   Bugs
   Dove
   Cross or any other Easter symbols (next page)
   Bottled fabric paint
   Small squirt bottle
   Water

❑ *To do:*

Cut paper patterns of hearts, eggs, butterflies, flowers, bugs, dove, cross, or any other Easter symbols.

To prevent paint from soaking through to the back of the project, place a grocery bag inside the tee shirt to be painted. Lay the shirt out on a flat surface. Place paper patterns on the shirt. In a small spray bottle mix a solution of half water and half fabric paint. Mist a light coat of paint from the spray bottle onto the shirt over the patterns. Leave the patterns in place to allow the misted paint time to lightly dry. Remove the patterns and allow the shirt to dry completely before wearing.

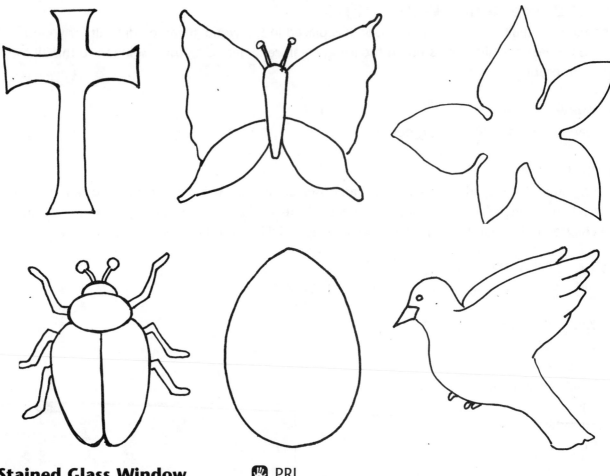

Stained Glass Window ✋ PRI

Use transparency paper to make stained glass windows for any holiday or season.

❏ *You will need:*
   Transparency paper
   Coloring book pictures
   Permanent markers

❏ *To do:*
Lay a piece of transparency film on top of a coloring book picture or clip art picture. Paperclip the corners so that it stays in place. Have the children color the picture that shows through on the transparency paper with permanent markers. (If possible run the transparency film through the copy machine to get uncolored pictures.) Tape the pictures on windows or punch a hole in the top for hanging.

❏ *More to do:*
Cut the transparency film into shaped ornaments, such as Christmas balls, trees, angels, Easter eggs, or rabbits. Have the children color them in and again hang on the window.

Star Lit Room  PRI

Children can count their blessings by awarding stars to those people in their lives who they feel are "heavenly." Light up a room with stars to represent these heavenly people.

❑ **You will need:**
    Stiff paper
    Scissors
    Markers

❑ **To do:**
To make a star trace a five-pointed star. Fold the star in half lengthwise and make a cut from the top point down as shown in diagram 1. Unfold the star and fold the triangle down on the shown dotted line in diagram 2, making a support for the freestanding star.

Provide a variety of colored stars cut out as described. Around the edge of the star, write to whom the star is awarded and the reason why. You may need to help younger children record this information. Display the stars all around the room with a sign that reads, "Stars awarded to heavenly people."

Star of Bethlehem 😊 ALL

A curly Christmas star.

❑ **You will need:**
    Heavy silver or gold paper (white tag will also work)
    5 silver or gold sparkly pipe cleaners
    Gold or silver curly ribbon
    Paper punch
    Pencil

❑ **To do:**
Enlarge, trace, and cut the star pattern provided. Punch a hole in the points of the star. Wrap the pipe cleaner around a pencil so that it is like a coil. Twist one end of the pipe cleaner to each hole in the star. String a piece of ribbon through the top hole to make a loop for hanging. Write, "Follow the Star," on the middle of the cutout.

317

S

Steps ☺ ALL

Keep in step with God. Try these stepping ideas to kick off the year or enhance a new unit. Make a movable staircase and bulletin board.

❑ *To say:*

One step, two step,
Red step, blue step.
With God's love we will go to the top,
With God's love we can't be stopped.
One step, two step,
Red step, blue step.
With God's love we will go far,
With God's love we can touch the stars.

❑ *You will need:*

Graduated sizes of cardboard boxes of all shapes
Wrapping paper
Construction paper
Magazine pictures of things that help us stay in step with God
Glue
Tape
Scissors

❑ *To do:*

Wrap the boxes with wrapping paper. On the sides of the boxes paste pictures the children have made, magazine pictures or words that illustrate the ways we stay in step with God. Have the children stack the boxes (no higher than the shortest child's shoulders) to make a staircase. Explain to the children that the steps are there to remind us of God's presence and love. They are symbolic or a physical reminder of God's love for us. Tell the children that they may stack the steps but not use them. Move the staircase around and rearrange the steps.

❑ *More to do:*

Cut out footprints of the children and the words, "Step by Step With God." Tape them to the floor or steps that you may have in your classroom. To hold the paper foot in place cut out a slightly larger piece of clear contact to cover it and fasten it to the floor. Make a staircase on the bulletin board with the name of each child on each step titled; "Step UP With God"

Sticker Tag   ☺ ALL

No matter what we do or where we go, God is always with us. We cannot hide from God's love for us. God is STUCK ON US. Play a game of sticker tag to convey the message.

❑ *You will need:*
   Stickers

❑ *To do:*
Invite the children to hide within a designated area. The teacher or a selected leader places a sticker on the children as they are located or found. The found children are given stickers and asked to help locate other hiding children. Once everyone is found and stickered, discuss how we cannot hide from God's love.

Stone Art   ☺ ALL

Rock'N'Roll Fun

On your next nature walk or trip to the playground have the children hunt for rocks for these little projects.

❑ *You will need:*
   Large smooth rocks
   Many smaller pebbles
   Glue
   Box covers
   Puffy paint

❑ *To do:*
Have the children wash and dry their rocks. With adult help have them write a God word on the rock: Hope, love joy, smile, etc. Add more painted decorations and dry.
Use the smaller pebbles to spell out the children's names on the inside of a box cover. Use generous amounts of clear drying glue and dry over night.

❑ *More to do:*
Spell out "Jesus" with the rocks in a box cover. Add other nature finds such as acorns, pinecones, and dried flowers to decorate.

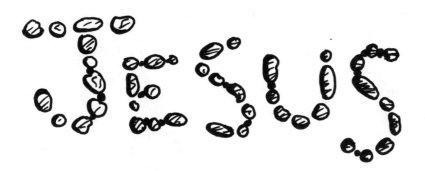

Stone Soup ☺ ALL

A timeless story and community-building activity.
Read the delightful story "Stone Soup" and plan a day to make soup with your class.

❏ *You will need:*
Crock-pot
Disposable spoons and bowls
Soup Recipe
1 cup carrots
1 cup celery
1cup onion
1 cup cubed potatoes
1 can of diced tomatoes
8 cups water
6 chicken or beef bouillon cubes
1 clean stone
Salt and pepper to taste
Combine in the pot and cook on high for 2 hours.

❏ *To do:*
Discuss working together and sharing with the children. Let them know that things usually go better when we cooperate and help one another out. Read the story, "Stone Soup." Talk about how the people in the story solved their problem. Take a nature walk and choose the perfect rock for your soup. Assign 1 ingredient of the soup for each person to bring. Work together to get the soup cooking and enjoy.
Here's a short summary in case you have trouble locating the story.
A poor man wandered into a village. He was very hungry but found nothing to eat. The people in the village were also poor and hungry. The man came up with a great idea to share with the village. He found a large pot in which he placed water and a large stone. The man invited each villager to add one item to the pot. The result was a wonderful, delicious pot of soup and no one went away hungry.

Story Smock ☺ PRE

A "wearable" story.
Use plastic table coverings to make the pictures to tell a story. The children wear the characters and make the story more interesting

❏ *You will need:*
Plastic table coverings
Scissors
Permanent markers

❑ *To do:*

Cut the table coverings into pieces about 12" wide by 36" long. Adjust to fit the size of the child.
Cut a hole in the middle to slip the child's head through, about 8" in diameter.
With permanent marker draw the characters or things that are part of the story you are telling to the front of the smock. For example, if you are telling the story of creation, draw a sun on one smock, water on another, etc. As you tell the story have the person with that character or scene stand up. Add movement and voice if necessary.

Story Wheel   😃 PRE

Telling the story without a book.
Make a story wheel for Bible stories you tell the children.

❑ *You will need:*

2 sheets of tag board
Scissors
Magazines
Glue
Metal paper fasteners
Metal washer (to put between the top of the fastener and the tag to
    make the wheel move more easily)

❑ *To do:*

Cut out two large matching circles from the tag board. Cut a 1/4 pie shape from one of the circles. Leave an inch of paper at the tip of the pie shape cut out so that there is room to poke the paper fastener through. Divide the whole circle into fourths. Use drawings, magazine pictures, symbols or clip art to tell the story. Glue these to the pie-shaped sections of the circle. Write the title of the story on the cutout circle and decorate. Line up the picture circle underneath the cutout one. Punch the paper fastener (with a metal washer under it) through the center of both circles. As you tell the story move the wheel to reveal the appropriate pictures.

❑ *More to do:*

Make mini story wheels out of paper plates for the children to take home.

String Art   ☺ ALL

Paint with a string to create a beautiful design.

❏ *You will need:*
Construction paper
Tempera paint
Heavy yarn or string
Pie tin

❏ *To do:*

Pour a small amount of paint in a pie tin. Wrap a piece of masking tape around one end of an 8"
piece of string. Using the taped end as a holder, run the yarn through the paint in the pie tin.
Carefully drag the string across construction paper to make fun designs. Provide more than one
string per pan of paint as well as a couple of different colors of paint.

❏ *More to do:*

Make waves for a sea scene by using blue paint only to make lines across the paper. After the
paint has dried glue paper cutouts of fish and other sea life to the picture. Follow the same plan
to make a sky or, with green lines going vertically, a field of grass.

Summer Survival Kit   ☺ ALL

For those fun summer outings with little ones.

Make up a backpack of items to take with you on your little summer outings. Whether you are
taking a walk around the block or a ride across town, you will find these things helpful.

❏ *You will need:*
Backpack
Disposable wet wipes
Band-Aids®
Sun screen
Bug repellent
Coins for a phone call
List of children's names, allergies and emergency phone numbers.
Packaged snacks just in case of a delay
Tissues

❏ *To do:*

Round up these items and pack them in a backpack. Be sure that this pack is kept together for
outings all year long.   An extra set of one size fits all clothes and a plastic bag may also be
helpful.

Sun Ball   PRI

Make a ball of sunshine to use with your creation, spring or summer time units. Send a ray of sunshine to someone special or someone who is blue.

❑ *You will need:*

Yellow nylon net

Yarn

Large plastic needle

Copy of the lyrics (below) to "You Are My Sunshine" on card stock.

You are my sunshine. My only sunshine.

You make me happy when skies are gray.

You'll never know dear how much I love you.

Please don't take my sunshine away.

Paper punch

❑ *To do:*

Nylon net may by purchased at fabric and craft stores. Cut the netting into strips that are 5" x 36". Lay two strips on top of each other on the table. Thread the needle with a 24" piece of yarn and tie a large knot at the end. Beginning at one end of the fabric, take big basting stitches down the middle, all the way to the end. You will be gathering the netting as you go. When the stitching is complete hold the two ends of yarn together and tie a tight knot. This will push the netting together into a tight ball. Trim the edges of the ball if it is uneven. Attach a copy of the song, "You Are My Sunshine," to the yarn on the ball. What a heart-warming gift for a grandparent.

❑ *More to do:*

Play a game similar to hot potato using the sun ball. Make a bunch of them to lay on the parachute and bounce around. Hide the sunshine in your classroom. The person who finds the sunshine gets to hide it for the next group.

Sunflower Pencil Top   🖐 PRI

Make a sunny summer pencil topper sure to bring a smile.

❏ *You will need:*
Unsharpened pencils
Green floral tape
Silk sunflowers
Twine
Card stock paper
Scissors

❏ *To do:*
Cut the stem of the flower so that it is about 3" long. Twist it around the top of a pencil.
Starting at the top of the pencil wrap the floral tape around the pencil and wire. Continue
wrapping until it is about an inch from the bottom of the pencil. Add a little note card that says,
"Sunny thoughts of you."

Talking Stick ☺ ALL

The talking stick comes from Native American tradition. The talking stick was passed from one person to another to indicate whose turn it was to talk. Only the person holding the stick could talk. When the stick was passed to you, you could keep it to talk or pass it to the next person if you didn't care to talk. Use the talking stick during gather times. What a great way to reinforce sharing, taking turns, and listening. Make one stick for your class or have the children make one for home. Be sure to send background information home.

❑ *You will need:*
Sticks 12" x 1/2"
Ribbon
Yarn
Feathers
Dried flowers
Bells

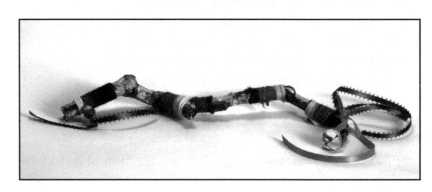

❑ *To do:*
Take a nature walk to find just the right sticks.   Decorate them with feathers, ribbon, yarn, dried flowers, and a jingle bell. Use the Talking Sticks during gather or snack time.

Teacher Care Package ☺ ALL

Beat the mid–season blahs with a little teacher survival kit.
Show appreciation to your teacher with these little survival kits. If possible make them with the children.

❑ *You will need:*
Zip lock sandwich bags
Hershey Hugs® and Kisses®
Small package of Lifesavers®
Band-Aid®
Wet wipe
Tea bag
Tissue
Gum
Jingle bell
Whistle (purchased from a party shop)

❑ **To do:**

Assemble the items for the bag and attach the following poem.

Thank you, teacher, for all the things you do each day,
You share your love and faith in God in oh so many ways.
With hugs and kisses we hope you know
Just how much we love you so.
Take these little treasures here,
So that you know we hold you dear.
A tissue for all the tears you make go away,
A band-aide for all of the bumps and bruises in a day.
A tea bag when you are able to take five,
A lifesaver for when you think you won't survive.
Wet wipes to clean up all the dirt and grime,
A piece of gum for all of those sticky times.
With bells and whistles and a great big shout,
You're the greatest teacher ever without a doubt.

Terrarium Garden   ☺ ALL

Make individual terrarium gardens for your creation or springtime units.

❑ **You will need:**
  One gallon milk jug
  Pebbles
  Potting soil
  Green or bedded plants
  Raffia
  Card stock with the following poem printed on it.

❑ **To do:**

Before planting with the children have staff cut out a 4" square panel on one side of the bottle. Have the children put pebbles in the terrarium first for drainage and then 2" – 3" of soil. Plant green or bedded plants such as, marigolds, petunias, or impatients. Add a bit of water. Place a couple of nature finds in the terrarium too. A rock, seashell, piece of drift wood, etc. would look great. Copy the little garden poem and attach it with raffia to the handle of the terrarium.

God bless the flowers,
God bless the trees.
God bless our garden,
And God bless me!

326

Thankful Cornucopias 🐨 PRE

Give the children visual reminders of things they are thankful for.

❑ *You will need:*

Brown construction paper
Yellow construction paper
Magazines
Glue

❑ *To do:*

Cut out a cornucopia for each child from the brown
construction paper. Collect a variety of small magazine
pictures that symbolize some of the things that the
children are thankful for. Have the children trace and cut
out their cornucopias. Then have them glue some of the
things they are thankful for on and around the open end of the cornucopia.

Thanksgiving Brown Bag Book 😊 ALL

Make Thanksgiving brown bag books to tell the story of the many things in our lives we have to
be grateful for. Each page of the book is a bag that holds pictures or symbols or the specific
things we are thankful for.

❑ *You will need:*

3 to 4 brown lunch bags per child
Yarn or ribbon
Stickers
Magazine pictures
If possible, photos of family, class, individuals
Construction paper
Scissors
Glue
Markers
Labels from soup cans, cereal boxes, etc.
Blue Mylar strips
Bean seeds

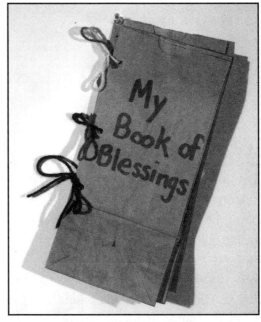

❑ *To do:*

Schedule extra help to prepare the bags for the children. Line up 3 to 4 brown lunch bags with
the open end up and folded bottom down. Punch 3 holes along the left side of the bags. Lace
ribbon or yarn through each set of holes and tie. Leave the ties loose enough so that the bags
can turn like pages in a book. On the first bag print, "My Book of Thanksgiving Blessings." On
each additional page write a category of things that we are grateful for. Example would be,
family, food, creation, animals, etc. Choose 2 o 3 to work on. Specific ideas for each of the
above categories are as follows. Print, "Thank you, God, for My family," on bag 2. Using a

paper doll cutout, have the children trace and cut enough for every member of their immediate family. With adult help print the names of each person on the paper dolls. On bag 3 print, "Thank you for the food we eat." Ask the children to bring in the wrappers or empty boxes of their favorite foods. Cut out the main pictures from the wrapper and boxes they brought in and put them in the bag. Print, "Thank you for the wonderful gifts of creation," on bag 4. For this bag cut out a sun, moon, and stars. For fun use Mylar confetti instead of the cutouts. For water use 6" strips of Mylar and cotton balls for clouds. Bean seeds, dried flower, pine cones, acorns etc. would also work for the creation bag. If you add a, "Thank you, God, for the animals bag," (page) have the children cut pictures out of magazines. When the books are completed have the children share one bag of their book with everyone else. Encourage the children to read and share their bag books at home.

❑ *More to do:*

Use brown bag books to do a book, "All About Me, to tell Bible stories or teach other concepts such as love.

Thanksgiving Gift Bags   ☺ ALL

A service project. Get the children excited about a service project for your local food pantry or shelf. Decorate brown grocery bags for the holidays with pictures, drawings, and uplifting messages of hope.

❑ *You will need:*
   Brown grocery bags
   Markers
   Magazine pictures
   Glue
   Scissors

❑ *To do:*

Use markers to draw pictures related to upcoming holidays or simply cheerful thoughts. Have the children search magazines for holiday pictures also. Recycle the pictures from Christmas and other holiday cards. Glue these to the bags. Older children will be able to print messages of encouragement and hope. Pass these on to your local food pantry or shelf for them to use as they distribute food.

Thanksgiving Show and Tell   ☺ ALL

Prepare the children for Thanksgiving a couple of weeks before the holiday by talking about things they are thankful for. Invite them to bring something from home that represents what they are thankful for.

❑ *You will need:*

A small table
Table covering
A sign with "Thanksgiving Table" printed on it

❑ *To do:*

Send home a note asking the parents to remind the children to bring something they are thankful for or a symbol of something they are thankful for (i.e., picture of family). Place the items on your table of thanksgiving. Gather around the table and one by one invite the children to talk about what they brought. When each child is done say, "Thank you, God, for the (name of item)." Comment on how many different things we have to be thankful for in our lives! Give thanks to God for all of the blessings in our lives.

Tie a Knot 🖐 PRI

While practicing tying a shoe, children can be reminded that "We are all bound together by God's love."

❑ *You will need:*

12-inch piece of cording or nylon rope

❑ *To do:*

Give each child the piece of cording. Demonstrate how to make the first simple knot used for shoe tying. Help the children hang the cording through a belt loop or buttonhole on their clothing. Then encourage the children to practice the simple knot throughout the day each time they see a kind action or when they do something nice for others. At the end of the day snip the knots away from the loop or buttonhole. Give the tied knots to the children to take as a reminder that God's love ties us together with others.

Time Capsule 🖐 PRI

Make time capsules at the beginning of the year with the children, bury them and then find them in the spring. The children love the mystery of burying or hiding and then seeing the changes and growth in themselves over the year.

❑ *You will need:*

Pringles® chip cans
Construction paper
Glue or tape
Stickers
Photo of each child
Blank index cards
A token or symbol of something
    important to each child

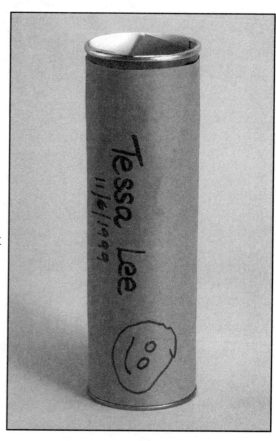

❑ *To do:*

Tell the children that you are going to start an activity that won't be finished until next spring. Explain that a time capsule is something people put together to reflect the signs of the times. They might put a newspaper, photograph, or toy in a special box. The box is then buried for a very long time. Some time capsules are buried for 100 years.

Let the children know that you are going to make time capsules. They will be buried or hidden until next spring and then dug up and discovered. It will be fun for the children to see how much they have grown and changed throughout the year.

❑ *More to do:*

Cover the chip cans with construction paper. Have the children print their names on the cans and decorate them with stickers. In each can, for each child, provide the following: a photo and/or self-portrait; an index card with a sample of the child writing his or her own name; another index card that has a question about God; and a picture or drawing of a favorite toy. Take a few days to compile this list of items. When everyone has filled her can talk about a good place to "bury" the cans for the year. The bell tower, attic, under a stairway, a shed are all good ideas. Take the time capsules to your special burial place together. Bundle them up in a large bag and label the bag with your class name and a "do not touch (or throw away)" sign. In the spring remember to "dig up," the time capsule. Take time to look through the contents and talk about the growth that has taken place. Have favorite toys changed? How about appearances? Review the God question. Can we answer it now that we have learned so much? Send the time capsules home and ask the children to share the contents with their parents.

To Do Bags   ☺ ALL

Mini lessons for home.

To Do Bags are special bags that go back and forth between home and school. They contain activities, books, puppets, stuffed toys, etc. that go along with lessons or topics you are working on in class. Not only will the bags enhance the work done in your program, they will involve parents and assist them in keeping up with what their child is doing.

❑ *You will need:*

Canvas bags
Storybooks
Coloring sheets
Puppets
Audiotapes

❑ *To do:*

The possibilities for To Do Bags are endless. Use your imagination and the resources you have available. Here are three examples of how you might want to fill your To Do Bags.

To go with a unit on self-esteem pack your bag with Joan Plum's book, "Pandy's Rainbow." Include a stuffed panda bear and coloring sheet. For Christmas send home a tape of Christmas songs and a card to color. The Clown of God is a favorite story. Send it home with a clown hat and 3 small rubber balls.

Be sure to send brief instructions for parents as well as the date the bag is to be returned. Another good idea is to attach a recipe card to the bag with a list of the contents so that parents know exactly what is to be returned.

T

Tool Belt 🐻 PRE

Make a tool belt that reflects the foundation of our Christian church.

❑ *You will need:*

Pelon strips 3" wide x 24" long
Markers
A variety of colored tag board
Scissors
Stapler
Large paper clips or paper fasteners

❑ *To do:*

Discuss the purpose of a tool belt with the children. Remind them that God gives each Christian special gifts and talents to share with the community. These allow us to build and grow together. Show the children the symbols for the Christian Tool Belt. Discuss the meaning or purpose for each one. To make the tool belt cut the pelon into strips 3" wide x 24" long. Print, "(name of the child)'s Christian Tool Belt," along the pelon. Enlarge and trace the patterns provided here, a heart to remind us to love one another, a band-aid to remind us to forgive, our hands for prayers and acts of kindness, our ears to listen to those around us. Use other symbols that might better fit with your group. Cut the symbols out of the tag board and staple them to the belt. To fasten the belt around the waist of the child, use a large paper clip or paper fastener.

Toy Blessing   PRE

Allow the children in your class to bring in one new toy after Christmas break. Have show and tell with the new toys and use this prayer.

❑ *To do:*

Have the children sit in a circle holding their new toys. Take turns showing the toys and answering questions such as, Who gave you the toy? Why do you like it? How does it work? Does it have a name? Etc.

After sharing, pray this little prayer:

Dear God,

Thank you for the gift of life and our families.

The gifts we receive are a sign of the love we have for one another.

Response: Bless us.

Our toys help us learn.

Response: Bless us.

Our toys are signs of happiness and love.

Response: Bless us.

Help us to use our toys wisely and share them with our friends.

Response: Bless us.

Thank you, God, for hearing us and being with us as we pray.

Response: Bless us.

Move around the circle and bless each child individually. Gently touch their heads and say, "God bless Joey and his new fire truck," or "God bless Sarah and her new panda bear."

Transparency Ornaments   PRI

Ornaments for all seasons.

Make ornaments for any holiday of the year with transparency paper and a bit of imagination.

❑ *You will need:*

Transparency paper
Paper punch
Ribbon or yarn
Wrapped candies, tissue paper balls, or shredded Mylar

❑ *To do:*

Use basic shapes about 6" in size of holiday symbols such as a star, bell, egg, pumpkin. With adult help trace and cut out two of the symbols you will be using. Holding the two symbols together, punch holes about 1/2" apart around the outside edge of the shape. Keep the holes lined up and hold the two pieces together while lacing through the holes with yarn or ribbon. A small piece of tape or paper clips will help to hold the two pieces together. Start near the top and end leaving a couple of holes undone so that you can fill the ornament. Use wrapped candy, shredded Mylar, or tissue paper balls to fill the ornament. If you'd like, use a combination of the three. If you are doing an Easter egg, put Easter grass in the bottom of the egg and foil wrapped candy. To finish the ornament, continue to lace to the end and tie a bow.

Treasure Box   ☺ ALL

Make little treasure boxes for the children to use at home to keep little treasures that they collect along the way.

❑ *You will need:*
    Paper egg cartons
    Tempera paint
    Puffy paint
    Beads
    Buttons
    Glitter
    Glue

❑ *To do:*
Have the children first paint the inside of the egg carton. Allow it to dry over night. Next open the carton flat and paint the top and bottom. After that has dried use puffy paint to write out each child's name on top. Continue to decorate the top of the box with beads, buttons, sequins, etc.

Treasure Hunt Exchange   ☺ PRE

This exchange will encourage young children to describe, identify, and label many of God's creations. A simple nature walk provides language development while admiring the work of God.

❑ *You will need:*
    Brown paper lunch bag for each child

❑ *To do:*
Provide a bag for each child to collect treasures in while on an outdoor walk. Upon the return from the walk collect the bags from the children. Ask the children to take turns reaching inside a bag and describing what they feel. Encourage the rest of the group to identify what the object might be. Then ask the describing child to reveal the object so everyone can label it.

Caution: Be sure to lay out some guidelines as to what may be placed in the bag. No living plants, animals, or insects should be collected.

❑ *More to do:*
Extend this activity to the families by encouraging the children to share the filled bags and play at home.

Tube Turkey Center Piece   ☺ ALL

Make tube turkeys to celebrate Thanksgiving.

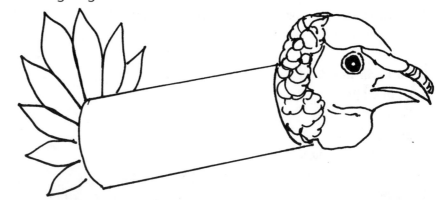

❑ **You will need:**
  Toilet tissue tube
  Colored tissue paper
  Construction paper
  Glue
  Scissors
  Markers

❑ **To do:**
Enlarge and trace the head pattern provided on red construction paper. Cut it out and draw eyes and outline the beak. Glue this to the inside of one end of the tube. Cut 4 sheets of different colored construction paper into 12" x 8" pieces. Round off into scallops one end of the long side of the paper. Gather and crinkle the non-scalloped end and stuff it in the end of the tube opposite the head. Fold the feathers up and fluff them out. Add a circle of tape in the area between the feathers and the tube to hold the feathers in place.

Tulip Card   ☺ ALL

Make this cute easy card for Mother's Day, May Day, or Easter. It is sure to warm hearts.

❑ **You will need:**
  1" - 1 1/2" wide spring colored fabric ribbon
  Stapler
  Glue
  Construction paper
  Pinking shears or scalloped edge scissors

❑ **To do:**
Cut the ribbon into 6" strips. Using pinking shears or other decorative edge scissors, round off the ends of the ribbon. Holding the ribbon in the middle, decorative side out, cross the two ends of the ribbon. Staple to hold in place. Cut one, two, or three ribbon tulips to glue to the front of a card. Use green construction paper or ribbon to make leaves and stem. With adult help write a greeting inside the card.

Turkey Lurkey ☺ ALL

With coffee filter feathers .
Make these fun and colorful turkey wall decorations. They'd also be neat on the front of a Thanksgiving card.

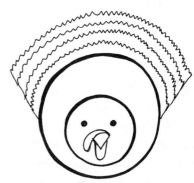

❑ *You will need:*
   Coffee filters
   Food coloring
   Small bowls
   Construction paper

❑ *To do:*

Enlarge, copy, and cut the turkey head and body provided. Use brown construction paper for the body/head piece and red for the wattle. Next fill small bowls with water and add a different color of food coloring to each. Fold two coffee filters into small squares. Carefully dip the corners of the folded squares into the colored water long enough for the water to soak in. Dip each corner into a different color. The children love seeing the colors run together. After dipping, unfold the coffee filters and allow them to dry flat, probably over night. When dry put two filters together. Fold them in half and adjust slightly so that there are 4 graduated rows of feathers. Staple in place near the center bottom of the fold. Glue the head/body piece to the center of the folded filters. Fluff up the feathers a bit and you have a turkey.

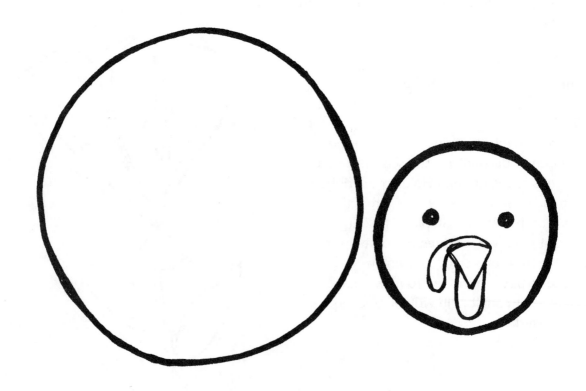

Turkey of Hands and Feet   ☺ ALL

The children will laugh with delight and love bringing this great turkey home for the holidays.

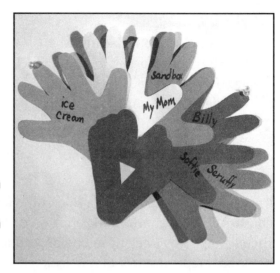

❑ *You will need:*

Brown construction paper
A variety of primary colored construction paper
Glue
Pencils
Scissors

❑ *To do:*

Have the children trace both of their feet on the brown construction paper. Cut the paper feet out. Glue together, overlapping the heels so that the toes will fan outward. Cut out eyes, beak, and wattle from construction paper and glue them on as shown in the picture. Cut out two legs and glue to the bottom of the turkey. Trace each child's hand on several colors of construction paper and glue to the back of the turkey to form the tail. Tell the children to print things that they are thankful for on the tailpieces of the turkey. Younger children will need your help.

Turkey Place Card Holder   ☺ ALL

Make turkey pinecone holders for your snack table or for the children to take home. Place a small card with a table prayer in the turkey instead of a name card.

❑ *You will need:*

Round, medium-size pinecones
Assorted colors of pipe cleaners
Brown clay
Card stock paper

❑ *To do:*

Lay the pinecone on its side to find out where it will balance best. Shape a brown or orange pipe cleaner to make the head. Place it into the pinecone with a bit of clay near the narrow end. Add a piece of red pipe cleaner to the head to make the waddle. Using different colored pipe cleaners, make feathers. Bend the pipe cleaners, match the ends, and twist them. Open up the loop at the other end and place with a little clay into the wide end of the pinecone.   Place a name or prayer card in the pinecone in front of the feathers.

Turkey Tray 　　　🐯 PRE
A fun table decoration for the Thanksgiving holiday

❑ *You will need:*
Washed pint-size milk cartons
Construction paper
Real feathers
Wooden ice-cream spoon
Markers
Tape

❑ *To do:*
Cut out the spout side of one side of the milk carton. Cover the rest of the carton with brown construction paper. Have the children draw facial features on the round end of the ice-cream spoon. Tape this face out to one of the long sides of the milk carton. To the opposite side, on the inside, tape a variety of multicolored feather cutouts. If possible add a few real feathers too. Add a prayer to the tray that says, "God, thank you for the many blessings we have to share." Encourage the children to use the tray at home for Thanksgiving goodies.

God, thank you for the many blessings we have to share.

Umbrella   😊 PRE

During the rainy days of April umbrellas pop up everywhere. Use this umbrella craft to send home the message that we are each covered by God's love.

❑ **You will need:**
  Paper plates
  Pipe cleaners
  Scissors
  Markers

❑ **To do:**
Cut the paper plate from the edge to the center. Overlap the paper plate at the cut to form a cone shape. On the outer edge of the cone print the message "Surrounded by God's love." On the inside of the umbrella print the names of the people each child says loves her or him.

Slide a pipe cleaner down the middle of the cone as shown in diagram. Twist a loop at the top to prevent the pipe cleaner from sliding down. Fold the opposite end of the pipe cleaner into a "hook" shape for the handle of the umbrella.

Under the Umbrella   😊 PRE

Just as an umbrella protects us from the rain, God's love provides shelter and protection from the hard things in life. We are safe in God's loving care.

❑ **You will need:**
  Tag board
  Markers
  Construction paper

❑ **To do:**
Enlarge and trace the umbrella pattern here.
Use cutouts and drawings to decorate each section.
Make hearts, stars, raindrops, flowers, etc.
Attach this little prayer:
    God's love is just like an umbrella,
    I know that God is always near,
    God will shelter and protect me
    I'm safe beneath God's loving care.
    Amen.

Universe Thank-You   ☺ ALL

Remind the children that God made the entire world, the entire universe, and that God created all creatures, things, planets, and beings.

❑ *To do:*

Clap in a rhythmic motion as you chant...

    Thank you, God, for the flowers and trees,

    Thank you, God, for the birds and bees,

    Thank you, God, for the moon and sun,

    Thank you, God, for the stars at night.

As children think of others, invite them to add verses. Conclude with, "God made them all for you and me!"

Ups and Downs of Life   ✋ PRI

Sometimes things happen in our lives that cause us to feel down. Then God sends the Spirit to lift us back up. Use this craft to talk about how we are lifted up when feeling down.

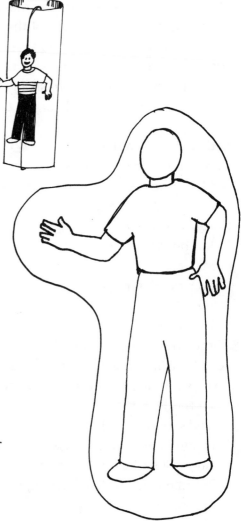

❑ *You will need:*

    Empty paper towel tube

    25" piece of yarn or string

    Paper person pattern

    Markers

    Scissors

    Stapler

❑ *To do:*

Use markers to decorate, then cut out the paper person pattern. Encourage the children to decorate the person to resemble their own color of hair, eyes, clothes, etc. Attach the head and feet of the person to the string with staples. Thread the string through the paper towel tube and tie the free ends together leaving the string looped inside the tube. The paper person should look as though it is climbing up or down the outside of the tube. Use a child's tube to demonstrate how the person can move down, as you ask a child one thing that causes him or her to feel down. (Example: My friend makes me feel bad when he won't play with me.) Then as you show how the paper person moves up the tube, ask the children how God helps to lift that person up. (Example: Another friend asks you to join in their game.)

Up, Up, and Away With God's Blessings ☺ ALL

Hot air balloons celebrate a special day with your group.

❏ *You will need:*
    Large round balloons
    Yarn
    Plastic berry basket
    Fabric or ribbon scraps

❏ *To Do:*

Lace scraps of ribbon, fabric, or paper in and out of the sides of the basket. Cut four 30" pieces of yarn and tie one end of each to each of the four corners of the basket. Gather the strings together about 6" above the middle of the basket and tie a knot. Spread the string evenly around the balloon and tie a knot on top. Add a couple of pieces of clear tape to hold the balloon in place. With the extra string at the top of the balloon, tie a loop for hanging. Fill the baskets with prayer suggestions or little treats.

❏ *More to do:*

Blow up balloons and tie them to a balloon stick (which may be purchased at a party store).   Put the balloon and stick in a ball of clay in a flowerpot. Print, "Grow in love with Jesus."

U.S.A. Cookie Cutter Planter ☺ ALL

A fun idea for Earth Day or the 4th of July. Plant grass seed in a cookie cutter for a fun reminder to cherish the land in which we have been blessed to live.

❏ *You will need:*
    U.S.A. cookie cutter
    Potting soil
    Grass seed
    Disposable plate
    Water spray bottle

❏ *To Do:*

Put the cookie cutter on the plate. Add potting soil to the inside of the cookie cutter. Sprinkle grass seeds on top and water with a spray bottle. Keep the seeds fairly moist by spraying with water. As the grass grows trim it with a scissors.

U

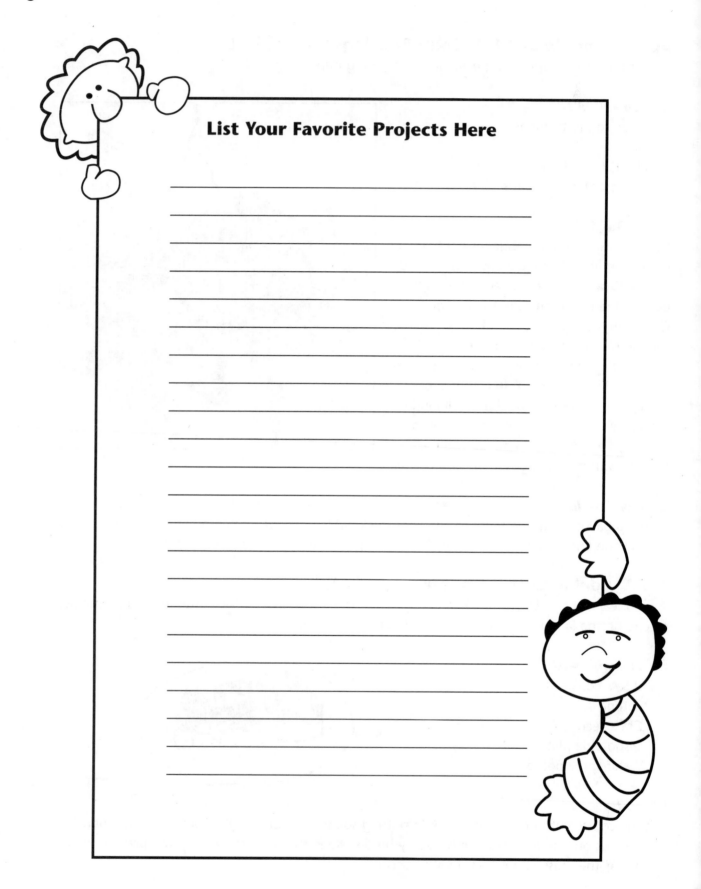

List Your Favorite Projects Here

Valentine ☺ ALL

St. Valentine was a man of courage. He had great love for others.

The Tradition of Valentine's Day comes from the fact that Valentine performed Christian marriages when it was outlawed to do so. He was put in jail for this. While in jail, Valentine became friends with the jailer's daughter who did kind things for him. Before Valentine died he sent the girl a note expressing his thanks for her kindness. He signed the note, "Your Valentine," hence the beginning of our Valentine traditions.

Valentine Antics 🐻 PRE

This lively game provides a lot of movement and fun.

❑ *You will need:*

  Several 12" hearts cut out of red poster board
  Pictures of things or animals that the children will recognize

❑ *To do:*

Glue a picture on each heart and then place them on the floor in a random arrangement.
Tell the children to sit along one wall until they hear their names called one by one with specific instructions. Call a child's name and add a specific instruction such as "Jamie, go and hop on the bunny five times." Then Jamie has to find the bunny heart and hop on it five times. Continue until everyone has had at least two turns. Finish the game by asking each child to bring you a card, until all have been returned to you.

Valentine Bandana Ideas ☺ ALL

Clean out your drawers and grab the red bandanas to use for your Valentine's celebrations.

You will need:

  Red bandanas
  One side fusible interfacing
  Doilies
  Construction paper

To do:

Cut the interfacing to fit a bandana. Iron the interfacing to the bandana to give it a little stiffness. Have the children trace and cut the hearts from the bandanas. Use the bandana hearts to make cards with construction paper and doilies.

Use this little poem in the cards you make.

> Roses are red,
> Violets are blue.
> You are so special,
> I love you.
> Roses are red,
> Violets are blue.
> God loves you
> And I do, too.

❑ *More to do:*

Cut the scraps from the hearts to make strips long enough to tie into bows. As a class, thank God for all of the people in your lives who love you. Tie a ribbon on a tree branch or wreath for those people. Observe all of the red color on that tree and how lucky we are to have so many people who love us.

❑ *More to do:*

For the Valentine's party cut the bandanas in half corner to corner to make a triangle for each child to wear around his neck. Use puffy paint to print, "Jesus loves (the name of the child.)" Be sure to dry overnight.

Use the bandanas to decorate the tables. Put them in baskets, use them for place mats, or tie them to chairs

Tie several bandanas together to make a long rope. Outline a heart on the floor with the bandana rope. Have the children sit around the heart for gather time or prayer.

Valentine Box of Fun   ☺ ALL

This game will give any Valentine party a spark of fun.

❑ *You will need:*

> Collection of a variety of small tokens such as small erasers
> Suckers
> Stickers
> Pencils
> A covered shoebox decorated with Valentines
> Tape or CD of lively music
> Children sitting in a circle

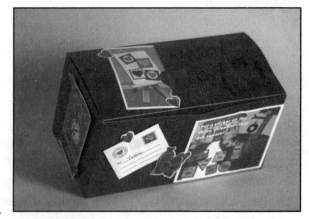

❑ *To do:*

Tell the children to pass the box around the circle while the music plays. When the music stops, the child who has the box may choose an item from the box. Play until every child has at least one item.

If any children get several items, encourage them to share what they have.

Valentine Box of Love ✋ PRI
A reminder of God's love for us.

❏ *To do:*
Wrap and decorate a box of love reminder that
God loves us and is always with us.
Include the following note:

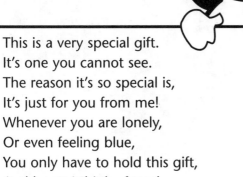

This is a very special gift.
It's one you cannot see.
The reason it's so special is,
It's just for you from me!
Whenever you are lonely,
Or even feeling blue,
You only have to hold this gift,
And know I think of you!
You never can unwrap it,
Please leave the ribbon tied.
Just hold the box close to your heart.
It's filled with LOVE inside.

❏ *You will need:*
Small boxes (the size jewelry comes in)
Wrapping paper
Ribbon
Bows
Tape

❏ *More to do:*
Write "LOVE" on the inside of the box. Fill it with more love with Valentine heart stickers, etc.
Have the children wrap and decorate the boxes. Wrap a ribbon around the box and tie a bow.
Attach the little love poem from above.

Valentine Bugs   👋 PRI

Love bugs are a sign of Valentine's Day. Share God's love with this token of love.

❑ *You will need:*
Hole punch
Messages of love written on piece of heart-shaped cardstock paper
Pipe cleaner
Heart-shaped pony beads
Colored barrel pony beads.

❑ *To do:*
Punch a hole in the corner of the heart-shaped message. Fold a pipe cleaner in half. Slide the pipe cleaner through the hole of the message, leaving the message at the fold. With the two ends of the pipe cleaner together, slide a barrel pony bead to the message. Next slide the heart to the barrel pony bead. Twist the pipe cleaner ends together, then separate the very ends to form the antennae of the "valentine bug."

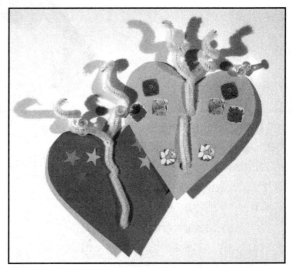

Valentine Heart Folder   👋 PRI

A perfect heart for holding Valentines.

❑ *You will need:*
Red paper (from the roll) sheets measuring 20" x 36"
Stickers
Glue
Tape
Marker

❑ *To do:*
Fold the paper the long way so that you have made a 10" by 18" rectangle. Cut a half circle across the top of one end of the fold. Then fold in half the short way. Put the new fold at the top of your table with the half circle cuts down. Take each corner top and fold to the center just as if you were making a newspaper hat. This fold makes two triangles. Fold the bottom edge of the paper to the line made by the triangles. Cut the outside fold of the triangles to about the same distance as the folded edge from the bottom so that you can make one more fold. Notice how you now have an upside down heart. Fold the flaps made from the last fold behind so that the edge is straight. Tape these flaps in place. Turn the heart right side up and round off the half circles if necessary. Decorate with stickers and drawings. What a neat place to keep all of those Valentine greetings!

Valentine Magnet Covered With Love ☺ ALL

Easy to make and lots of fun, this large Valentine will be a big hit!

❑ *You will need:*
Tag board
Variety of pink and red fabric pieces
Glue
Scissors
Markers
Magnet rolls

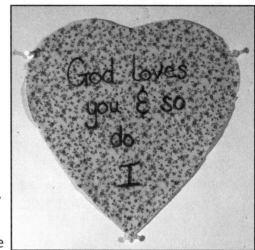

❑ *To do:*
Give each child a 12" square piece of tag board and a 12"
square piece of fabric. Have the children glue the fabric
onto the tag board. Then help the children cut the square
into a heart shape. Tell them to print, "God loves you & so do I" on the Valentines. Put two
magnet pieces on opposite sides on the back of the heart for hanging on the refrigerator at home.

Valuable Gems ☺ ALL

Encourage your children to see the blessings that God has given them as valuable as priceless gems.

❑ *You will need:*
Variety of brightly colored construction paper
Glitter
Sequins
Buttons
Patterns of gems
Styrofoam or paper burger boxes
(Most fast food chains will donate
enough for your class to use)
Glue
Scissors
Markers

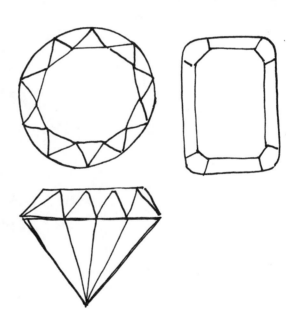

❑ *To do:*
Discuss all of the wonderful people and things
that God has blessed us with. Sometimes we take these people and things for granted when really
they are like precious gems to us.
Give the children patterns of gems to trace and cut out. Encourage them to decorate each gem
and then print someone or something they value on the gem such as Dad, Mom, My dog, etc.

❑ *More to do:*
Have the children decorate the burger boxes with stickers, glitter, contact paper shapes. Print "My
treasures" on the treasure chest with permanent marker.

Vine and Branches   ☺ ALL

Tell the children that Jesus is like a vine and we are like the branches because it is through Jesus, the vine that we the branches can grow to become better people.

❑ *You will need:*

    8" – 10" of artificial vine
    Yarn
    Patterns for symbols of things that help you grow in faith
      (i.e., praying hands, Bible, church, family)
    A variety of colors of construction paper
    Yarn
    Paper punch

❑ *To do:*

Trace and cut out symbols of ways through which we can get to know Jesus better. Examples would be praying hands, a church, a Bible, or people. Punch a hole in the top of each and string yarn through. Tie on the vine. Tell the children that it is important to learn more about Jesus, our vine, better through all of these ways.

Wagon Prayer 😊 ALL

Have prayer time in lots of different places with this on the move idea.

❏ *You will need:*

Wagon
Bible
Religious articles such as a cross
Picture
Nature finds
Class prayer cloth, etc.

❏ *To do:*

With the help of the children arrange the prayer table items on the wagon. Be sure things are fairly secure so that they don't fall when moving. Take your wagon to different areas of your building for prayer: under a stairway, the kitchen, or a hallway. Outside sit under the slide or jungle gym. How about the front steps or a corner of the parking lot? Take turns pulling the wagon from place to place. To keep interest, change the items on the prayer wagon with the seasons or holidays.

Walking Stick 🦁 PRE

Make a walking stick with the children to remind them that we are on the move and growing close to God.

❏ *You will need:*

Cardboard tubes from wrapping paper
Glitter
Sticker
Markers
Ribbon
Jingle bells

❏ *To do:*

Talk with the children about the ways in which we grow closer to God. Remind them that we need to attend church, pray, help others, etc. With adult help print some of these things on the stick. Also print, "Walking With God," and the child's name. Decorate the sticks with drawings and stickers. Punch a hole near the top of the stick and lace the ribbon with a jingle bell through it.

Wall Prints ☺ ALL

Children will love this opportunity to compare their handprints from the beginning of the year to those at the end of the year.

❑ *You will need:*

Poster board with a line down the middle.
Paper plates
Tempera paint

❑ *To do:*

Print the date and year at the top of the left section of the poster board. Put small amounts of paint on paper plates. Carefully press each child's hands into one color of paint. Place his hands on the left side of the poster board and press down. Save the right side of the poster board to repeat this activity at the end of the year. The children will be able to compare their handprint growth. Print the children's names next to their handprints.

Waste Basket for the Sick ☺ ALL

If you have a child or family member who has been ill for an extended length of time here is a practical gift idea.

❑ *You will need:*

Two brown paper grocery bags
Markers
Stickers
Magazine pictures
Scissors
Glue

❑ *To do:*

Cut a hole in the bottom of bag one. Invite classmates or family members of the ill person to decorate bag one using the stickers, magazine pictures, and glue. Be sure to decorate the bag so that the bottom of the bag is the top when complete. Write positive and prayerful messages on the decorated bag with the markers. Open bag two and place it inside the decorated bag to form a paper wastebasket as shown in the diagram.

Watering Jug 😊 ALL

Make a usable and fun watering jug for your spring gardeners.

❑ *You will need:*

1 gallon milk jug
Raffia
Stickers
Contact paper
Permanent markers

❑ *To do:*

With an ice pick or compass point punch 5 or 6 holes in the top side of a milk jug opposite the handle. Decorate the jug with stickers or cut outs from contact paper. With permanent marker write, "Sprinkle God's Love." Tie a raffia bow to the handle of the jug.

Watermelon Art 🙂 PRE

Watermelon, a favorite fruit, is a tasty reminder of the many gifts God gives us to enjoy throughout the summer.

Watermelon Necklace

❑ *You will need:*

Pink and black fun foam
Glue
Scissors
Black yarn
Black permanent marker
Compass point to punch holes

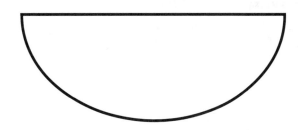

❑ *To do:*

Enlarge, trace, and cut out the pattern provided. Cut the half circle watermelon slice from pink fun foam. Use a green permanent marker to draw the rind on the round side of the slice. Cut out seeds from the black foam and glue to the pink. Punch a hole on the straight side about 1/2" from the edge. On the back of the water melon slice write, "Thank you, God, for watermelons." Lace yarn through the hole to make the string for hanging.

Watermelon Wall Hanging

❑ *You will need:*

Paper plates

Pink tempera paint

Green and black construction paper

Glue

Scissors

Black yarn

Sponges

Pie tin

Thank you God for summer sun,
It glows and warms everyone.
Watermelon grows big and sweet,
Thank you God for such a delicious treat.
Amen.

❑ *To do:*

Cut the paper plate in half. Put the pink paint in a pie tin and sponge paint the half plate. Allow this to dry. Cut out and glue black seeds and a green rind to the watermelon. Punch a hole in the top for hanging. Attach this rhyming prayer:

Thank you, God, for the summer sun,

It glows and warms everyone.

Watermelon grows big and sweet,

Thank you, God, for such a delicious treat.

Amen.

Web Weaving 　　　✋ PRI

Build community by tossing a ball of yarn back and forth and forming a web. As Christians we are all individuals, unique and different, and yet we are all are connected by our belief in God and the love God has for us.

❑ *You will need:*

Ball of yarn

❑ *To do:*

Have the children sit in a circle. One person holds the end of the ball of yarn. He or she then gently tosses the ball to someone else while still holding the end. The person who catches the first toss holds on to a piece of yarn and then tosses it again. Repeat this until a web is formed. As you observe the web with the children talk about how they are still themselves, individuals and yet connected by the web. Reverse the process and try to roll the ball of yarn up again.

Weight of the World Can Be Lifted 👋 PRI

At times we feel we are carrying the weight of the world. Life's disappointments and challenges sometimes feel too heavy to bear alone. But God has given us people in our lives to help ease everyday burdens. We only need to turn to these people for support. To discuss these concepts, play a game of "hopscotch pick-up."

❏ *You will need:*
   Garden stones
   Sidewalk chalk

❏ *To do:*
Use sidewalk chalk to draw a hopscotch pattern. Place a garden rock or stone on each hopscotch space. Invite the group of children to stand around the outer edge of the pattern, waiting to be called upon when needed. Then encourage a child to pick up each stone as they hop in the space. When the hopping child has more stones than he can carry, he may call to the group for assistance. Use this opportunity to talk about the people God sends into our lives to assist us day to day. The child then continues to hop through the remainder of the pattern. After they have completed the hopscotch they should replace the stones for the next child to try. (Whether hopping on one foot or skipping over spaces, this activity is easy to adapt to fit the motor skills of the children playing.)

❏ *More to do:*
After experiencing this game a few times, children may be ready to label each stone as a difficulty in life. As the stone is lifted, older children might identify a difficulty in life.

Welcome Wall Hanging 😊 ALL

Let everyone know you're glad they are here.
Make a welcome sign that the children help decorate the first few days of class.

❏ *You will need:*
   7 - 12" x 10" squares of pelon
   Markers
   Stickers
   Sequins
   Glitter
   Buttons
   Glue

W	E	L	C	O	M	E

❏ *To do:*
On individual squares of pelon, print the letters to spell W-E-L-C-O-M-E. Each day of class set out one panel for the children to decorate with markers or another craft medium such as buttons, sequins, glitter, etc. Set out a different craft item a day. At the end of class time, hang up the newly completed letter. By the end of the first 7 days of class not only will the word welcome be spelled out, but also the children will feel it. Welcome God to your year with a class prayer after the banner is complete and hung.

What If Game PRI

Perfect to help children think about positive responses to a variety of situations. Ask them what they think Jesus would want them to do.

❏ *To do:*

Ask "what if" questions such as:

What if Collin took away the toy that Tahra was playing with?

What if your mom is talking to another person and you have a question?

What if one person was to push or hit another?

Wheeling With God ALL

Like the hub of a wheel that supports the spokes, God is at the center of our lives. Like a hub God is always at the center of what we think, say, and do. The spokes of the wheel can be thought of as the many parts of ourselves, our community, and our world that make us who we are: our parents, friends, teachers, sunshine, rain, plants, animals, etc. All are gifts from God that help us as we roll through life. Enjoy these wheeling good ideas with your children.

Bulletin Board

❏ *You will need:*

Bulletin board

Construction paper

Yarn

Large Styrofoam ball

Straw

Photos of each child

❏ *To do:*

Label the bulletin board, "Wheeling Through the Summer With God." Enlarge and copy the art provided here. Have the children color the pictures. Make a large wheel the size of the bulletin board. Use yarn for the outside rim and spokes. Cut the Styrofoam ball in half and pin or tape it to the middle of the wheel for the hub. Print, "God is the hub of our lives," on a pennant. Tape the pennant to a straw and stick it in the Styrofoam ball. Staple the art colored by the children to the spokes of the wheel and staple the photos of the children around the rim.

❏ *More to do:*

Wheeling activities

Have a bike/wagon parade around the block or parking lot. Decorate with balloons and crepe paper.

Plant a garden in a wagon. Add a sign that says, "Wheeling and Growing with God."

Window Cling   ☺ ALL

A clear window carries the Good News of the Holy Spirit for all to see inside and outside.

❑ *You will need:*
Scissors
Heavy clear vinyl
Permanent marker
Hole punch
Ribbon

❑ *To do:*
Cut a free form shape from a piece of heavy clear vinyl about 6" x 4". Using a permanent marker print the words "Holy Spirit" on the vinyl. Punch holes around the bottom edge. Tie 8" colored ribbon strips in each hole. Cling to a sunny window.

Windsock   PRI

God sends the Spirit to move through each of us allowing us to live together in God's love. As a group create a community fish-shaped windsock.

❑ *You will need:*
Brown paper lunch bag
Tissue paper
Glue
Scissors
Hole punch
String

❑ *To do:*
Take a flat folded lunch bag (with the bottom cut out) and draw a fish outline as shown. Cut the fish shape out being careful not to cut on the folds. Use a marker to make a fish eye on both sides of the lunch bag. Decorate the bag by gluing colorful tissue paper scales all over the body of the fish. Open the bag so air may move through the bag. Punch two holes at the top of the bag so a string may be used to hang the windsock in a window. When the windows are open and wind moves the fish, remind the children the Spirit moves through each of us.

Windsock Prayer Reminder ☺ ALL

Make an ice-cream bucket wind sock for home. Every time the family remembers to pray, a streamer is added to the bottom edge of the bucket.

❑ *You will need:*
   Ice cream buckets
   Contact paper
   Scissors
   Plastic strips (cut from plastic table cloths) or Mylar strips
   Masking tape

❑ *To do:*

Cut out the bottom of the ice-cream bucket. Cover the bucket with any patterned contact paper. Write, "Remember to pray," on the side of the bucket. Cut several strips of plastic about 1" wide x 24" long. Send these home in an envelope with instructions to tape them to the inside of the bucket when prayers are shared. When streamers are hung from the bucket, hang it outside to enjoy in the wind.

Wind Wands ☺ ALL

Celebrate the wind with these wind wands while making its power more visible.

❑ *You will need:*
   Dead tree branch
   Pieces of bright colored ribbon or yarn
   And a windy day

❑ *To do:*

After some strong March winds have passed through your neighborhood, as a class look for a dead tree branch that has been blown down. Bring the branch back to class and decorate it with strands of colorful ribbons. Tie pieces of the ribbons to the bare branches. Then take a walk around the neighborhood waving the branch through the air. Let the children take turns waving the "wind wand" in the air as they describe ways they see the effects of the wind – helps to fly kites, moves the sails of boats, makes a flag fly, etc.

Winter Garden ☺ ALL
Bring some beauty into your classroom with the gifts God has given us.

❑ *You will need:*
    A large porous rock
    Six tablespoons of water
    Six tablespoons of bluing
    One tablespoon of ammonia
    Food coloring
    A flat, shallow bowl

❑ *To do:*
Mix the salt, water, and bluing, let it set for about an hour. Stir the salt mixture and add the ammonia. Place the rock in the center of the flat bowl and pour the mixture over the top. Sprinkle a few drops of food coloring over the rock. Set the bowl in a sunny place. Beautiful crystals will grow in your winter garden for several weeks.

Wrapped Yarn Ornaments ☻ PRE
Make wrapped yarn ornaments for the Christmas tree.

❑ *You will need:*
    A variety of different colored yarn
    Tag board
    Paper punch

❑ *To do:*
Enlarge and copy the Christmas symbols provided here. Trace these to the tag board and cut them out. Tape a strip of yarn to the ornament and begin to wrap. The children can change colors of yarn and direction of wrapping. Punch a hole in the top and lace a piece of yarn through it for hanging.

Wrapper Collage ☺ ALL

A reminder of our own uniqueness.

Have the children bring in the wrapper of their favorite snack or treat to be part of a poster titled, "We are each wrapped a little differently, but we all have God in us," poster.

❑ ***You will need:***

Poster board
Glue
Wrappers from favorite snacks or treats
Markers

❑ ***To do:***

Have the children write their names on their snack wrappers. Around the edge of the poster board write, "We are each wrapped a little differently, but we all have God within us." Glue the wrappers to the center of the poster. Be sure to talk about the things that are alike about us and the things that make us different.

Wreath ☺ ALL

A clay wreath for Advent.

Make an Advent wreath from modeling clay.

The four Advent (birthday) candles make this idea a big hit.

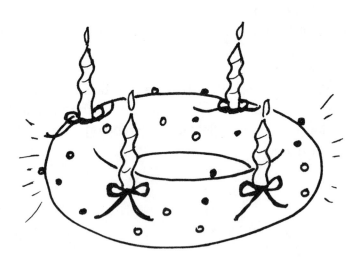

❑ ***You will need:***

4 birthday cake candles
Beads
Sequins
Narrow ribbon
Plastic covers or plastic disposable plates
Modeling clay
2 cups flour
1 cup salt
2 cups water
2 teaspoons cream of tarter
1 tablespoon oil
Green food coloring

Combine ingredients and cook over medium heat stirring constantly until it becomes stiff.

❑ ***To do:***

Mix up a recipe of the dough. Use about 1/2 - 3/4 cup of dough for each wreath. Put the dough on a plate or cover and have the children shape it into a wreath. Add sequins or beads for decoration. Tie a ribbon around each candle and put them in the wreath. Send home a note cautioning parents to remind the children that the candles may not be lit unless Mom or Dad do it.

Wreaths for Christmas ☺ ALL

Evergreen Christmas wreathes have traditionally been symbols of God's everlasting love. The circle is unending just as the love of God for each of us.

❑ *You will need*:

Paper plate
Magazine pictures of people
Photos of child's family
Glue
Ribbon
Hole punch

❑ *To do:*

Cut the center out of the plate leaving a paper wreath. Cover the underside of the plate with glue and the magazine pictures. Then glue on the picture of the child's family members. Punch two holes at the top of the wreath. Tie a ribbon bow through the holes at the top of the wreath. Use this wreath project to talk about how all people share in God's unending love.

❑ *More to do:*

Before sending the finished wreaths home to the families, display the wreaths on a bulletin board in the shape of a large circle. Title the bulletin board, "We all play a part in God's unending love!"

List Your Favorite Projects Here

X Commandments 👋 PRI

God gave us the Ten Commandments to help us remember to love God and others. A copy of their own will remind the children that this is the way we are asked to live.

❑ *You will need:*

Large rocks
Tacky glue
Copies of the Ten Commandments (using a tablet shape as below)

❑ *To do:*

Review and discuss the commandments. Give each child a rock and a copy of the commandments. Have the children cut around the paper tablet and glue it onto the rock. Encourage them to keep the rock in a place they will see it often.

Ten Commandments

Don't have any gods except me.
Be careful how you use God's name.
Remember to rest and worship on God's day.
Honor and obey your parents.
You must not kill anybody.
Stay with your husband or wife.
Never tell a lie.
Do not steal things from others.
Don't be jealous of your neighbor's family.
Don't be jealous of what your neighbor has.

X's and O's Pencil Topper 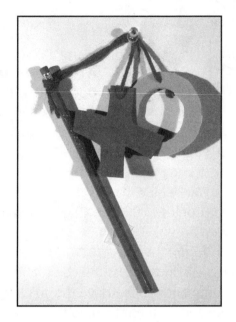 PRI

A Valentine's gift with hugs and kisses.

❑ **You will need:**
  Unsharpened pencils
  Fun foam
  String
  Masking tape

❑ **To do:**

Use the pattern here to cut out an X and O from fun foam for each child. With a compass point put a hole through each letter. Lace a separate piece of string 6" long through each hole and tie a knot. Tie the ends of both strings to the top of the pencil. Wrap tape around the strings to secure them.

Xylophone Prayer 🐻 PRE

Encourage spontaneous prayer by playing the xylophone.

❑ *You will need:*

Xylophone

❑ *To do:*

Invite the children to pray by giving them a prayer theme such as people in our lives. Tell the children to sit quietly as they think about whom they would like to pray for. Choose one person to play a note on the xylophone as the children offer spontaneous petitions. For example, you are praying for special people in the lives of the children: Begin with "Dear God, be with us as we pray." (ting) "Please take care of my Grandma because she is sick." (ting) or, "Thank you for sending my Uncle Bob home safe from the Army." (ting) Have the same person play for each prayer. Be sure to pray this often enough so that everyone gets a turn.

X–tra! X–tra! Read All About It! Jesus Christ Is Born! 🐻 PRE

Make up a newspaper with the Good News of Jesus' birth. "Read all about it!"

❑ *You will need:*

Newspapers
12" x 18" white construction paper
Markers

❑ *To do:*

Make copies or write, "Good News!   Jesus Christ is born!" on white construction paper. Glue this to the top page of a newspaper. Have the children draw the picture to go with the headline. Roll the finished product up and send home.

List Your Favorite Projects Here

_____

_____

_____

_____

_____

_____

_____

_____

_____

_____

_____

_____

_____

_____

_____

_____

_____

_____

_____

_____

_____

Year Book ☺ ALL

Memories of the time you spend together.
Keep track of the highlights of your year by beginning a Yearbook, scrapbook of your class.

❑ *You will need:*
Camera and film
Scrapbook or notebook with blank papers
Markers
Construction paper

❑ *To do:*
Decorate the cover of your notebook with the name of your class. Use stickers or a class picture also. Plan to put photos, programs, art projects, or pictures drawn by the children in the scrapbook. Little ones love to see pictures of themselves and their friends. At the beginning of the year, ask parents to donate film for your particular camera. Ask parents to take turns developing rolls of film. Or, check with your local pharmacist and see if they will donate the film and processing.
Leave the scrapbook out in your prayer corner or bookshelf for all to see.

Yell, Yelp, Yodel for God ☺ PRE

When energy levels are high use this cheer of praise!

Yell, yelp, yodel for God
I am happy as can be,
The dear Lord loves me, loves me,
I'm as happy as can be.
Yell, yelp, yodel for God.
I'm as happy as can be,
The dear Lord made me special,
I'm as happy as can be.
Yell, yelp, yodel for God
I'm as happy as can be,
The dear Lord is always with me,
I'm as happy as can be.

Yo-yo Play   PRI

When life seems down, God sends the Spirit to lift us back up.

❑ *You will need:*

Yo-yo

❑ *To do:*

Demonstrate how a yo-yo moves up and down. As you show the children how it works, talk about how God sends the Spirit to bring us up when we feel down. As the yo-yo moves down the string, give examples of feeling low or down (example: When it is too cold to go outside). As the yo-yo moves up the string, present uplifting solutions to the low-down feelings (example: Mom asks if we want to invite a friend over to play).

❑ *More to do:*

Invite a child to present a low-down feeling and encourage others to identify the uplifting work of the Spirit.

Yule Log   PRI

A Scandinavian tradition.

There is a Scandinavian tradition of tossing a log in the fire during the holiday season as sign of gratitude for the year that has passed and for the blessings of the year that is to come. Make these with the children to give or take home at Christmas or New Year's.

❑ *You will need:*

Large sticks 1" x 8"
Small pine cones, holly, evergreen branches, dried flowers, etc.
Raffia
Blank index cards

❑ *To do:*

Take a nature walk to find large sticks (logs would be too big to handle for little ones.) Glue or tie with raffia the pine cones, holly, dried flowers, etc. to the center of the stick. Tie a raffia bow around the stick also. Print the following prayer to the index cards and attach to the Yule log. Families may choose to burn their log or use it as a table blessing.

❑ *More to do:*

Yule Log Prayer
Dear Lord,
Thank you for the blessings of the past year.
We have loved and grown, laughed and cried,
Always keeping you by our side.
Help us to always remember you are always near,
Protect us and bless us and those we hold dear.
As we look ahead to a brand new year.

Zaccheus 🦁 PRE

Introduce the children to this friend of Jesus and teach them an important lesson. (cf. Luke 19:1-10)

❏ *To do:*

Jesus was coming though the town. (Walk in place)

Poor Zacchaeus was too short to see. (Extend hand to show short)

Then he remembered that big sycamore tree. (Point to brain)

If he climbed to the top, he would be sure to see. (Pretend to climb a tree)

He climbed the tree and waited for Jesus to come by. (Shade your eyes and look from side to side)

Jesus called to Zacchaeus, Come down! (Motion with arm to come)

I'm going to your house today!

Zacchaeus learned a lot from Jesus. (Shake head yes and point to heart)

How to treat others in a better way. (Shake hands with another)

Zebra Welcome 🦁 PRE

Start your gather time with this fun cheer. What a great way to get everyone excited about a brand new day. Make a Zebra puppet, a stand-up Zebra, and cheerleading pompoms to go with the cheer.

❏ *To do:*

Hey, Mr. Zebra, what do you say?

Today's going to be a mighty fine day!

Together we will learn and work and play,

as our teachers and parents show us the way.

With friends whom we love,

and the dear Lord up above.

A prayer in our heart,

we are ready to start.

Zebra Puppet

❑ *You will need:*

White sock
Black felt
Glue
Scissors
Black yarn

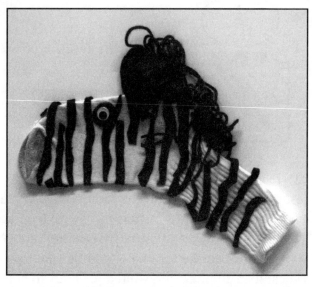

❑ *To do:*

Use the white sock for the head of the puppet. Glue strips of felt to the face and neck. Add facial features. Use the black yarn to make a mane. Wrap the black yarn around a flattened toilet tissue tube until thick. Gently slide the wrapped yarn off the tube, gather at the center, and tie a knot leaving at least 10" of yarn on the end of the knot. Use these ties to fasten the yarn mane to the head. Make 3 to 5 yarn balls to make the mane thick. Thread a large needle with the yarn tails to sew it to the sock. Have the children take turns using the puppet when you say the cheer at gather time.

Stand Up Zebra

❑ *You will need:*

Cardboard
Snap clothespins
Black and white tempera paint

❑ *To do:*

Enlarge and copy the zebra pattern provided here. Trace the zebra onto the cardboard and cut out. Paint both sides of the zebra all white and then add the black stripes. Paint the clothespins black. When all the paint has dried clip a clothespin to the front and back sets of legs and let the zebra stand up by himself.

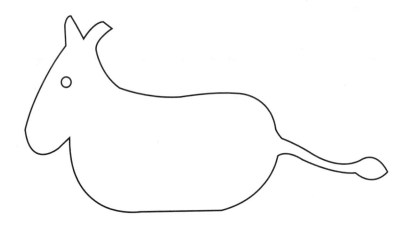

Zebra Pompoms
Black and White Zebra Pompoms

❑ *You will need:*
  Newspaper
  Masking tape
  Scissors

❑ *To do:*
Lay the newspaper (about 6 sheets) on table with the fold at the top. Cut 1" strips from the opposite end of the fold, stopping 3" from the fold. Carefully roll the folded end tightly to make a handle for the pompom. Wrap masking tape around the end to hold in place. Make one pompom per child to use during your opening.

Zingers   😊 ALL
Good news notes for home.
Every now and then send home a Zinger, a positive note to parents about their child. Highlight an accomplishment, an act of kindness, or interesting insight the child might have had.

❑ *You will need:*
  Copy of the zinger certificate
  Construction paper

❑ *To do:*
Enlarge and copy the zinger certificate provided here. Use the same colored paper, etc., so parents and children know good news is on the way. After filling out the certificate, mount it to a piece of construction paper, add a sticker or little gift like a bookmark or pencil.

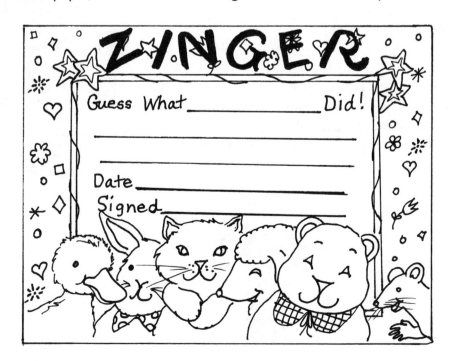

Zip Up and Share   ☺ ALL

To show others you care.

Use a zip-up bag for the children to use to share with one another. Show and tell items, treats, or small gifts such as pictures drawn by the children or a book to read.

❑ **You will need:**

    1-gallon plastic zipper bags
    Permanent markers
    Instructions for parents

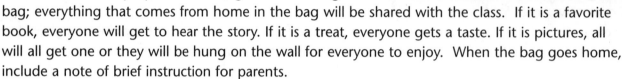

❑ **To do:**

Print, "Our Class Zip Up and Share Bag." Talk to the children about the purpose of the bag. It is a sharing bag; everything that comes from home in the bag will be shared with the class. If it is a favorite book, everyone will get to hear the story. If it is a treat, everyone gets a taste. If it is pictures, all will all get one or they will be hung on the wall for everyone to enjoy. When the bag goes home, include a note of brief instruction for parents.

Zipper Charm   ☺ PRE

For outside of jackets that keep us warm, make this little zipper charm.

You will need:

    Plastic covers from coffee cans or margarine tubs
    Permanent marker
    Puffy paint
    Scissors
    Metal key ring or plastic lacing

To do:

Trace and cut out the cross pattern provided here on a plastic cover. With a compass point, poke a hole at the top of the cross. Put the metal key ring through the hole. Decorate the cross with permanent marker of puffy paints. Remind the children that wherever they zip up to go Jesus is with them.

Zippy the Zoo Keeper   ☺ ALL

As the children act out the animals in this rhyme, they will love Zippy and giggle out loud.

❑ *To do:*

Zippy the zookeeper is very kind,
but lately he's having a terrible time.
The words from his mouth, they all start with z,
and the animals aren't quite sure where they should be.
The zhales and the zeals who swim with ease,
are suddenly hanging upside down in trees.
The zions and zears who love to growl and roar,
are making like birds and trying to soar.
The znakes and zizzards who rarely make a sound,
are jazzing and jiving and marching all around town.
The ziraff and the zippos who always toe the line,
are suddenly complaining and starting to whine.
We know you love your animal friends,
but this mix up of names has got to end.
Zippy sat down and thought and he thought,
I know I can get rid of "Z" thing I caught.
He took a really deep breath and he sat down so still,
and concentrated hard and used all of his will.
And before Zippy knew it the names came out right,
and this nonsense did not go on for another night.
The animals were all as happy as can be,
that their names were not starting with letter, "Z."
And in closing it's not too hard to believe,
that old Mr. Zebra was the most relieved.

Zoo Animal Cards   🐨 PRE

Play a matching game with these animal cards. Or, play a concentration game or use them when you tell the Zippy Story.

❑ *You will need:*
    Cardstock paper
    Markers
    Clear contact
    Scissors

❑ *To do:*

Enlarge and copy the animal cards provided here. Have the children help color them with markers and then cover them with clear contact. Cut out the cards and use.
Put the animals on tongue depressors to use when telling the Zippy Story.

Z

❏ *More to do:*

To play concentration, you will need two sets of cards. Lay the cards face down on the floor. The children take turns turning over the cards two at a time. If there is no match, they turn the cards back over. The next child then takes a turn. The children must remember what has been turned over and then they need to match them up.

Zoo Heigh Ho the Derry Oh   ☺ ALL

Just for fun, sing this one!

❏ *To do:*   ♪

Sing to the tune of "The Farmer in the Dell."

> *The animals in the zoo,*
> *The animals in the zoo,*
> *Heigh ho, in the zoo,*
> *The animals in the zoo.*
> *The monkey climbs like this,*
> *The monkey climbs like this,*
> *Heigh ho, in the zoo,*
> *The monkey climbs like this.*
> *The elephant waves his trunk,*
> *The elephant waves his trunk,*
> *Heigh ho, in the zoo,*
> *The elephant waves his trunk.*
>> Invite the children to add more verses.

Notes

Notes

Notes

Notes